PHILOSOPHY OF LOGICS

PHILOSOPHY OF LOGICS

SUSAN HAACK

Reader in Philosophy, University of Warwick

CAMBRIDGE UNIVERSITY PRESS

CAMBRIDGE
LONDON   NEW YORK   NEW ROCHELLE
MELBOURNE   SYDNEY

Published by the Press Syndicate of the University of Cambridge
The Pitt Building, Trumpington Street, Cambridge CB2 1RP
32 East 57th Street, New York, NY 10022, USA
296 Beaconsfield Parade, Middle Park, Melbourne 3206, Australia

First published 1978
Reprinted 1979 1980

Printed in Great Britain at the
University Press, Cambridge

Library of Congress Cataloguing in Publication Data

Haack, Susan.
Philosophy of logics.

Bibliography: p.
Includes index.
1. Logic. I Title.

BC1.H15   160   77-17071

ISBN 0 521 21988 4 hard covers
ISBN 0 521 29329 4 paperback

for RJH

ACKNOWLEDGMENTS

This book is based, in large part, on lectures in the philosophy of logic given at the University of Warwick since 1971. Thanks are due to all the colleagues and friends with whom I have discussed the issues raised here; especially to Nuel Belnap, Robin Haack, Peter Hemsworth, Paul Gochet, Dorothy Grover, Graham Priest and Timothy Smiley for detailed comments on draft material. I am indebted, also, to my students, who have taught me a great deal; and to Jeremy Mynott, for editorial advice and support.

CONTENTS

PREFACE

The century since the publication of Frege's *Begriffsschrift* has seen a tremendous growth in the development and study of logical systems. The variety of this growth is as impressive as its scale. One can distinguish four major areas of development, two in formal, two in philosophical studies: (i) the development of the standard logical apparatus, beginning with Frege's and Russell and Whitehead's presentation of the syntax of sentence and predicate calculi, subsequently supplied with a semantics by the work of e.g. Post, Wittgenstein, Löwenheim and Henkin, and studied metalogically in the work of e.g. Church and Gödel; (ii) the development of non-standard calculi, such as the modal logics initiated by C. I. Lewis, the many-valued logics initiated by Łukasiewicz and Post, the Intuitionist logics initiated by Brouwer. Alongside these one has (iii) philosophical study of the application of these systems to informal argument, of the interpretation of the sentence connectives and quantifiers, of such concepts as truth and logical truth; and (iv) study of the aims and capacities of formalisation, by those, such as Carnap and Quine, who are optimistic about the philosophical significance of formal languages, by those, such as F. C. S. Schiller and Strawson, who are sceptical of the pretensions of symbolic logic to philosophical relevance, and by those, such as Dewey, who urge a more psychological and dynamic conception of logic over the prevailing one.

I see some philosophical significance in the fact that these developments took place in parallel rather than in series; for it is salutary to remember that 'non-standard' logics have developed alongside the standard systems, and that there have always been critics, too, not only of specific formal systems, but of the aspirations of formalisation itself.

Developments in the four areas I have distinguished were not, of course, independent of each other; and I see philosophical significance, also, in the interplay between them. For example, although some of the key ideas of both modal and many-valued logics were anticipated by MacColl as early as 1880, their systematic formal development came, respectively, in 1918 after the canonical formalisation of non-modal calculi in *Principia Mathematica*, and in 1920 after the provision of truth-table semantics for 2-valued logic. However, the motivation for the development of non-standard calculi derived not only from the mathematical appeal of the prospect of extensions and modifications of classical logic, but also from philosophical criticism: in the case of modal logics, of the claim of the material conditional to represent implication, and, in the case of many-valued logics, of the assumption that every proposition is either true or else false. And one development in non-standard logic prompted another: doubts about the success of modal logics in formalising the intuitive idea of entailment led to the development of relevance logics, while the mathematical appeal of modal systems encouraged the development, by analogy, of epistemic, deontic and tense logics; or again, reflection on the philosophical motivation for many-valued logics led to the idea of supervaluations. Formal innovations, in turn, have given a new dimension to philosophical questions originally raised by standard calculi: as, for instance, issues about the interpretation of quantifiers and their relation to singular terms arose in a new and acute form when the intelligibility of modal predicate logic was challenged; or, as old worries about whether logic deals with sentences, statements or propositions turned out to be implicated in the challenge to bivalence posed by many-valued systems. Sometimes new formal systems have even challenged, explicitly or implicitly, and more or less radically, accepted assumptions about the aims and aspirations of formal logics: relevance logic, for instance, questions not only the adequacy of the material and strict conditionals but also the classical conception of validity; the distinctive character of Intuitionist logic derives in part from a challenge to the 'logicist' presumption of the priority of logic over mathematics; and fuzzy logic breaks with the traditional principle that formalisation should correct or avoid, but not compromise with, vagueness. And, as the last example reminds one, new formal developments have sometimes aspired to overcome what both supporters and critics of formal logic had taken to be its inherent limitations – such as its supposed incapacity, stressed by both Schiller and Strawson, to deal with the pragmatic features which affect the acceptability of informal reasoning, perhaps overcome, at least in part, by the 'formal pragmatics' initiated by Montague.

My concern, in this book, is with the philosophy, rather than the history, of logic. But my strategy has been devised with an eye to the history of the interplay of formal and philosophical issues which I have just sketched. I begin with a consideration of some problems raised by the standard logical apparatus – the interpretation of sentence connectives, sentence letters, quantifiers, variables, individual constants, the concepts of validity, truth, logical truth; I turn, from ch. 9 onwards, to a consideration of the way some of these problems motivate formal innovations, 'extended' and 'deviant' logics, and to the ways in which these new formalisms lead, in turn, to a re-evaluation of the philosophical issues; and I conclude, in the final chapter, with some questions – and rather fewer answers – about the metaphysical and epistemological status of logic, the relations between formal and natural languages, and the relevance of logic to reasoning.

And two recurring themes of the book also reflect this historical perspective. What seem to me to be the vital philosophical issues in logic are focussed by consideration (i) of the plurality of logical systems and (ii) of the ways in which formal calculi bear on the assessment of informal argument. More specifically, I shall be urging that, in view of the existence of alternative logics, prudence demands a reasonably radical stance on the question of the epistemological status of logic, and that the interpretation of formal results is a delicate task in which judicious attention to the purposes of formalisation is highly desirable.

I have tried to produce a book which will be useful as an introduction to the philosophical problems which logic raises, which will be intelligible to students with a grasp of elementary formal logic and some acquaintance with philosophical issues, but no previous knowledge of the philosophy of logic. But I haven't offered simple answers, or even simple questions; for the interesting issues in philosophy of logic are complex and difficult. I have tried instead to begin at the beginning, to explain technicalities, and to illustrate highly general problems with specific case studies. To this end I have supplied, for those new to the subject, a glossary of possibly unfamiliar terms used in the text, and some advice on finding one's way about the literature; while, for those anxious to go further, I have included a generous (but I hope not intimidating) bibliography. The response of my students has encouraged me to believe that it is unnecessary, as well as undesirable, to oversimplify. I have aspired – though the result, I fear, inevitably falls short of the aspiration – to produce a book which may be of some use to the student, and at the same time of some interest to the teacher.

It is, I find, irritating to be unsure whether, or how, an author has modified views he previously put forward; but, on the other hand, it is tedious to be subjected to frequent discussions of an author's earlier mistakes. By way of compromise, therefore, I indicate here, briefly, where, and how, I have modified the ideas put forward in *Deviant Logic*. First: I have, I hope, made the distinction between metaphysical and epistemological questions about the status of logic rather clearer; and this has led me to distinguish more carefully between the question of monism versus pluralism, and the question of revisability, and to support a qualified pluralism rather than the monism somewhat confusedly assumed in *Deviant Logic*. Second: I have come to appreciate that the consequences for ontology of the substitutional interpretation of the quantifiers are somewhat less straightforward than I used to suppose; and this has led me to a more subtle, or at any rate more complex, account of the respective roles of quantifiers and singular terms. I dare say, though, that I shall have missed some old mistakes, besides making some new ones.

NOTATION AND ABBREVIATIONS

A, B ...	metavariables, ranging over sentence letters
p, q ...	sentence letters
$-$	negation ('it is not the case that')
$\vee$	disjunction ('or'); sometimes called 'vel'
$\&$	conjunction ('and'); 'ampersand'
$\rightarrow$	material implication ('if')
$\equiv$	material equivalence ('if and only if')
x, y ...	individual variables
$(\exists)$	existential quantifier ('at least one')
$(\ )$	universal quantifier ('for all')
$(\imath x)$ ...	definite description ('the x such that...')
F, G ...	predicate letters (R, ... for polyadic predicates)
a, b ...	singular terms
$=$	identity
L	necessarily
M	possibly
$\prec$	strict implication
$\Rightarrow$	relevant implication
$\Rrightarrow$	entailment
$\urcorner$	Intuitionist negation
$\{\ \}$	set
$\{x\|...x\}$	the set of xs which are...
$\langle\ \rangle$	sequence (ordered pair, triple ... n-tuple)
$\in$	set membership
$\|...\|$	the value of ...
$<$	less than
$>$	greater than

$\leqslant$	less than or equal to
$\geqslant$	greater than or equal to
iff	if and only if
wff	well-formed formula
V.C.P.	vicious circle principle
$\vdash$	syntactic consequence
$\vDash$	semantic consequence
MPP	*modus ponens* (from A and $A \rightarrow B$ to infer B)
RAA	*reductio ad absurdum*

I

'Philosophy of logics'

There is no mathematical substitute for philosophy.
Kripke, 1976

1 Logic, philosophy of logic, metalogic

The business of philosophy of logic, as I understand it, is to investigate the philosophical problems raised by logic – as the business of the philosophy of science is to investigate the philosophical problems raised by science, and of the philosophy of mathematics to investigate the philosophical problems raised by mathematics.

A central concern of logic is to discriminate valid from invalid arguments; and formal logical systems, such as the familiar sentence and predicate calculi, are intended to supply precise canons, purely formal standards, of validity. So among the characteristically philosophical questions raised by the enterprise of logic are these: What does it mean to say that an argument is valid? that one statement follows from another? that a statement is logically true? Is validity to be explained as relative to some formal system? Or is there an extra-systematic idea that formal systems aim to represent? What has being valid got to do with being a good argument? How do formal logical systems help one to assess informal arguments? How like 'and' is '&', for instance, and what should one think of 'p' and 'q' as standing for? Is there one correct formal logic? and what might 'correct' mean here? How does one recognise a valid argument or a logical truth? Which formal systems count as logics, and why? Certain themes recur: concern with the scope and aims of logic, the relations between formal logic and informal argument, and the relations between different formal systems.

The sphere of the philosophy of logic is related to, but distinct from, that of metalogic. Metalogic is the study of formal properties of formal logical systems; it would include, for instance, proofs (or disproofs) of their consistency, completeness or decidability. Philosophy of logic likewise concerns itself with questions about formal logical systems – but with philosophical rather than purely formal questions. Take the relations between the standard, 2-valued, and many-valued sentence calculi as an example: the philosopher will want to know in what, if any, sense many-valued logics are alternatives to 2-valued logic; whether one is obliged to choose between many-valued and 2-valued calculi, and if so, on what grounds; what would be the consequences for the concept of truth if a many-valued system were adopted, and so forth. Metalogical results may well help one to answer questions of this kind: for instance, it is presumably a necessary, though not a sufficient condition of a many-valued logic's being a serious alternative, that it be consistent; and it may be pertinent to questions of their relative status that (most) many-valued logics are contained in 2-valued logic (i.e. that all their theorems are theorems in 2-valued logic, but not vice-versa). A second difference is that philosophy of logic is not wholly occupied with questions about formal logics; informal argument, and the relations between formal system and informal argument, are also within its sphere. The development of formal systems, indeed, greatly increases the depth and rigour of logical studies; but the study of informal argument is often an indispensable preliminary to such developments, and success in systematising informal arguments a test of their usefulness. It is pertinent that Frege, one of the pioneers of modern formal logic, was prompted to develop his *Begriffsschrift* (1879) because he needed a less ambiguous and cumbersome medium than German in which to give properly rigorous arithmetical proofs.

The locution 'philosophy of logic' is, I think, much to be preferred to 'philosophical logic', which is apt to convey the unfortunate impression that there is a peculiar, philosophical way of doing logic, rather than that there are peculiarly philosophical problems about logic. (I observe that, unlike 'philosophical logic', 'philosophical science' and 'philosophical mathematics' have never gained currency.) My examples have already shown, however, that philosophical interest attaches to the fact that there is not just one, but a plurality of formal logics; and so 'philosophy of logics' is, I hope, better yet.

2 The scope of logic

Among the problems of the philosophy of science are questions about the scope of science: what domains of knowledge (or 'knowledge') are to count as sciences? – for example, should alchemy, or astrology, or sociology, or psychology count as *bona fide* sciences? And what grounds could be given for including or excluding a given domain of inquiry? Similarly, among the problems of the philosophy of logic are questions about the scope of logic, and hence about the scope of the philosophy of logic: what is a logic? which formal systems are systems of logic? and what makes them so?[1]

Because I have to begin somewhere, I shall take for granted an intuitive idea of what it is to be a formal system. But I shall indicate what range of formal systems I have in mind when I speak of formal *logics*.

It is relevant to distinguish, at the outset, between *interpreted* and *uninterpreted* formal systems: uninterpreted, a formal system is just a collection of marks, and cannot, therefore, be identified as a formal logic rather than, say, a formalisation of a mathematical or physical theory. The claim of a formal system to be a logic depends, I think, upon its having an interpretation according to which it can be seen as aspiring to embody canons of valid argument: I count many-valued 'logics' as logics, for example, because they have interpretations according to which their values are 'truth-values', their variables sentences, their operators negation, conjunction etc. (They also have *other* interpretations – e.g. in terms of electrical circuits; the isomorphism between the logical and the electrical interpretations is relevant to the way computers work. See Rescher 1969 p. 61 for references.) So, in speaking of various formalisms as logics, I shall be making an implicit appeal to their usual interpretations.

In deciding which formalisms to count as logics I have adopted, for the present, the hospitable policy of giving the benefit of any doubt – subsequently, though, I shall give some attention to arguments why systems I have *included* ought to be *excluded*. One reason for this policy is that it lessens the danger of dismissing a formal system as 'not really a logic', when one ought to be asking seriously whether it is a good or useful system. I fear for instance that Quine (1970 ch. 5),

---

[1] The significance of such questions as these will, I hope, become increasingly apparent as the book proceeds. Readers who find this section hard going may prefer to return to it at the end of the book.

who excludes second-order predicate calculus because of what he takes to be its commitment to an ontology of abstract, intensional objects – properties – may have succumbed to this danger. (Similarly, I should distrust definitions of what it is for something to be a work of art which encouraged evasion of questions about *bad* works of art.) Anyway, as formal logics I shall include:

'traditional' logic – Aristotelian syllogistic

'classical' logic   – 2-valued sentence calculus
                         predicate calculus[1]

'extended' logics – modal logics
                         tense logics
                         deontic logics
                         epistemic logics
                         preference logics
                         imperative logics
                         erotetic (interrogative) logics

'deviant' logics   – many-valued logics
                         Intuitionist logics
                         quantum logics
                         free logics

'inductive' logics

The intention is to distinguish between formal logics and systems of, say, arithmetic or geometry, or axiomatisations of biology, physics and so forth. The demarcation is not based on any very profound ideas about 'the essential nature of logic' – indeed, I doubt that there is any such 'essential nature'. But it is not wholly arbitrary; it corresponds reasonably well, I hope, to what writers on philosophy of logic usually have in mind when they speak of 'logics'; and it has, at least, the following pragmatic rationale.

Those formal systems which are known as the 'standard' or 'classical' logic (and taught in courses in elementary formal logic) must surely count as logics if anything does. It then seems appropriate to admit also as logics those formal systems which are analogous to these. Among such 'analogous' systems I include: extensions of classical logic, systems, that is, that add new logical vocabulary ('necessarily' and 'possibly' in modal logics, 'it used to be the case

---

[1] In accordance with the 'benefit of the doubt' policy, I take this to include identity theory (i.e. axioms or rules for '=') and second-order predicate calculus (i.e. quantification binding 'F'...etc. as well as 'x'...etc.) besides first-order predicate calculus.

that' and 'it will be the case that' in tense logics, 'ought' and 'may' in deontic logics, 'knows' and 'believes' in epistemic logics, 'prefers' in preference logics) along with new axioms or rules for the new vocabulary, or which apply familiar logical operations to novel items (imperative or interrogative sentences); deviations of classical logic, i.e. systems with the same vocabulary but different (usually more restricted) axioms or rules; and inductive logics, which aim to formalise a notion of support analogous to, but weaker than, logical consequence. Their similarity to classical logic – not just formal similarity, but also similarity in purpose and intended interpretation – makes it natural to regard these systems as logics. (Alternatively, I could have begun with traditional Aristotelian logic, of which the modern 'classical' logic is an extension, and proceeded from there by a similar process of analogy.)

However, the idea of a system's being sufficiently similar to the classical logic is obviously pretty vague; and one might reasonably wonder whether the scope of logic could be delimited in some less pragmatic, and more precise, fashion.

The traditional idea that logic is concerned with the validity of arguments as such, irrespective, that is, of their subject-matter – that logic is, as Ryle neatly puts it, 'topic-neutral' – could be thought to offer a principle on which to delimit the scope of logic. On this account those systems which are *applicable to reasoning irrespective of its subject-matter* would count as logics. This idea is one with which I sympathise; I doubt, though, that it is really appreciably more precise than the notion of analogy to classical logic with which I began. What does it mean, first, to say that a formal system is 'applicable' to reasoning on such-and-such subject-matter? Presumably, that its principles are intended to be true of such reasoning. And now what is one to understand by 'irrespective of its subject-matter'? It could be suggested that while sentence and predicate calculi are indifferent to subject-matter, arithmetic, for example, is not topic-neutral because it is specifically about numbers; but this raises awkward questions about 'about' (is first-order predicate calculus 'about individuals'?). It is suggested, again, that logic applies to reasoning irrespective of its subject-matter because it is concerned with the *form* of arguments rather than their *content*. Again, I think, the idea is helpful, though it is still imprecise. How is one to distinguish between the form of an argument and its content? Tense logic is applicable to tensed sentences, imperative logic to imperative sentences, and the tense or mood of a sentence could, not implausibly, be regarded as a matter of its form rather than its content; but other cases are less straight-forward – the idea of form would need refinement before it was clear that a sentence's being about belief was a matter of form, but its being about numbers a matter of content, for example.

However, the vagueness of the idea of topic-neutrality and the related distinction between form and content isn't necessarily objec-tionable; as I said, I am doubtful that logic has a precisely specifiable 'essential character'. When I judged that modal logics, for example, are enough like classical logic to be included within the scope of logic, I was implicitly relying on the idea that the adverbs 'necessarily' and 'possibly' are topic-neutral enough to count as 'new *logical* vocabu-lary'. So the idea of topic-neutrality can certainly help to fortify one's intuitions about what formal systems are relevantly analogous to classical logic. It is also significant that where to draw the line between logics and other formal systems is more doubtful and more contro-versial in some cases than in others. For example: some mathematical theories, notably set theory, are very general in application, and seem to have strong affinities to logic; while epistemic or preference logics seem more specific as to subject-matter than the standard logical formalisms, and not to have quite so strong a claim to inclusion. Briefly, one gets more doubtful about the exclusion of a 'mathe-matical' formalism, the more general its application, and more doubt-ful about the inclusion of a 'logical' formalism, the less general its application; this suggests that topic-neutrality is vague *in the right way*.

These ideas will prove important subsequently. The distinction between form and content will receive some closer scrutiny when, in the next chapter, I discuss the thesis that the validity of an argument depends upon its form; and the idea that logic is characteristically topic-neutral will be relevant when, in ch. 12, I tackle the question of monism versus pluralism in logic, i.e. whether there is, so to speak, one correct logic, or whether different logics might each be appro-priate to different areas of discourse.

Sometimes a purely formal, metalogical criterion is suggested to demarcate logical from other formal systems. Kneale, for instance, urges that only *complete* systems be allowed within the scope of logic. The upshot of adopting such a criterion would be to restrict my hospitable list; since second-order predicate calculus is not complete in the usual sense, it would, by these standards, be excluded. This proposal has the advantage of precision; one is entitled to ask, though, what rationale it could have – why should completeness be the criterion of a system's being a logic? Kneale (1956 pp. 258–9) argues like this: the fact that a theory is incomplete shows that its basic concepts cannot be fully formalised, and this, in view of the essentially formal character of logic, justifies excluding such theories from its scope. So, interestingly, Kneale is proposing completeness as the test of a system's being 'purely formal'; he connects the precise idea of completeness with the vaguer notion of topic-neutrality. However, I fear that Kneale's argument may depend upon an equivocation over 'formal': the sense in which the incompleteness of set theory shows its basic concept, membership, not to be 'formal' is, simply, that that concept cannot be completely characterised by a set of axioms and rules which yield all the truths which involve it essentially; it is not obvious why it should be thought to follow that such a concept is not 'formal' in the sense that it belongs to the content rather than the form of arguments.

My feeling is that the prospects for a well-motivated formal criterion are not very promising (but cf. p. 19 n. below). Another example supports this hunch: if one placed particular weight on the role of logic as a guide to reasoning, as a means of assessment of informal arguments, one might see some point in requiring that logical systems be decidable, that there be a mechanical procedure for settling whether or not a formula is a theorem. But this would restrict the scope of logic very severely indeed, for though sentence calculus is decidable, predicate calculus is not.

It is notable that practically every non-standard 'logic' has, at some time, been subject to criticism on the ground that it isn't really a logic at all; which raises the suspicion that a restrictive view of the scope of logic may disguise a conservatism that would be questioned if it were more openly proclaimed.

Nevertheless, it may prove instructive to look at some arguments for excluding systems which, in accordance with the 'benefit of the doubt' policy, I have included. Dummett has urged (1973 pp. 285–8; and cf. Kneale and Kneale 1962 p. 610) that epistemic 'logics' aren't really logics, because belief and knowledge are ineradicably vague notions. It is true that an important element in the motivation for the formalisation of logic has been to increase precision, and consequently vagueness is normally to be avoided in the logician's choice of constants, though it is more debatable whether vagueness absolutely debars a concept from logical employment. Of course, the logician's treatment of 'not' or 'and' or 'or' or 'if' already involves a not inconsiderable tidying-up of informal negation, conjunction, etc. (cf. ch. 3 §2); the issue is not, I think, simply whether 'knows' and 'believes' are vague, but whether their vagueness is ineradicable, whether, that is, they *necessarily* resist regimentation. And it must be conceded that the epistemic logics to be found in the literature (cf. Hintikka 1962) are somewhat disappointing, and for a reason to which Dummett draws attention: that one is apt to find an axiom to the effect that if *s* believes that *p*, and *q* follows from *p*, then *s* believes that *q*. The ordinary, vague concept of belief, in other words, gets replaced by a logical understudy, perhaps called 'rational belief', which allows the construction of a formally interesting system, but quite severely limits its relevance to informal arguments about belief.

Others, again, Leśniewski for instance, have suggested that many-valued systems shouldn't really count as logics (see Rescher 1969 p. 215). It is true that some many-valued systems were devised and investigated out of purely formal interest, or for purposes of computer technology; but it is also true, and important, that such pioneers as Łukasiewicz and Bochvar quite clearly regarded themselves as presenting logical systems as alternatives to the classical apparatus. Still, the claim of a formal system to be a logic depends, I allowed, on its having a certain kind of interpretation; and a reason that might be given for excluding many-valued systems is that they require too radical a change in the theory of truth, or perhaps of truth-bearers, to be sufficiently analogous to classical, 2-valued logic. How much weight one gives to this kind of argument depends, obviously, on how radical one believes the effect of many-valuedness on the concept of truth to be (cf. Haack 1974 ch. 3 for relevant discussion).

I gave both epistemic and many-valued systems the benefit of the doubt about their status as logics. In each case, however, the doubts that are raised are based on considerations the relevance of which I concede: in the case of epistemic logics, the difficulty of eliminating the vagueness of the new operators; in the case of many-valued logics, the difficulty in supplying an appropriate interpretation of the new values. The relevance of these considerations is that they throw into question the strength of the analogy of epistemic or many-valued 'logics', in respect of purpose and interpretation, to classical logic. My inclination, nevertheless, is to admit these systems as logics, at the same time, of course, submitting their credentials as alternatives to classical logic to stringent scrutiny. This tolerance will help to counteract any conservatism inherent in the procedure of delineating logic by analogy with the classical systems.

What difference does it make, one might reasonably ask, exactly how one delimits the scope of logic? Sometimes the issue has been thought crucial to a philosophical thesis; the case of *logicism* provides an interesting example.

Logicism is the thesis (suggested by Leibniz, but worked out in detail by Frege) that arithmetic is reducible to logic: that is, that arithmetical statements can be expressed in purely logical terms, and arithmetical theorems can then be derived from purely logical axioms.[1] Given that a certain set of formulas can, in the sense explained, be reduced to a certain other set, whether this counts as 'reducing arithmetic to logic' will depend on whether the former set is allowed adequately to represent arithmetic, and whether the latter set is properly described as 'purely logical'. In the case of logicism, there is room for doubt on both scores. It may be urged that Gödel's incompleteness theorem shows that it is not possible to derive all the truths of arithmetic from any set of axioms, and so, *a fortiori*, not possible to derive them from any set of purely logical axioms. Or, more to the present point, it may be urged that the axioms to which Frege reduced the Peano postulates for arithmetic are not 'purely logical' but, since they include set-theoretical principles, mathematical. Quine, for example, urges (1970 pp. 64ff.) that set-theory should not be counted as part of logic. But his reasons are less than conclusive: he points out that there are alternative set-theories, but there are also alternative logics (cf. chs. 9–12 below); and he objects to the heavy ontological commitments which set-theory carries, but the criterion of ontological commitment he employs is open to question (see ch. 4 §2).

So here is a case when the fate of a philosophical theory seems to depend on the demarcation of logic. But isn't it rather dismaying to think that the truth of logicism should depend on so pragmatic a question as I have taken that of the scope of logic to be? Not, I think, once one goes a little deeper, and asks why it should be thought to

---

[1] Frege devised the first fully worked-out formal logical system as a preliminary, as he hoped, to establishing the truth of logicism by actually deriving the Peano postulates for arithmetic from his logical axioms. He developed the logical apparatus in 1879, supplied the appropriate logical definitions of arithmetical terms in 1884, and the derivations in 1893 and 1903; see Carnap 1931 for a straightforward introduction to the logicist philosophy of mathematics.

matter whether arithmetic is really purely logical. The really important issue is, or so it seems to me, obscured by putting the question as
if the scope of logic were the key point. Why did Frege think it was
important to show that arithmetic is reducible to logic? The motivation for logicism was at least in part epistemological; the principles
of logic, Frege thought, are self-evident, so that if the laws of arithmetic can be shown to be derivable from them, they are thereby
shown to be epistemologically secure – they acquire innocence by
association, so to speak. It turned out, however, that Frege's logic
(or 'logic') was inconsistent – Russell's paradox (cf. ch. 8) is derivable in it. Frege's response to the discovery of the inconsistency
was to concede that he'd never really thought that the relevant axiom
was *quite* as self-evident as the others – a comment which may well
induce a healthy scepticism about the concept of self-evidence. The
relevance of this story to present concerns, though, is this: that since
Frege's basis – logic or not – hasn't the epistemological standing he
thought, the epistemological point of his programme is lost regardless
of the decision about the demarcation of logic.

One thing, at least, should be quite clear by now: that whether or not
a formal system should count as a logic is itself a question which
involves quite deep and difficult philosophical issues. It is all to the
good that the pervasiveness of philosophical problems in logic be
evident at the outset. For the very rigour that is the chief virtue of
formal logic is apt, also, to give it an air of authority, as if it were above
philosophical scrutiny. And that is a reason, also, why I emphasise the
plurality of logical systems; for in deciding between alternatives one is
often obliged to acknowledge metaphysical or epistemological pre-
conceptions that might otherwise have remained implicit.

2

Validity

1 Assessing arguments

Arguments are assessed in a great many ways; some, for instance, are judged to be more persuasive or convincing than others, some to be more interesting or fruitful than others, and so forth. The kinds of assessment that can be made can be classified, in a rough and ready way, like this:
  (i)   logical: is there a connection of the appropriate sort between the premises and the conclusion?
  (ii) material: are the premises and conclusion true?
  (iii) rhetorical: is the argument persuasive, appealing, interesting to the audience?
I have given only the vaguest indication of the kinds of question characteristic of each dimension of assessment, but a rough indication should be adequate for present purposes. The separate category given to rhetorical considerations is not intended to suggest that the validity of an argument, or the truth of its premises, is quite irrelevant to its persuasiveness; it is intended, rather, to allow for the fact that, though if people were completely rational they would be persuaded only by valid arguments with true premises, in fact often enough they *are* persuaded by invalid arguments or arguments with false premises, and *not* persuaded by sound (cf. p. 14 below) arguments (see e.g. Thouless 1930, Stebbing 1939, Flew 1975, Geach 1976 for discussion of, and advice on how to avoid, such failures of rationality).

In what follows I shall be almost exclusively concerned with the first, logical, dimension of assessment. Within this dimension, in turn, I need to distinguish different standards of assessment which may be employed: an argument, that is, may be judged to be *deductively valid*, or *deductively invalid* but *inductively strong*, or neither. Deductive standards, as this indicates, and as we shall see in more detail later, are more stringent than inductive ones – the connection between premises and conclusion has to be, as it were, tighter for deductive validity than for inductive strength.[1]

Sometimes it is suggested (e.g. Barker 1965, Salmon 1967) that there are *two kinds of arguments*, deductive arguments, on the one hand, and inductive arguments, on the other. This 'distinction', at least as it is usually explained, only confuses matters. One is told that 'deductive arguments' are 'explicative' or 'non-ampliative', that is, they 'contain nothing in the conclusion not already contained in the premises'. If this is, as it seems to be, intended as an explanation of what it is for an argument to be *deductively valid*, it is apt to turn out either false, if 'contains nothing in the conclusion not already contained in the premises' is taken literally (for while 'A and B, so A' meets this condition, 'A, so $A \vee B$', which is also deductively valid, does not) or else trivial, if 'contains nothing in the conclusion not already contained in the premises' is taken metaphorically (for what is the test for '$A \vee B$' being *implicitly* 'contained in' 'A', if not that '$A \vee B$' follows deductively from 'A'?). 'Inductive arguments', by contrast, one is told, are 'ampliative' or 'non-explicative', that is to say, 'their conclusions go beyond what is contained in their premises'. This makes matters worse, because it cannot be taken, symmetrically with the explanation of 'deductive argument', as an explanation of what it is for an argument to be inductively strong. For all it says about inductive arguments is that they are not deductively valid; but not all deductively invalid arguments are inductively strong.

So I (with Skyrms, e.g. 1966 ch. 1) prefer to put the matter this way: it is not that there are two kinds of argument, but that arguments may be logically assessed by different, deductive or inductive, standards; they may be deductively valid, inductively strong, or neither. And this makes it clear what the next questions should be: What is an argument? What conditions must an argument meet if it is to count as deductively valid or inductively strong?

What is an argument? Well, one recognises that some stretches of discourse are intended as supporting a conclusion by means of premises, as arguing to a conclusion from premises; in informal dis-

---

[1] Some writers, notably Peirce and, more recently, Hanson, think there are other logical standards, 'abductive' standards, as well. Cf. Haack 1977b for some relevant discussion.

course in natural languages this intention may be signalled by marking the passage from one statement to another by means of such locutions as 'so', 'hence', 'it follows that', 'because' and so forth; in formal logic, by the presentation of a string of formulae with an indication on each line that it is claimed to follow by such-and-such a rule of inference from such-and-such a previous line or lines. What one judges to be valid or invalid, though, can be thought of simply as a stretch of discourse: if one is considering formal argument, a sequence of wffs of a formal language, or, if one is considering informal argument, a sequence of sentences (or perhaps statements or propositions; cf. ch. 6) of natural language. (Similarly, some of the things people say are intended assertively – the speaker means to claim their truth – and others are not; but it is *what is said* that is true or false.)

2 Deductive validity: with some brief comments about inductive strength
Validity in a system

Within a formal logical system, validity can be defined both syntactically and semantically, i.e. in terms of the axioms or rules of the system, and in terms of its interpretation. I will represent a formal argument as a sequence of well-formed formulae (i.e. grammatical sentences of a formal language; hereafter 'wffs') $A_1 \ldots A_{n-1}, A_n,$ ($n \geqslant 1$) of which $A_1 \ldots A_{n-1}$ are the premises, and A_n the conclusion. *Syntactic validity* can then be explained along the following lines:

> $A_1 \ldots A_{n-1}, A_n$ is valid-in-L just in case A_n is derivable from $A_1 \ldots A_{n-1}$, and the axioms of L, if any, by the rules of inference of L.

This is usually represented: $A_1 \ldots A_{n-1} \vdash_L A_n$.
Semantic validity can be explained along the following lines:

> $A_1 \ldots A_{n-1}, A_n$ is valid-in-L just in case A_n is true in all interpretations in which $A_1 \ldots A_{n-1}$ are true.

This is usually represented: $A_1 \ldots A_{n-1}, \vDash_L A_n$.
The 'L' in '$\vdash_L$' and '$\vDash_L$' serves to remind one that both these conceptions of validity are *system-relative*.

Corresponding to the syntactic and semantic ideas of validity of sequences of wffs are the ideas of theoremhood and logical truth, respectively, of wffs. You may have noticed that I allowed the possibility of arguments consisting of just one wff (sometimes these are

called 'zero-premise conclusions'). If the ideas of validity just
sketched are applied to this special case, the upshot is:

> A is valid-in-L (is a *theorem* of L) just in case A follows
> from the axioms of L, if any, by the rules of inference
> of L ($\vdash_L A$)

and

> A is valid-in-L (is a *logical truth* of L) just in case A is
> true in all interpretations of L ($\vDash_L A$).

I have represented theoremhood and logical truth as, as it were,
special cases of, respectively, syntactic and semantic validity. It would
also have been possible to approach the matter the other way round,
and explain validity as theoremhood of the corresponding conditional.
The former approach has the advantage of stressing logic's concern
with the connection between premises and conclusion, which is why
I chose it.

How do the syntactic and semantic ideas fit together? Well, one
naturally aspires to have a formal system in which just those wffs
which are syntactically valid are semantically valid (soundness[1] and
completeness results show that theoremhood and logical truth
coincide).

Extra-systematic validity

The conceptions of validity, syntactic and semantic, considered thus far, are system-relative and apply only to formal arguments. What is going on, though, when one judges an informal
argument to be valid? One is claiming, I take it, that its conclusion
follows from its premises, that *its premises couldn't be true and its
conclusion false*. (If, besides being valid, an argument has true
premises – and so, being valid, true conclusion too – it is said to be
sound.) When, intuitively, we judge some ordinary, informal arguments good and others bad, something like this conception of validity
is probably being deployed. Of course, judging an argument 'good' is
apt to involve *more* than judging it valid; but we recognise that
validity is an important, though not the only, virtue of an argument.

The question arises, whether there is also an informal, extra-
systematic conception corresponding to the system-relative notions
of theoremhood and logical truth. I think that there is, though I sus-

---

[1] A different sense of 'sound', applying not to logical systems but to
arguments, will be defined below.

pect that it is somewhat less developed and central than the extra-systematic idea of validity (another reason for treating logical truth as a special case of validity rather than vice-versa). The extra-systematic idea of a valid argument as one such that its premises couldn't be true and its conclusion false, adapted to the case of a single statement (as the formal definitions were adapted to the case of 'zero-premise conclusions') yields the notion of a statement that couldn't be false – the notion, in other words, of a necessary truth. And something like this idea is indeed to be found at the informal level. For example, one judges that some statements are 'tautologous'; this, in the non-technical sense, means that those statements are trivially true, they just (as the etymology of 'tautologous' suggests) say the same thing twice, and consequently they couldn't be false. The informal notion of a tautology, of course, is broader than the technical usage, which includes only logical truths of *truth-functional* logic. And the informal idea of a necessary truth is also broader than the formal idea of a logical truth (cf. ch. 10 § 1). It should occasion no great surprise that these informal conceptions have themselves been refined with the development and study of formal logical systems.

But what is one to say of the connection between the system-relative conceptions of validity, applicable to formal arguments, and the extra-systematic conception, applicable to informal arguments? Something like this: formal logical systems aim to formalise informal arguments, to represent them in precise, rigorous and generalisable terms; and an acceptable formal logical system ought to be such that, if a given informal argument is represented in it by a certain formal argument, then that formal argument should be valid in the system just in case the informal argument is valid in the extra-systematic sense.

Logica utens and logica docens
In fact, there is likely to be a quite complex process of adjustment. One may begin to develop a formal system on the basis of intuitive judgments of the extra-systematic validity of informal arguments, representing those arguments in a symbolic notation, and devising rules of inference in such a way that the formal representations of informal arguments judged (in)valid would be (in)valid in the system. Given these rules, though, other formal arguments will turn out to be valid in the system, perhaps formal arguments which represent informal arguments intuitively judged invalid; and then one may

revise the rules of the system, or one may, instead, especially if the rule is agreeably simple and plausible and the intuition of informal invalidity not strong, revise one's opinion of the validity of the informal argument, or else one's opinion of the appropriateness of representing that informal argument in this particular way. And once a formal logical system becomes well-established, of course, it is likely that it will in turn tutor one's intuitions about the validity or invalidity of informal arguments. Following Peirce (who in turn borrowed the terminology from the medieval logicians) one may call one's unreflective judgment of the validity of informal arguments the *logica utens*, the more rigorous and precise judgments developed as, through reflection on these judgments, formal systems are devised, the *logica docens*. The picture is somewhat like fig. 1.

logica utens	*logica docens*
informal arguments	formal arguments

symbolic
representation
of informal
argument

extra-systematic	system-relative
validity	validity

Fig. 1

Some writers have doubts about the adequacy of the extra-systematic conception of validity as I explained it above. What, specifically, they object to in the idea that an argument is valid if it is impossible for its premises to be true and its conclusion false, is the 'and'. On this account, if the premises of an argument are impossible, or if its conclusion is necessary, then, since *a fortiori* it is impossible that its premises should be true *and* its conclusion false, that argument is valid; and this is so, of course, even if its premises are quite irrelevant to its conclusion. Proponents of 'relevance logic' therefore challenge this conception of validity; and because of this challenge they urge the adoption of a non-classical formal logic which requires relevance of premises to conclusion (see Anderson and Belnap 1975 §22.2.1, and cf. ch. 10 §7); so their dissatisfaction with the usual informal conception of validity is intimately connected with their challenge to classical logic. (Conventionally, considerations of relevance are apt to be relegated to the rhetorical rather than the logical dimension of assessment of arguments.)

Inductive strength

Inductive strength could be characterised, syntactically or semantically, relatively to formal systems of inductive logic. However, since there is no formal system of inductive logic which has anything approaching the kind of entrenchment that classical deductive logic enjoys, the extra-systematic idea has, in the case of inductive strength, an especially central role. The idea is that an argument is inductively strong if its premises give a certain degree of support, even if less than conclusive support, to its conclusion: if, that is, it is *improbable* that its premises should be true and its conclusion false. (Notice that if one puts it this way all deductively valid arguments would count as inductively strong; deductive validity will be a limit case of inductive strength, where the probability of the premises' being true and the conclusion false is zero.)

It is worthy of notice, however, that in his characterisation of the extra-systematic idea of inductive strength Skyrms (1966 pp. 9–11) insists on the formulation: 'it is improbable, *given that* the premises are true, that the conclusion is false', because he doesn't want to allow that the high probability of its conclusion or the low probability of its premises should be sufficient, of themselves, for the inductive strength of an argument. Significantly, then, his view of inductive strength is closely analogous to the relevance logicians' conception of deductive validity.[1]

3 Formal logical systems: the 'L' in 'valid-in-L'

I distinguished, above, system-relative conceptions of validity applicable to formal arguments and an extra-systematic conception applicable to informal arguments. An adequate account of the former – of validity-in-L – will obviously require some explanation of how one identifies and individuates formal systems. The problem may be illustrated by considering the sentence logic to be found in, say, *Principia Mathematica* (Russell and Whitehead 1910) and *Beginning Logic* (Lemmon 1965): if one was concerned with the difference

---

[1] Notoriously, of course, there is a problem about the justification of induction. Nothing in what I have said shows that there *are* any arguments which are (deductively invalid but) inductively strong. In fact, I think that deduction and induction are more symmetrical than is generally supposed; cf. Haack 1976a.

between two-valued and many-valued logics, one would naturally regard them as alternative formulations of the *same* (two-valued) system, whereas if one was concerned with the contrast between axiomatic and natural deduction techniques (see below, p. 19), one might take them as examples of *different* systems.

For the sake of having some suitably neutral terminology, I shall call a specific presentation of a system a 'formulation' of a logical system. Now, differences between formulations are of two main kinds: differences in vocabulary, and differences in axioms and/or rules of inference. I shall first sketch some significant differences between formulations, and then offer two accounts of 'the same system', one broader and one narrower.

Notational variants

Typographically different expressions may be used for the same operations (e.g. for the same truth-functions). Among the commonest current notational variants one finds:

for negation:	$-p$, $\sim p$, $\bar{p}$, Np
for disjunction:	$p \vee q$, Apq
for conjunction:	$p \,\&\, q$, $p \cdot q$, $p \wedge q$, Kpq
for material implication:	$p \rightarrow q$, $p \supset q$, Cpq
for material equivalence:	$p \equiv q$, $p \leftrightarrow q$, $p \sim q$, Epq
for universal quantification:	(x), $(\forall x)$, Λx, Πx
for existential quantification:	$(\exists x)$, (Ex), Vx, Σx

The last notation, in each case, is Polish notation, which has the advantage of being bracket-free; operators precede the formulae they govern, and scope is determined without brackets.

Alternative primitive constants

Different sets of constants are equivalent in expressive power; e.g. '&' and ' — ' or '∨' and ' — ' to express 2-valued truth-functions, '(∃x)' and ' — ' or '(x)' and ' — ' for existential and universal quantification. Some formulations take e.g. '&' and ' — ' as primitive and define '∨' and '→'; others take '∨' and ' — ' as primitive and define '&' and '→', and so forth. *Principia Mathematica*, for example, has only negation and disjunction as primitive, whereas *Beginning Logic* has negation, disjunction, conjunction and material implication.

Axiomatic and natural deduction formulations

An axiomatic system of logic (e.g. *Principia Mathematica*) includes, besides one or more rules of inference, a privileged set of wffs, the axioms, which may be used at any point in an argument, and the truth of which is unquestioned in the system. The axioms are included among the theorems of the system, since, trivially, they are derivable from themselves. (An axiomatic system must have at least one rule of inference, since no derivations or proofs would be possible without the means to move from one wff to another.)

A natural deduction formulation (e.g. *Beginning Logic*), by contrast, relies just on rules of inference. (A rule of assumptions will enable one to get started without the need of axioms from which to begin.) It is worth observing that natural deduction rules have an indirect, even quasi-metalogical character; consider the rule of vel elimination: if you have derived C from assumption A (plus possibly other assumptions) and derived C from assumption B (plus possibly other assumptions), you may derive C from the assumption that $A \vee B$ (plus any other assumptions used in deriving C from A and from B).[1]

Sometimes axioms not known to be true, or even known to be false, are adopted simply with the aim of investigating their consequences. A famous example comes from the history of geometry. Saccheri took the contradictory of Euclid's parallel postulate as an axiom, hoping to show that the result was an inconsistent system, and hence, that the parallel postulate was deducible from Euclid's other axioms. Since this postulate is actually independent of the others, he didn't succeed in this aim. (Cf. the discussion of Prior's rules of inference for '*tonk*', ch. 3 §2.)

The very same valid arguments and theorems can be generated either axiomatically or by means of natural deduction rules: by the axioms of *Principia Mathematica* or the rules of *Beginning Logic*, for instance. But, of course, this is not to say that the difference between natural deduction and axiomatic techniques is of no significance. Kneale for example argues (1956 §4) that natural deduction formulations better reflect the central concern of logic with the validity of

---

[1] Cf. Blanché 1962 and Prawitz 1965 for detailed discussion of, respectively, axiomatic and natural deduction techniques. The pioneer natural deduction presentation, in Gentzen 1934, includes one axiom. Gentzen also devised a metalogical calculus, the sequent calculus; see Hacking 197+ for an interesting attempt to demarcate the scope of logic formally by reference to the sequent calculus.

arguments. An unfortunate effect of the axiomatic formulation of the *Begriffsschrift* and *Principia*, Kneale suggests, was a shift of attention from validity of arguments to logical truth of wffs. And Blumberg suggests (1967 p. 24) that natural deduction formulations highlight the difference between formal logic and other formal theories, such as geometry or biology, say, which require special axioms relating to their special subject matter, over and above a common basis of logical rules of inference. I agree in stressing logic's concern with arguments, and I agree that with natural deduction presentations of formal logic this concern is thrown into relief. However, since validity of arguments and logical truth of formulae are intimately connected, an axiomatic formulation needn't necessarily distort one's perspective. (Carnap 1934 points out that one can think of axioms as rather peculiar rules of inference, to the effect that one may infer the given wff from any premises or none at all.) And the distinction between logical and other formal systems needn't be lost in an axiomatic presentation of logic, either, since there remains room for a distinction between *logical* and *proper* (i.e. geometrical, biological or whatever) axioms. It is pertinent that some instrumentalist philosophers of science have urged that one regard scientific laws rather as rules than as axioms.

Alternative axioms and/or rules

If two formulations are notational variants, their axioms and/or rules will differ at least typographically; again, if they take different constants as primitive, each will, usually, employ its primitive constants in its axioms and/or rules. (Sometimes, though, a system is formulated in such a way that defined constants appear in the axioms/rules; in *Principia* only '$-$' and '$\vee$' are primitive, but '$\to$' also appears in the axioms.)

Some formulations employ *axiom schemata* rather than axioms and a substitution rule. The difference is that between having, say, the axiom:

$$(p \to q) \to ((q \to r) \to (p \to r))$$

and the rule that any substitution instance of an axiom is a theorem, and having the schema:

$$(A \to B) \to ((B \to C) \to (A \to C))$$

where the use of the 'metavariables' 'A', 'B', 'C' indicates that no matter what wff of the language is put for these letters, the resulting wff is an axiom.

Quite apart from divergences of notation and presentation already mentioned, different formulations may simply have different sets of axioms/rules, even when notational differences are allowed for: their sets of axioms/rules may overlap or even be entirely distinct. As an example, compare Mendelson's and Meredith's axiom schemata, both in '−' and '→', for 2-valued sentence calculus:

Mendelson's set:
1. $(A \to (B \to A))$
2. $((A \to (B \to C)) \to ((A \to B) \to (A \to C)))$
3. $((-B \to -A) \to ((-B \to A) \to B))$

Meredith's:
1. $((((A \to B) \to (-C \to -D)) \to C) \to E) \to$
$$((E \to A) \to (D \to A))$$

(And see Prior 1955 pp. 301ff., Mendelson 1964 pp. 40–1 for alternative axiom sets.)

The example just given is of alternative axiom sets for the 2-valued sentence calculus; the alternative formulations yield just the same sets of theorems and valid inferences. Another way in which formulations may differ is that they may result in different theorems or valid inferences; for example, Intuitionist sentence logic lacks some classical theorems, including double negation and excluded middle.

At this point I have sufficient material to return to my original problem, when to treat alternative formulations as formulations *of the same system*. I shall suggest two accounts of 'the same system', one broader and one narrower, each suitable for certain purposes.

The narrower sense: L_1 and L_2 are alternative formulations of the same system if they have the *same axioms and/or rules of inference* once allowance has been made for differences of notation (e.g. replacing '&' by '.') and of primitive constants (e.g. replacing '$p \mathbin{\&} q$' by '$-(-p \lor -q)$').

The broader sense: L_1 and L_2 are alternative formulations of the same system if they have the *same theorems and valid inferences* once allowance has been made for differences of notation and of primitive constants.

An example: the formulations of *Principia Mathematica* and of

Beginning Logic are formulations of different systems in the narrower sense (one has axioms plus *modus ponens*, the other only rules of inference) but of the same system in the broader sense (they generate the same theorems and inferences).

These two senses of 'same system' will help, I hope, to reconcile some conflicting intuitions. The narrower of these senses seems suitable to use in the definitions of validity-in-L, whereas the broader will be more useful in contrasting, for example, 2-valued and many-valued logics. An advantage of the narrower sense for the account of validity is that it avoids a circle which otherwise threatens, in which 'theorem' and 'valid inference' are defined relatively to a system, and 'system' relatively to sets of theorems and valid inferences.

The narrower sense will also be useful for the discussion of inconsistent formulations. Since, except in some unconventional systems, anything whatever follows from a contradiction, in virtue of the theorem '$A \rightarrow (-A \rightarrow B)$', all inconsistent systems will count as the same system in the broader sense. The narrower sense enables one to respect the intuition that some but not all inconsistent formulations are nevertheless of considerable philosophical interest; an example would be Frege's, in which Russell's paradox is a theorem.

4   Validity and logical form

One cannot tell whether an informal argument is (in the extra-systematic sense) valid merely by investigating the truth-values of its premises and conclusion. If the argument has true premises and false conclusion, that shows that it is *in*valid; but if it has true premises and true conclusion, or false premises and true conclusion, or false premises and false conclusion, that doesn't show that it's valid. For it is valid only if it *couldn't* have, not just *doesn't* have, true premises and false conclusion. A technique that is often useful to show that an argument is invalid, even though, as it happens, it doesn't have true premises and false conclusion, is to find another argument *which is of the same form* and which does have true premises and false conclusion. For example, to show that: 'Either Gödel's proof is invalid, or arithmetic is incomplete, so arithmetic is incomplete', though it has true premise and true conclusion, is nevertheless invalid, it could be pointed out that the structurally similar argument: 'Either $7 + 5 = 12$ or dogs meow, so dogs meow' has true premise and false conclusion. This, of course, is a better method of showing invalidity than of showing validity; if one can't find an argument of the same form with true premises and false conclusion, that isn't conclusive proof that an argument is valid (cf. Massey 1974).

What one seeks, to show an argument is invalid, is a *structurally similar* argument with true premises and false conclusion; and this suggests that there is some truth in the dictum that arguments are valid or invalid 'in virtue of their form'. And formal logical systems are devised to represent in a schematic, generalised way the structure which we judge to be shared by a group of informal arguments, and to be the basis of their validity or invalidity. This is apt to suggest, in turn, a picture of informal arguments as having a unique, recognisable structure, as composed, as it were, of a skeleton, the expressions which constitute its form, clothed in flesh, the expressions which constitute its content; and of the formal logician as simply devising symbols to represent the 'logical constants', the structural components. But this oversimplifies. A better picture, I think, is this. One recognises structural similarities between informal arguments, similarities characteristically marked by the occurrence of certain expressions, such as 'and' or 'unless' or 'every'. (But one shouldn't expect each informal argument necessarily to have a unique place in this pattern.) The formal logician selects, from among the expressions whose occurrence marks structural similarities, those which (for various reasons, truth-functionality, for instance; cf. ch. 3 §2) are promising candidates for formal treatment.

This picture – sketchy as it is – already begins to explain why it should be that attempts to specify which expressions of English should be counted as 'logical constants' should have a tendency to conclude with a somewhat uncomfortable admission that not all suitably 'topic-neutral' expressions (Ryle 1954), not all the expressions which seem to be essential to the validity of informal arguments (von Wright 1957) are represented in the symbolism of formal logic; for instance, 'several' is as topic-neutral as, and may be as essential to an argument as, 'all'; the formal logicians' equipment includes an analogue of the latter but not of the former. Compare Quine's enumeration of the logical constants: ' . . . basic particles such as "is", "not", "and", "or", "unless", "if", "then", "neither", "nor", "some", "all", etc.' (1940 p. 1); it is notable that the list comprises just those English expressions that can comfortably be represented within the classical sentence and predicate calculi, and that it excludes 'necessarily' and 'possibly', for instance, no doubt because of Quine's scepticism about the intelligibility of modal logic. The 'etc.', of course, helps not at all, since one is given no indication what would count as a permissible addition to the list.

The relation between informal arguments and their formal representations is, as this would lead one to expect, not straightforwardly one–one. An informal argument may be appropriately represented in different ways in different formalisms; for instance:

> Every natural number is either greater than or equal to zero, and every natural number is either odd or even, so every natural number is either greater than or equal to zero and either odd or even

could be correctly represented in sentence calculus as:

$$\frac{p}{q}$$

and in predicate calculus as:

$$\frac{(x)\,Fx\,\&\,(x)\,Gx}{(x)\,(Fx\,\&\,Gx)}$$

(Notice that the availability of alternative representations needn't depend upon any ambiguity in the original, though if an informal argument *is* ambiguous that will naturally mean that it has more than one formal representation; cf. Anscombe's splendidly ambiguous 'if you can eat any fish, you can eat any fish'.)

'p, so q' is invalid, but '$(x)Fx\,\&\,(x)Gx$, so $(x)\,(Fx\,\&\,Gx)$' is valid; and since the latter reveals more of the structure of the original, informal argument than the former one might be tempted to think that the best formal representation will be the one that exhibits the most structure. But my informal argument can be represented, again in the symbolism of predicate calculus, with further structure revealed, as:

$$\frac{(x)\,(Fx\,\vee\,Gx)\,\&\,(x)\,(Hx\,\vee\,Ix)}{(x)\,((Fx\,\vee\,Gx)\,\&\,(Hx\,\vee\,Ix))}$$

It is clear that there is a sense in which this exhibits more structure than one needs; it is preferable to think of the optimal formal representation as the one which reveals the least structure consistently with supplying a formal argument which is valid in the system if the informal argument is judged extra-systematically valid. This is Quine's *maxim of shallow analysis* (1960a p. 160): 'where it doesn't itch, don't scratch'.

In the interplay between *logica utens* and *logica docens*, I suggested (p. 16), one may judge it worthwhile to sacrifice pre-formal judgments of validity to smoothness of formal theory, or modify one's formal theory to accommodate assessments of informal arguments, or – and it is this point I want to pursue here – to revise one's view of the appropriate way to represent an informal argument in formal logic. One criterion by which one judges whether an informal argument is correctly represented by a given formal argument is that intuitive judgments of validity be respected. For example, one's confidence that 'Somebody is Prime Minister and somebody is Queen, so the Prime Minister is Queen' is invalid would lead one to resist representing it by a formal argument valid in predicate calculus, as:

$$a = b$$
$$\frac{a = c}{b = c}$$

and to require something like the invalid:

$$\frac{(\exists x)\ Fx\ \&\ (\exists x)\ Gx}{(\imath x)\ Fx = (\imath x)\ Gx}$$

If, on the other hand, one judges an informal argument to be valid, one will seek a representation by means of a valid formal argument. For example, within the confines of the standard predicate calculus, adverbially modified predicates are normally represented by means of new predicate letters, so an argument like:

The President signed the treaty with a red pen.
So, the President signed the treaty.

would be represented as:

$$\frac{Fa}{Ga}$$

where 'a' represents 'the President', 'F' represents 'signed the treaty with a red pen' and 'G', 'signed the treaty'. This, of course, is an invalid argument in predicate calculus; and so, in view of the presumed validity of the original, informal argument, it has been urged that some more perspicuous means of representing adverbial modification, which does not simply obliterate the logical connection between an adverbially modified predicate and its unmodified form, be devised. Davidson, for example (1968a), proposes a representation along the lines of:

$$\frac{(\exists x)\ (x \text{ was a signing of the treaty by the President}}{(\exists x)\ (x \text{ was a signing of the treaty by the President})} \text{ and } x \text{ was with a red pen)}}$$

which, like the original, is valid. Notice that this supplies the original argument with a representation within the standard predicate calculus by quantifying over events and treating adverbs as predicates of events; another possibility would be to extend the standard formalism, e.g. by the addition of predicate operators to represent adverbs. In the case of modal adverbs, 'necessarily' and 'possibly', this kind of extension of the vocabulary of formal logic has already taken place.

Some philosophers of logic have urged the claims of a neater picture, according to which each informal argument has a unique logical form – perhaps not immediately recognisable – which the correct symbolic representation will exhibit. Such a view was held, for instance, by Wittgenstein and by Russell during their logical atomist periods (see e.g. Russell 1918, Wittgenstein 1922; and cf. comments on Russell's theory of descriptions in ch. 4 §3); for they aspired to devise a unique, ideally perspicuous language in which logical form would be perfectly exhibited. More recently, Davidson has taken a similar stance: for Davidson, the logical form of an argument is its representation in a formal language for which truth can be defined in accordance with the constraints imposed by Tarski's theory (ch. 7 §5). Russell thought that the grammatical form of a sentence was apt to be misleading as to its logical form; some recent writers, impressed by Chomsky's postulation of a deep grammatical structure underlying, but perhaps quite different from, surface grammatical structure (see Chomsky 1957), have suggested that the logical form of an argument could be identified with its deep grammatical structure (see e.g. Harman 1970). The relevant deep grammatical/logical structure would have, presumably, to be universal as between languages, since otherwise one would be in danger of allowing that an argument could be, say, valid in Hebrew but invalid in Hindi; and it is, to my mind, doubtful whether one is entitled to expect that linguists will eventually discover a sufficiently rich, universal, grammatical structure. So I cannot be altogether optimistic about the prospects for this – admittedly gratifyingly tidy –

picture. But nonetheless I see no reason for dismay at the inter-dependence between intuitive, informal judgments of validity, hunches as to the essential structural features of informal arguments, and the development of formal logical systems. Rather, one might even feel some satisfaction at the way this explains why the central questions in philosophy of logic should cluster around the issue of the fit between informal arguments and their formal representations: an issue which, with respect to connectives, quantifiers and singular terms, the next three chapters will investigate more thoroughly.

3

Sentence connectives

1 Formal considerations

I shall begin by sketching some important formal features of the sentence connectives, and proceed to a consideration of some philosophical questions about the meanings of the connectives.

Adequate sets of connectives: functional completeness

The connectives – '$-$', '&', '$\vee$', '$\rightarrow$', and '$\equiv$' – of classical sentence calculus are truth-functional: the truth-value of a compound sentence formed by means of them depends only on the truth-values of its components. A set of connectives is *adequate* if it can express all truth-functions. There are 16 (2^{2^2}) 2-valued truth-functions of two arguments.[1] Each of the sets $\{-, \rightarrow\}$, $\{-, \vee\}$, $\{-, \&\}$, $\{|\}$, and $\{\downarrow\}$ ('$A|B$' is 'not both A and B' and '$A{\downarrow}B$' is 'neither A nor B') is adequate to express them all. A formal system is *functionally complete* if it has an adequate set of connectives. For instance, *Principia*, with '$-$' and '$\vee$' as primitive, is functionally complete, whereas the implicational fragment of sentence calculus, with '$\rightarrow$' alone, is not. Many formulations – e.g. Lemmon 1965 – have more connectives than are needed for functional completeness. It is because there are alternative adequate sets of connectives that one has formulations of sentence calculus with different sets of primitives. Given any adequate set, the other connectives can be defined. For example, with '$-$' and '$\rightarrow$' as

[1] *viz*:

A	B	1	2	3	4	5	6	7	8	9	10	11	12	13	14	15	16
t	t	t	t	t	t	t	t	t	t	t	f	f	f	f	f	f	f
t	f	t	t	t	t	f	f	f	f	t	t	t	t	f	f	f	f
f	t	t	t	f	f	t	t	f	f	t	t	f	f	t	t	f	f
f	f	t	f	t	f	t	f	t	f	t	f	t	f	t	f	t	f

primitive, '$A \vee B$' can be defined as '$-A \to B$', and then '$A \& B$' as '$-(-A \vee -B)$'; with '$|$' or '$\downarrow$' primitive '$-A$' can be defined as '$A|A$' or '$A\downarrow A$'. Some formulations employ a constant, 'F', which is always to have the value f, and define '$-A$' as '$A \to F$'. In each case the correctness of the definitions can be checked by comparing the truth-tables of *definiens* and *definiendum* and observing that they correspond to the same truth-function.

Characteristic matrices: decidability

A matrix, or set of truth-tables, M, is *characteristic* for a system S iff all and only the theorems of S are designated on M, and all and only the valid inferences of S are designation-preserving in M. Any value may be designated, but usually the point is to designate the 'truth-like' value, or, perhaps, in the case of many-valued logics, values; in 2-valued logic, of course, 't' is designated. A wff is designated on M iff it takes a designated value whatever assignment is made to its atomic parts; a rule, from $A \ldots A_n$ to infer B, is designation-preserving iff B takes a designated value whenever all of $A \ldots A_n$ do. For example, the 2-valued truth-tables are characteristic for classical sentence calculus.

Finite truth-tables provide a *decision procedure*, that is, a mechanical method for determining, for any wff of the system, whether it is a theorem.

Many-valued logic

Of course, it would be possible to devise many-valued matrices characteristic for 2-valued sentence calculus. I call 2-valued sentence logic '2-valued' rather than 'many-valued' because this is the smallest number of values which can supply a characteristic matrix. By an 'n-valued logic' I shall understand a system which has a characteristic matrix with n values and no characteristic matrix with m values for $m < n$. Some of the systems I referred to as 'deviant' have finite characteristic matrices; not unexpectedly, one motivation for devising such systems has been the belief that some sentences within the scope of logic are neither true nor false, but either are truth-valueless, or, perhaps, have an intermediate truth-value: a belief which will receive closer attention in ch. 11. Other deviant systems, such as Intuitionist and some quantum logics, have no finite but only infinite characteristic matrices. In what follows, 'many-valued logic' will mean 'n-valued logic for $2 < n < \infty$', except when I specifically speak of *infinitely* many-valued systems.

In an n-valued logic, any given place in a truth-table can be occupied by any of n values, so, since the truth-table for a k-place connective has n^k entries, the number of truth-functions of k arguments in an n-valued logic will be n^{n^k} – a number which increases enormously with small increases in n. Łukasiewicz's 3-valued logic, with ' $-$ ', ' $\&$ ', ' $\vee$ ', ' $\rightarrow$ ' and ' $\equiv$ ', is functionally incomplete; Słupecki showed that it becomes functionally complete with the addition of a new 1-place connective T (for '*tertium*') such that 'TA' takes the intermediate value whatever the value of 'A'. As is to be expected, the familiar interdefinability relations are apt to break down in many-valued logic; for example, in Łukasiewicz's 3-valued logic '$A \vee B$' does not, as in 2-valued logic, have the same truth-table as '$-A \rightarrow B$'; it can be defined, instead, as '$(A \rightarrow B) \rightarrow B$'.

2   The meanings of the connectives
Formal languages and informal readings

One can look at the sentence calculus from, as it were, four levels:

(i)   the axioms/rules of inference
(ii) the formal interpretation (matrices)
(iii) the ordinary language readings of (i)
(iv) the informal explanation of (ii)

(i) is the level of syntax; levels (ii) and (iv) are dubbed by Plantinga 1974 pp. 126–8 'pure' and 'depraved' semantics, respectively. Levels (i) and (ii), being formal, are agreeably manageable; but levels (iii) and (iv), though trickier, are no less important. I observed in ch. 1 that the identification of a system as a system of logic requires appeal to its (intended?) interpretation. To identify a system as a sentence calculus one does not only need to know the axioms/rules and their formal interpretation by means of matrices; one also needs to know that the values are to represent truth and falsity, the letters 'p', 'q', etc. to represent sentences, ' $-$ ' negation, '$\&$' conjunction, '$\vee$' disjunction, and so forth. One's understanding of the connectives must presumably derive somehow from some or all of these levels.

One's view about how the connectives get their meaning will affect one's attitude to a number of issues. For instance, it has been held that the connectives in deviant logics differ in meaning from the typographically identical connectives of classical logic, so that when a deviant logician denies '$A \vee -A$', say, what he denies is not, contrary to appearances, what the classical logician asserts when he asserts '$A \vee -A$'. One argument for this 'meaning-variance' thesis (cf. ch. 12 §1) would be that the meaning of the connectives is given simply by the axioms/rules and/or matrices of the system (levels (i) and (ii)), from which it follows that the connectives of a many-valued logic must differ in meaning from those of 2-valued logic, since the axioms/rules and the matrices differ. Another dispute concerns the appropriateness of the English readings of the connectives, how accurately, for instance, 'and' represents '&', or 'if', '$\rightarrow$'. What seems to be at issue here is whether the axioms/rules are true/truth-preserving, and the matrices correct, if thought of as characterising the English expressions used as readings: whether, since '$A \& B$' takes t iff 'A' takes t and 'B' takes t, 'A and B' is true iff 'A' is true and 'B' is true. This in turn raises another question: does it matter if there is a discrepancy?

'*tonk*'

Prior has argued that the meanings of the connectives cannot derive from the axioms/rules of the system in which they appear, nor from their truth-tables, but must be given by their English readings. (If he were right, of course, the 'meaning-variance' view of many-valued logics, mentioned above, would be refuted.) Prior (1960, 1964) presents a purported *reductio ad absurdum* of the thesis that there are 'analytically valid inferences', inferences, that is, the validity of which arises solely from the meanings of the logical constants contained in them. According to this thesis, the inference from '$A \& B$' to 'A' is analytically valid, for the meaning of '&' is completely given by the rules of inference of &-introduction and &-elimination. Prior argues that 'in this sense of "analytically valid" any statement may be inferred, in an analytically valid way, from any other statement' (1960 p. 130). Suppose the meaning of '*tonk*' to be given by the rules of inference:

> (T1) from 'A' to infer 'A *tonk* B' ('*tonk*-introduction')
> (T2) from 'A *tonk* B' to infer 'B' ('*tonk*-elimination')

Using these rules, $A \vdash B$, for any A and B:

> (1) A assumption
> (2) A *tonk* B (1), (T1)
> (3) B (2), (T2)

So, of course, a system with (T1) and (T2) would be inconsistent. Nothing vital depends on Prior's using rules of inference rather than axioms; the axioms '$A \rightarrow (A \; tonk \; B)$' and '$(A \; tonk \; B) \rightarrow B$', with the rule to infer B from $A \rightarrow B$ and A (*modus ponens*, hereafter MPP) would lead to equally alarming consequences; see Prior 1964 p. 192.

Prior believes himself to have shown that the notion of an analytically valid inference is a confusion, and that 'an expression must have some independently determined meaning before we can discover whether inferences involving it are valid or invalid' (1960 pp. 129–30).

Prior argues that since the rules (T1) and (T2) cannot give the meaning of '*tonk*' the meanings of the connectives cannot, in general, be given by the axioms/rules in which they occur. However, one might reply that (T1) and (T2) fail to specify the meaning of '*tonk*' for the sufficient reason that they are *defective* rules. They allow that $A \vdash B$ for any A and B; and no system in which anything is derivable from anything has any prospect of discriminating acceptable from unacceptable inferences (cf. Belnap 1961, Stevenson 1961). Prior has not shown that acceptable rules of inference could not give the meaning of connectives occurring in them.

I suggested earlier that a major objective of the construction of formal systems of logic is to give axioms/rules such that the informal inferences expressible in the language of the formalism which are intuitively judged valid in the extra-systematic sense are valid in the system. L_T would be so defective that it has no prospect of success in this enterprise.

Aims of formalisation

Some more needs to be said, however, about the way formal logical systems aim to represent intuitively valid inferences. One could think of a formal logical system as being devised in something like the following way. Some informal arguments are intuitively judged to be valid, others invalid. One then constructs a formal language in which the relevant structural features of those arguments can be schematically represented, and axioms/rules which allow the intuitively approved, and disallow the intuitively disapproved, arguments. This, of course, is at best a *very* sketchy 'rational reconstruction' and is not intended as detailed, serious history. Still, while I concede that formal logics have sometimes been devised simply out of mathematical curiosity, I think that something like the process I have described was at work when, for instance, Frege devised his

Begriffsschrift. Of course, the standard logical languages are now so familiar that one is no longer very conscious of how and why they were first constructed. But the same process can be seen in recent attempts to devise new formalisms for hitherto neglected kinds of argument; see, for example, the procedure adopted by D. K. Lewis 1973 in devising his analysis of counterfactuals.

Well, supposing that this is roughly right, what is its significance for questions about the meanings of the connectives? Something, I think, like this: first, *both* the syntax and pure semantics (levels (i) and (ii)) *and* the informal readings and depraved semantics (levels (iii) and (iv)) may be expected to contribute to the meanings of the connectives; for part of the object of the enterprise is to have levels (i) and (ii) adequately represent (iii) and (iv).

However, if formal logic faithfully followed informal arguments in all their complexity and vagueness there would be little point in formalisation; one aims, in formalising, to generalise, to simplify, and to increase precision and rigour. This means, I think, that one should neither expect nor desire a direct formal representation of all the informal arguments judged, extra-systematically, to be valid. Rather, pre-systematic judgments of validity will supply data for the construction of a formal logic, but considerations of simplicity, precision and rigour may be expected to lead to discrepancies between informal arguments and their formal representations, and even in some cases perhaps to a reassessment of intuitive judgments. One uses intuitive judgments of some arguments to construct a formal theory which gives verdicts, perhaps quite unexpected verdicts, on other arguments; and one might eventually sacrifice some of the original judgments to considerations of simplicity and generality. These points relate, of course, to the interdependence of one's judgments of the correctness of a translation of an informal argument into a formal language and one's pre-systematic view of its validity, remarked in ch. 2. (An example would be the standard rendering of 'All Fs are Gs' as '$(x) (Fx \rightarrow Gx)$', which is true if its antecedent is false, i.e. if there are no Fs. It is pretty doubtful whether one would pre-systematically have agreed that, say, all unicorns are purple, and pretty certain that one would not have agreed that all unicorns are purple *and* all unicorns are orange.)

One should recognise, then, that a failure on the part of a formal system to represent *all* the knobs and bumps of the informal arguments it systematises is not necessarily objectionable. On the other

hand, one must be wary of assuming that *all* adjustments are acceptable; one needs to ask whether the gains in simplicity and generality
compensate for the discrepancy. Some of the knobs and bumps of
English may be important. These remarks may seem disagreeably
vague; I shall try to make them more specific by considering a couple
of examples.

Why do the usual formal logics have, for example, ' & ', to be read
'and', but no formal analogue of 'because' or 'but'; and '($\exists$ ...)', to
be read 'at least one', but no formal analogue of 'several' or 'quite a
few'? Two features of the favoured expressions suggest themselves:
truth-functionality and precision.

' & ' is truth-functional; and truth-functions are especially readily
amenable to formal treatment – notably, they allow the possibility of
a mechanical decision procedure. This is no doubt why the formal
logician has an analogue of 'and' but none of 'because' or 'but';
'and', in at least a large class of uses, is truth-functional, whereas the
truth-value of '*A* because *B*' depends not only on the truth-values of
'*A*' and '*B*', but also on whether *B* is a reason for *A*, and the truth-
value of '*A* but *B*' also upon whether the combination of *A* and *B* is
surprising. 'At least one' and 'all' are not truth-functions (though in
the special case of a finite universe they are equivalent to '*Fa* $\vee$ *Fb* $\vee$
... $\vee$ *Fn*' and '*Fa* & *Fb* & ... & *Fn*' respectively). But they are –
unlike 'several' and 'quite a few' – precise. It is notable that one
common reading of '($\exists$ ...)', 'some', is vaguer than '($\exists$ ...)' itself;
'at least one' is a more accurate reading. (Other sciences share logic's
tendency to precisify and idealise; compare the extensionless points
of geometry or the frictionless surfaces of mechanics.)

However, while it is clear that truth-functional and precise expressions are preferable from the point of view of simplicity and rigour to
non-truth-functional or vague expressions, it is not so clear that this
preference is overriding. For non-truth-functional operators – '*L*'
and '*M*' for 'necessarily' and 'possibly', for example – *are* used by
formal logicians. Von Wright has suggested (1963) a system with a
sentence connective '*T*', to be read 'and then', which preserves the
temporal sense which 'and' sometimes has in English.[1] And, while
the standard predicate calculus restricts itself to 'all' and 'at least

---

[1] A related point is that the standard logical apparatus is insensitive to
temporal considerations; one is usually advised to understand its
'*p*'s and '*q*'s tenselessly. Some proposals for temporal logics are
discussed in ch. 9 § 3.

one', Altham (1971) has devised a logic with quantifiers for 'many' and 'few'.

The desirability of truth-functionality is quite uncontroversial; but it is equally clear that a logic restricted to truth-functions would be unacceptably limited. How essential precision is to the formal logical enterprise is more controversial. Dummett's objection to allowing epistemic 'logics' as genuinely logics, you will recall, was that 'knows' and 'believes' are inherently vague. Other logicians, however, have deliberately made use of vague ideas. For example, in an analysis of counterfactual conditionals ('If it had been the case that *A* it would have been the case that *B*') D. K. Lewis (1973, especially ch. 4) proposes to employ the admittedly vague idea of similarity between possible worlds (roughly, 'in all those possible worlds most similar to the actual world, but in which *A*, *B*'); he defends his compromise with vagueness by observing that the vagueness of the *analysans* is unobjectionable since the *analysandum* is itself vague. Zadeh, with his 'fuzzy logic' (see e.g. 1975), proposes an even more radical departure from logic's traditional concern with precision. I doubt whether such departures are justified by their results so far, but much more argument would be needed to show that this doubt is well-founded; cf. ch. 9 §4.

'&' *and* 'and', '∨' *and* 'or', *etc.*

Of the readings 'not' (of ' − '), 'and' (of '&'), 'or' (of '∨') and 'if ... then ---' (of '→'), Strawson has remarked (1952 p. 79) that 'the first two are the least misleading' and the remainder 'definitely wrong'. Certainly there are discrepancies.

Whereas ' − ' in sentence calculus is a sentence-forming operator on sentences, 'not' in English may negate either an entire sentence or else its predicate. This distinction (between 'external' and 'internal' negation) has been thought important for the understanding of allegedly meaningless sentences; for instance, it has been suggested that 'Virtue is not triangular', like 'Virtue is triangular', is meaningless, whereas 'It is not the case that virtue is triangular' is true. It has also been observed that in colloquial speech double negations do not always 'cancel out', but may be used as emphatic negatives. 'And', as I have already observed, is sometimes used in the sense of 'and then', whereas '&' is indifferent to temporal order.

Some have argued that 'or' has two senses, one inclusive and the other exclusive; but this would not be too serious a divergence from the '∨' of sentence calculus, since an exclusive disjunction could be defined as '$(A \lor B) \& - (A \& B)$'. A second argument for a discrepancy between 'or' and '∨' appeals to the fact that, in ordinary speech, it might well be seriously misleading to assert, say, 'John has the book or Mary has it' if one was in a position to assert 'John has the book'. However, it could be held that the oddity of the analogue of the rule of ∨-introduction (from 'A' to infer '$A \lor B$') in ordinary discourse is rather a matter of what Grice has called *conversational implicature* than of validity. According to Grice's account, a speaker conversationally implies that B if *his asserting that A* gives his hearer reason to believe that he believes that B. Since asserting 'A or B' when one is entitled to assert 'A' (or 'B') contravenes one of Grice's principles of conversational candour: that one should not make a weaker when entitled to make a stronger assertion – a speaker who asserts 'A or B' conversationally implies that he doesn't know whether it is A or B which is true. This explanation, since it doesn't concern the truth-values of assertions, allows one to agree that 'A or B', like '$A \lor B$', is true just in case 'A' is true or 'B' is true, and so would explain away the apparent discrepancy.

The discrepancies between '→' and 'if' have generally been thought the most serious. It seems to be pretty much agreed that if 'If A then B' is true, then '$A \to B$' is true, but it is highly controversial whether, if '$A \to B$' is true, 'If A then B' is true. Faris (1962) argues that 'If A then B' is derivable from '$A \to B$', so that '$A \to B$' and 'If A then B' are interderivable, if not synonymous. He assumes that a necessary and sufficient condition for the truth of 'If A then B' is *condition E*: there is a set S of true propositions such that B is derivable from A together with S. If '$A \to B$' is true, Faris goes on, there is a set of true propositions, namely, the set of which '$A \to B$' is the sole member, from which, with A, B is derivable; so E is satisfied, and 'If A then B' is true. Faris' argument has been attacked at various points; understandably, the objectors seem confident that the conclusion is mistaken, but less certain where exactly the flaw is in the argument (see e.g. Baker 1967, Clark 1971, L. J. Russell 1970). It may be worth observing that Faris' argument depends heavily on a notion of 'derivability' which spans natural and formal languages in a somewhat irregular manner. Other writers have argued that the apparent discrepancies between '→' and 'if' are rather a matter of conversational implicature than of truth-conditions. Their explanation would go something like this: it's not that 'If A then B' is false if 'A' is false or 'B' true but rather that when there is no connection between 'A' and 'B' it would be pointless and misleading to assert 'If A then B' if one was entitled to assert '$-A$' or 'B' (see e.g. Johnson 1921, Moore 1952). Others, again, have suggested that 'if' has several uses in English, one of which may correspond closely to '$\rightarrow$', but the others of which require a different representation (see e.g. Mackie 1973 where nine uses, and six accounts, of English conditionals are distinguished).

Modern logic offers, in fact, more than one kind of conditional. The material conditional, which I have been discussing so far, is truth-functional; and '$A \rightarrow B$' is true if either 'A' is false or 'B' is true. So it has the theorems:

$$A \rightarrow (B \rightarrow A)$$
$$-A \rightarrow (A \rightarrow B)$$
$$(A \rightarrow B) \vee (B \rightarrow A)$$

These are the 'paradoxes of material implication'. The 'paradoxes' result if one reads '$\rightarrow$' as 'if' or 'implies'; C. I. Lewis comments that the third of the above theorems says that if one takes any two sentences at random from a newspaper, either the first will imply the second, or the second the first. Reflection on these 'paradoxes' led Lewis to propose a stronger conditional, '$A \dashv B$' where '$\dashv$' is *strict* implication, defined as 'Necessarily $(A \rightarrow B)$'. 'Necessarily $(A \rightarrow B)$', given the standard semantics for modal logic, is supposed to be true if B is true in all possible worlds in which A is true. Other implication relations, modelled on strict implication, have been offered in analysis of counterfactuals (see Stalnaker 1968, D. K. Lewis 1973).

However, strict implication has its own paradoxes; briefly, just as a false proposition materially implies any proposition, and a true one is materially implied by any proposition, so an impossible proposition strictly implies anything, and anything strictly implies a necessary proposition. Relevance logicians consequently propose a stricter conditional yet, which requires a relation of relevance between antecedent and consequent (see Anderson and Belnap 1975 §1). These logicians object to calling '$\rightarrow$' 'material implication', as well as to reading it 'If ... then ---'; 'immaterial negation', they suggest, would be no more inappropriate. They also extend their critique of truth-functional logic to disjunction – remember that in the standard system '$A \rightarrow B$' is equivalent to '$-A \vee B$' – arguing that the informal 'or' is, like 'if', intensional.

One issue here is which conditional best corresponds to 'if'; to which, of course, the answer may be that different formal conditionals correspond best to different uses or senses of 'if'. Another is, granted that material implication, being truth-functional, is the simplest of the formal conditionals, whether resort to strict or subjunctive or relevant conditionals brings advantages to compensate for the loss in simplicity. And here, I think, the purposes for which formalisation is undertaken may be crucial. If one is concerned only to represent formally the valid arguments which are used in mathematics, for example, it might be that a truth-functional implication would be adequate; though even this is disputable (cf. Anderson and Belnap 1975 §3). If, on the other hand, one is also concerned to represent arguments in empirical science, it may be that, since science is apparently deeply committed to dispositions, and so to subjunctive conditionals ('*x* is soluble' or 'If *x* were put in water, it would dissolve') one is apt to need something stronger; but this too is disputable (see e.g. Goodman 1955, or Quine 1973 pp. 8–16). So the significance of the discrepancies between 'if' and '→' will depend on the answers to at least two further questions: for what purpose(s) is the formalisation intended? and, does that purpose require something stronger than the material conditional? Both – as we shall see in the course of a closer examination of the strict and relevant conditionals in ch. 10 – are deep and difficult questions.

4

Quantifiers

1 The quantifiers and their interpretation

'$(x) Fx$' is usually read long the lines of 'For all x, Fx', and '$(\exists x) Fx$' along the lines of 'For some x, Fx' or, more accurately, 'For at least one x, Fx'; '$(...)$' is generally known as the *universal*, '$(\exists ...)$' as the *existential*, quantifier. A variable inside the scope of a quantifier, such as 'x' in '$(\exists x) Fx$', is said to be *bound*, a variable not bound by any quantifier, such as 'x' in 'Fx', or 'y' in '$(\exists x) Rxy$', to be *free*. A formula with one or more free variables is called a (1-, 2- ... n-place) *open sentence*, a formula without free variables a *closed sentence* (or 'o-place open sentence'). So prefixing a quantifier, '(x)' or '$(\exists x)$', to an open sentence, such as 'Fx', with just 'x' free, yields a closed sentence, '$(x) Fx$' or '$(\exists x) Fx$'; in general, prefixing a quantifier binding one of its free variables to an open sentence with n free variables yields an open sentence with $n-1$ free variables.

Some formulations of the predicate calculus have *singular terms*, 'a', 'b', 'c' ... etc. as well as variables; these are individual constants, each denoting some specific individual. By dropping a quantifier and replacing the variable(s) it bound by singular terms, one obtains an instance of the quantified formula, as e.g. '$Fa \to Ga$' is an instance of '$(x) (Fx \to Gx)$'. One could think of bound variables as playing a role analogous to that of the pronouns which, in natural languages, secure cross-reference, and of singular terms as playing a role analogous to that of the proper names which, in natural languages, refer to individuals (but cf. ch. 5).

In modern logic, as I've just indicated, quantifiers and singular terms belong to quite different syntactical categories. Frege, who invented quantification theory (Frege 1879; the quantifiers were also devised, independently, by Peirce and Mitchell; see Peirce 1885) laid great stress on the importance of shifting attention from the subject–predicate distinction to the function–argument distinction. One consequence of this, essential to the adequacy of the formalism to represent mathematical argument, is to allow for relations, since one can have functions of more than one argument. Another, which is most relevant to our present purposes, is to allow for second-level functions, the category of the quantifiers. For instance, to say that three-legged dogs exist, according to Frege, is to say that the concept *three-legged dog* is not empty; the quantifier '(∃ ...)' is a concept which applies to concepts, a second-level function (see Frege 1891, 1892). However, some writers have thought that natural language quantifiers, 'some', 'all', 'every' and so forth, behave very much like names. Russell, for instance, once tried to treat these 'quantifiers' as 'denoting phrases'; 'some boy' was like 'John' except for denoting an 'ambiguous' individual; but subsequently he settled for an account in the Fregean style (Russell 1903; and cf. criticisms in Geach 1962). Later writers, notably Montague 1973, have pursued the idea of treating quantifiers as name-like (and cf. Hintikka's defence of this approach in 1976, and the comments by Fogelin and Potts). I, however, shall have to confine my discussion to the regular, 'Fregean' quantifiers.

In *first-order* predicate calculus only 'individual' variables, 'x', 'y' ... etc., may be bound by quantifiers; in *second-order* calculi 'F', 'G' ... etc. may also be bound, as in '$(x)(F)Fx$'. A sentence letter, 'p', 'q' ... etc., can be thought of as a limit case of a predicate letter; 'R' in 'Rxy' is a 2-place predicate, 'F' in 'Fx' a 1-place predicate, and 'p', in 'p', a 0-place predicate. So quantified sentence calculus, which allows quantifiers binding 'p', 'q' ... etc., as in '$(p)(p \lor -p)$', is a kind of second-order calculus. Calculi with different styles of variable, each varying over different kinds of thing, such as a formalism with one style of variable for natural, and another for real, numbers, are known as *many-sorted* theories.

With the help of the quantifiers numerical statements – 'There are n xs which are F' – can be formulated. 'There is *at least one* x which is F' is:

$$(\exists x)\ Fx$$

and 'There is *at most one* x which is F' is:

$$(x)\,(y)\ (Fx\ \&\ Fy \to x = y)$$

(if this isn't obvious, observe that you could read the above formula as 'If there are two Fs, they're the same'); so 'There is *exactly one x* which is F' is:

$$(\exists x)\,(Fx \;\&\; (y)\,(Fy \to x = y))$$

and 'There are *exactly two x*s which are F' is:

$$(\exists x)\,(\exists y)\,(Fx \;\&\; Fy \;\&\; x \neq y \;\&\; (z)\,(Fz \to z = x \lor z = y))$$

and so forth.[1] Less specific numerical quantifiers, such as 'many' and 'few', have also received formal treatment (Altham 1971), along the lines of 'at least n' and 'at most n' for variable n.

The distinctions made in the previous chapter between the *informal readings* of the symbols of a formal language (level (iii)), their *formal interpretation* (level (ii)), and the informal explanation offered of the formal semantics (level (iv)), applies, of course, to the quantifiers as well as the sentence connectives. Whereas in the case of the connectives the main controversy centred around the question, how adequately the truth-functional connectives represent their English analogues, in the case of the quantifiers a key issue concerns their appropriate formal interpretation. It is often observed that the universal quantifier is analogous to conjunction:

$$(x)\, Fx \equiv Fa \;\&\; Fb \;\&\; Fc \;\&\; \dots \text{ etc.}$$

and the existential quantifier to disjunction:

$$(\exists x)\, Fx \equiv Fa \lor Fb \lor Fc \lor \dots \text{ etc.}$$

Indeed, for a theory for which the domain is finite (e.g. where the variables range over the members of the British government) a universally quantified formula is equivalent to a finite conjunction and an existentially quantified formula to a finite disjunction. However, for a theory with an infinite domain (e.g. where the variables range over the natural numbers) quantified formulae can be represented only by infinitely long conjunctions or disjunctions – the '... etc.' is ineliminable. So an acceptable interpretation will have to supply the

---

[1] Part of the logicist programme consisted in the definition of the natural numbers as certain sets; 0 as the set of 0-membered sets, 1 as the set of 1-membered sets, ... n as the set of n-membered sets, for instance. Notice how this defines the *nominal* use of numbers (as in '$9 > 7$') in terms of the *adjectival* use (as in 'There are 9 planets'), which can, as I have just explained, be expressed in terms of quantifiers and identity.

requisite generality. And in fact two distinct styles of interpretation have been offered for the quantifiers. The *objectual interpretation* appeals to the *values* of the variables, the objects over which the variables range:

$(x) Fx$ is interpreted as 'For all objects, x, in the domain, D, Fx'

$(\exists x) Fx$ is interpreted as 'For at least one object, x, in the domain, D, Fx.'

The domain may be restricted, i.e., D may be specified as a set of objects assigned as the range of the variables – as it might be, the natural numbers, persons, fictional characters, or whatever; or it may be unrestricted, i.e., D is required to be 'the universe', i.e., all the objects there are. The restricted domains assigned on the model-theoretic approach aren't necessarily subsets of 'the universe', though; the set of fictional characters, for instance, wouldn't be (ch. 5 §4). The *substitutional interpretation* appeals, not to the values, but to the *substituends* for the variables, the expressions, that is, that can be substituted for the variables:

$(x) Fx$ is interpreted as 'All substitution instances of '$F \ldots$' are true'

$(\exists x) Fx$ is interpreted as 'At least one substitution instance of '$F \ldots$' is true.'

The objectual interpretation is championed by – among others – Quine and Davidson; the substitutional interpretation by – among others – Mates and Marcus. Both interpretations have a pretty long history; Russell's explanations of the quantifiers, for instance, are sometimes of the one and sometimes of the other character. However, it would be fair to say, I think, that the objectual interpretation is generally thought of as standard, the substitutional as a challenger whose credentials stand in need of scrutiny. There are, as this suggests, two possible views about the status of the two styles of interpretation: that they are rivals, only one of which can be 'right'; or that they may both have their uses. I, in the company of e.g. Belnap and Dunn 1968, Linsky 1972, Kripke 1976, shall take the second, more tolerant, view of the matter.

But this is *not* to say that nothing hangs on which interpretation is chosen. On the contrary, the choice may have important philosophical consequences. I shall not be able to consider all the ramifications in detail; I shall, however, sketch an account of the crucial role played by the objectual interpretation in Quine's ontological views. This will be worthwhile both for the sake of illustrating the metaphysical issues which are apt to be entangled with questions about the interpretation of formal languages, and also with a view to showing subsequently (ch. 10) how Quine's ideas about quantification and ontology effect his attitude to the intelligibility of modal logic.

2 Metaphysical interlude: Quine on quantification and ontology

Ontology may be characterised as that part of metaphysics which concerns the question, what kinds of thing there are. Quine's views on ontology may be seen as the product of two key ideas, the ideas expressed in two of his best-known slogans: '*to be is to be the value of a variable*' and '*No entity without identity*' (see fig. 2). The first slogan introduces Quine's *criterion of ontological commitment*, a test of what kinds of thing a theory says there are; the second introduces his *standards of ontological admissibility* – only those entities should be tolerated for which adequate criteria of identity can be supplied. I shall concentrate on the first of these ideas, the criterion of ontological commitment, for it is to this that Quine's support for objectual quantification is primarily relevant.

One or two brief comments on the second idea will, however, be useful. Criteria of identity give conditions for things of a given kind to be identical, as: sets are the same if they have the same members, or as: two physical objects are the same if they occupy the same spatio-temporal position. Notice that the requirement that only those kinds of entity be allowed for which criteria of identity can be given is rather strong (we're pretty confident that there are people, for instance, but there is a notorious problem about supplying criteria of personal identity). Quine holds that intensional (meaning) notions are hopelessly unclear; consequently, identity conditions stated in intensional terms are not, by Quine's standards, adequate; and so kinds of supposed entity which can only be individuated by appeal to meaning – properties or propositions, for example – are not, by his standards, admissible.

The criterion of ontological commitment

What, then, is Quine's criterion of ontological commitment, and how is it connected with the objectual interpretation of the

44

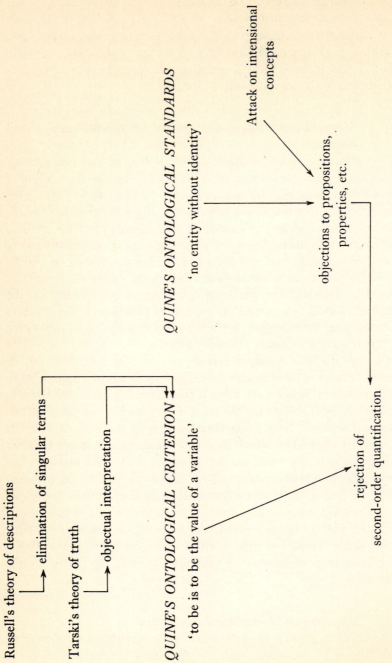

Russell's theory of descriptions → elimination of singular terms

Tarski's theory of truth → objectual interpretation

QUINE'S ONTOLOGICAL CRITERION
'to be is to be the value of a variable'

QUINE'S ONTOLOGICAL STANDARDS
'no entity without identity'

Attack on intensional concepts

objections to propositions, properties, etc.

rejection of second-order quantification

Fig. 2

quantifiers? The criterion is put in various, not always equivalent, forms:

> *entities of a given sort are assumed by a theory if and only if some of them must be counted among the values of the variables, in order that the statements affirmed in the theory be true.* (1953a p. 103)
>
> to say that a given existential quantification presupposes objects of a given kind is to say simply that the open sentence which follows the quantifier is true of some objects of that kind and none not of that kind. (1953a p. 131)

The idea is – roughly – that one tells what a theory says there is by putting it in predicate calculus notation, and asking what kinds of thing are required as values of its variables if theorems beginning '$(\exists x)...$' are to be true. (So a theory in which '$(\exists x)$ (x is prime and $x > $ 1,000,000)' is a theorem is committed to the existence of prime numbers greater than a million, and *a fortiori* to the existence of prime numbers and to the existence of numbers.) It is obvious that the criterion applies only to *interpreted* theories. It is important, also, that the criterion is to apply only when the theory is expressed in *primitive notation*; if quantification over numbers is only an abbreviation for quantification over classes, for instance, then the theory is committed to classes but not to numbers. Quine's criterion is a test of what a theory says there is, not of what there is. *What there is* is what a *true* theory says there is. The refusal to admit intensional entities acts as a sort of preliminary filter; theories which say there are intensional entities are not, in Quine's view, really intelligible, so *a fortiori* they are not true.

Quine's explanation of his criterion leaves a good deal to be desired. As Cartwright observes in 1954, some formulations – the first one quoted above, for instance – employ such locutions as 'has to', 'must', 'require'; yet these are intensional idioms, and Quine officially urges that these should be shunned. Quine has explicitly claimed that his criterion is extensional (1953a pp. 15, 131);[1] and some formu-

---

[1] He allows that when the criterion is applied to a theory not in quantificational form, an intensional element will be introduced in the form of an appeal to a correct translation of that theory into predicate calculus (1953a, p. 131). This concession, together with Quine's thesis of the indeterminacy of translation (1960a ch. 2) leads to the thesis of *ontological relativity* (1968). But my present concern is whether the criterion itself can be put in an extensional way.

lations – the second quoted above, for instance – are given purely in extensional terms. The question is whether extensional formulations are adequate. Scheffler and Chomsky (1958) argue rather persuasively that they are not. The problem is how to understand the condition 'the open sentence which follows the quantifier is true of some objects of a certain kind and none not of that kind' in the extensional formulation. If it is read '∃ objects of kind k such that the open sentence is true of them and of none not of that kind', it follows that it is impossible to say that a theory says there are objects of kind k, without *oneself* saying that there are objects of kind k, for '∃ objects of kind k...' itself involves ontological commitment. But if it is read 'If the open sentence is true of any objects, it is true of some objects of kind k and of none not of that kind', it follows that any theory which is committed to anything that doesn't exist is thereby committed to everything that doesn't exist, for if the antecedent is false, the conditional is true. But if the criterion cannot be adequately stated extensionally it fails by Quine's own standards. Someone who didn't share Quine's scruples, of course, might find the criterion acceptable notwithstanding its intensional character. But there are further questions to be asked about the reasons Quine offers for the criterion.

One important reason why Quine locates ontological commitment in the variables is that he thinks that the *eliminability of singular terms* shows that the ontological commitment of a theory cannot reside in its names. This raises two questions: is Quine right to claim that singular terms are eliminable? and, is he right to think that if they are, ontological commitment must be carried by bound variables? I shall take these questions in turn.

Quine's proposal for the elimination of singular terms has two stages: first, singular terms are replaced by definite descriptions, and then the definite descriptions are eliminated in favour of quantifiers and variables.

(i) In the case of some proper names at least, one can supply a definite description which denotes the same thing: 'the teacher of Plato' for 'Socrates', for example. To avoid the difficulties which might sometimes be encountered in finding an ordinary predicate reliably true of just the individual denoted by a name, Quine proposes the construction of artificial predicates, and defines 'a' (as, 'Socrates') as '$(\imath x)\ Ax$' (as, 'the x which socratises'). One could think of the new predicate, 'A', Quine suggests, as meaning '$= a$' (so '... socratises' means '... is identical with Socrates'). However this unofficial comment is not to be thought of as *defining* the new predicates, for the whole point of introducing them is to get rid of names altogether; it is merely an intuitive explanation of predicates which must be taken as primitive.

(ii) The second stage is to use Russell's theory of descriptions to eliminate the definite descriptions which now replace singular terms. This eliminates definite descriptions in favour of quantifiers, variables, and identity (details in ch. 5 §3), thus:

> The x which is F is G = df. There is exactly one F and whatever is F is G

i.e. in symbols:

$$G((\imath x)Fx) = \text{df.} \ (\exists x)\,((y)\,(Fy \equiv x = y) \ \& \ Gx)$$

Thus, sentences containing names (as, 'Socrates took poison') can be replaced by sentences containing descriptions ('The x which socratises took poison'), and then by sentences containing only quantifiers and variables ('There is just one x which socratises and whatever socratises took poison').

Quine draws the conclusion (1953a p. 13) that, since 'whatever we say with the help of names can be said in a language which shuns names altogether', it cannot be names, but must be the quantified variables, which carry ontological commitment.

The thesis of the eliminability of singular terms has come in for criticism (see e.g. Strawson 1961). But the real doubt concerns, not so much the formal feasibility of Quine's proposal, as its philosophical significance. The fact that Quine can supply an appropriate definite description to replace a name only by the use of predicates which, though officially unanalysable, are unofficially explained with the help of names ('A' means '$= a$') scarcely reassures one that the eliminability of singular terms really shows them to be ontologically irrelevant.

Equally unsettling is the discovery that not only singular terms, but also quantifiers and variables, are eliminable. In the *combinatory logic* due to Schönfinkel and Curry – and, ironically enough, explained by Quine himself in 1960b – variables are supplanted by predicate operators called 'combinators'. The predicate operator '*Der*', for 'derelativisation', turns an n-place predicate into an $(n-1)$-place predicate. If 'F' is a 1-place predicate, say '... is a dog', '*Der F*' is an o-place predicate – a closed sentence – 'Something is a dog'; if

'...*R*---' is a 2-place predicate, say '... bites ---', '*Der R*' is a 1-place predicate, '... bites something', and '*Der Der R*' a 0-place predicate, 'Something bites something'.

'*Inv*', for 'inversion', reverses the order of the places of a 2-place predicate; so '((*Inv R*)..., ---)' means '---*R*...'. '*Ref*', for 'reflexive', turns a 2-place predicate into a 1-place reflexive predicate; so '*Ref R*' means '... has *R* to itself'. The procedure is generalised to polyadic predicates and to compound predications; and the upshot is a translation without quantifiers of the formulae of quantification theory, in which inversion provides for permutation of the order of variables, reflexion for repetition of variables, and derelativisation for quantification.

Quine concedes that his criterion doesn't apply directly to combinatory logic, but observes that it can be applied indirectly, via the translation of combinatory into quantified formulae. But this is only to obscure the issue, which is that if the eliminability of singular terms were a good reason for denying that they carry ontological commitment, the eliminability of quantifiers should presumably be as good a reason for refusing *them* ontological significance.

This makes clearer, I think, the very considerable importance which Quine's insistence on the *objectual interpretation of the quantifiers* has for his ontological criterion. Though the same theory could be expressed using singular terms as well as quantifiers, or combinatory operators instead of quantifiers, its quantificational form reveals its ontological commitments most transparently, Quine thinks, because *a sentence of the form '(∃x)...' says that there is something which...*

> To insist on the correctness of the criterion...is, indeed, merely to say that no distinction is being drawn between the 'there are' of 'there are universals', 'there are unicorns', 'there are hippopotami' and the 'there are' of '(∃x)', 'there are entities *x* such that...'

And deviation from the objectual interpretation would threaten the criterion:

> To contest the criterion...is simply to say either that the familiar quantificational notation is being used in some new sense (in which case we need not concern ourselves) or else that the familiar 'there are' of 'there are universals' et al. is being used in some new sense (in which case again we need not concern ourselves). (1953a p. 105)

On the objectual interpretation '$(\exists x)\ Fx$' means that there is an object x, in the domain, D, which is F. Now, if one takes D to be 'the universe' – everything there is – which, it seems, is what Quine assumes, then, indeed, '$(\exists x)\ Fx$' means that there is an (existent, real) object which is F; cf. Quine's use of 'entity' in the passage just quoted.

If '$(\exists x)\ Fx$' *means* 'There is an (existent) object which is F' then, if it is a theorem of a theory that $(\exists x)\ Fx$, then that theory says that there is an object which is F; and if one says that there are Fs, one is committed to there being Fs. The objectual reading of the quantifier does indeed locate ontological commitment in the bound variables of a theory. Perhaps I may rewrite Quine's slogan: to be said to be is to be the value of a variable bound by an objectual quantifier; it's less memorable, but truer, that way! Notice, though, that Quine's criterion now begins to look oddly oblique: as if one discovered that a theory which says there are so-and-so's is ontologically committed to so-and-so's by first translating it into predicate calculus notation, and then appealing to the objectual interpretation of the quantifiers to show that its existential theorems say that there are so-and-so's.

The serious work has to be done in deciding which *ostensibly* existential assertions of a theory need remain in primitive notation, and which are eliminable by suitable paraphrase. An example would be Morton White's proposal (1956) to reduce 'There is a possibility that James will come', which seems to assert the existence of possibilities, to 'That James will come is not certainly false', which does not. (There are still tricky philosophical questions to be asked about the significance of paraphrase here, though I shan't pause over them now; but see Alston 1958 for a critique of the idea that paraphrase may eliminate ontological commitment, and cf. Lewis 1973 ch. 4, where it is assumed that paraphrase *preserves* ontological commitment.)

Substitutional quantification and ontology

The substitutional interpretation does not give a negative answer to ontological questions; rather, it *postpones* them. On the substitutional account, '$(\exists x)\ Fx$' means 'Some substitution instance of '$F\ldots$' is true'; questions of existence now depend upon the conditions for the truth of the substitution instances. If, for instance, 'Fa' is true only if 'a' is a singular term which denotes an (existent) object, then there will have to be an object which is F if '$(\exists x)\ Fx$' is to come out true; but it is not *inevitable* that the truth-conditions for the appropriate substitution instances will bring an ontological commitment. An example: the presence in predicate calculus of theorems such as:

$$(\exists x)\, Fx \vee - Fx$$

which on the objectual interpretation says that there is at least one object which is either F or not F, i.e. that there is at least one object, is embarrassing if one thinks it oughtn't to be a matter of *logic* that *anything* exists. Would a substitutional interpretation avoid the existential commitment of the embarrassing theorems? Well, on that interpretation the theorem means that:

At least one substitution instance of '$F \ldots \vee - F \ldots$' is true. If only names which denote an object are admitted as substituends, then on this interpretation too predicate calculus will require at least one object. But if non-denoting terms, like 'Pegasus', are allowed as substituends, then ontological commitment may be avoided. This illustrates the way that substitutional quantification *defers* ontological questions, shifting them from the quantifiers to the names. Quine is apt to suggest that this relocation of existential questions is a deplorable evasion of metaphysical responsibility! But I shall suggest subsequently that it may have advantages.

Since on the substitutional reading '$(\exists x)\, Fx$' means that at least one substitution-instance of '$F \ldots$' is true, if this metalinguistic quantifier is interpreted objectually, it will be committed to the existence of the appropriate expressions, the substitution-instances. But this will not be so if it too is interpreted substitutionally.

3   The choice of interpretation

Is one interpretation of the quantifiers the 'correct' one? Or may one choose between the two according to one's purposes? And if so, what are the strengths and weaknesses of each?

Substitutional quantifiers and truth

Which interpretation of the quantifiers is adopted will make a difference to the definition of truth for quantified sentences. I'll be brief now, since there will be more sustained discussion in ch. 7 §§5 and 6. If the quantifiers are interpreted substitutionally, then the truth of quantified formulae can be defined directly in terms of the truth of atomic formulae (as, ''$(\exists x)\, Fx$' is true iff some substitution instance of '*F*...' is true'); if the quantifiers are interpreted objectually the definition of truth will be less direct. Now Tarski proposes, as a 'material adequacy condition' on definitions of truth, that any acceptable definition must have as consequence all instances of the '(T)-schema': 'S is true iff *p*', where 'S' names the sentence '*p*'; and Wallace 1971 fears that if a substitutional interpretation is adopted the definition of truth will not meet this requirement. But Kripke has argued (1976) that Tarski's condition isn't violated; and anyway there may be reservations about the requirement itself. So I shall assume that the substitutional interpretation isn't objectionable on *this* score.

Too few names?

This leaves the question of whether the substitutional and objectual interpretations are always equally suitable. The answer is, pretty clearly, no. It is of course a requirement on an acceptable interpretation that the theorems of the theory being interpreted come out true. The substitutional interpretation will obviously make existentially quantified wffs true only if suitable substituends are available. For instance, '$(\exists x)(Fx \lor -Fx)$' is a theorem in first-order predicate calculus; in a formulation with quantifiers but no singular terms, however, the substitutional interpretation could not, for want of appropriate substitution-instances, make such a wff come out true (so that the elimination of singular terms will preclude a substitutional account). Another situation in which a substitutional interpretation would be precluded would be a formal system in which '$(\exists x) Fx$' was a theorem but for every substitution instance '$-Fa$' was provable; for the substitutional interpretation couldn't make the quantified theorem true without making at least one of its instances true (this possibility is discussed by Quine 1968; and cf. Weston 1974).

Tense

Its supporters argue, however, that sometimes the substitutional interpretation offers advantages over the objectual. For instance, Marcus suggests that a substitutional reading will avoid difficulties about tense. Strawson had asked (1952 pp. 150–1) how to represent 'There was at least one woman among the survivors': 'There is (was?) at least one *x* such that *x* is (was?) a woman and...'? I think it unlikely that this problem will be solved by a substitutional reading: 'At least one substitution instance of '...' is (was?) true'. It is true, and important, that tense matters to the (in)validity of informal arguments, and that the usual logical apparatus is insensitive to tense (cf. ch. 9 §3); but the substitutional interpretation doesn't seem to help.

Modality

Marcus also suggests, with, I think, more justice, that substitutional quantification could resolve some problems about the interpretation of modal predicate logic. From the presumably true sentence:

Necessarily (the Evening Star = the Evening Star)

by presumably valid predicate calculus reasoning there follows:

($\exists x$) Necessarily (x = the Evening Star)

that is, on the objectual interpretation,

There is at least one object, x, such that necessarily x is identical with the Evening Star.

But this is hard to understand; indeed, Quine bases upon it an argument that the whole enterprise of modal predicate logic is misguided; for what is this object which is necessarily identical with the Evening Star? Not the Evening Star; for that is the Morning Star, and the Morning Star isn't necessarily, but only contingently, identical with the Evening Star. But Quine's awkward questions are avoided by reading the bothersome sentence substitutionally:

At least one substitution instance of 'Necessarily (. . . = the Evening Star)' is true

when it seems (since 'Necessarily (the Evening Star = the Evening Star)' is true) unproblematically true.

The substitutional interpretation also seems to offer certain advantages when one turns to second-order quantification.

Second-order quantification

If, as on the objectual interpretation, '($\exists x$)...' says that there is an object such that..., and '(x)...' that for all objects, ..., then it is to be expected that the appropriate substituends for bound variables should be expressions whose role is to denote objects, that is to say, singular terms. Quine, indeed, sometimes defines a singular term as an expression which can take the position of a bound variable. On the substitutional interpretation, however, quantification is related directly not to objects, but to substituends; and so there is no particular need to insist that only expressions of the category of singular terms may be bound by quantifiers. The substitution class could be the class of singular terms, but could equally be the class of predicates, or the class of sentences...etc.

On the objectual interpretation, therefore, just as a first-order quantification like:

   1. $(\exists x)\, Fx$

says that there is an object (individual) which is F, a second-order quantification, like:

   2. $(\exists F)\, Fx$

says that *there is an object (property) which x has*, and:

   3. $(\exists p)\,(p \rightarrow -p)$

says that *there is an object (proposition) which materially implies its own negation*. The natural restriction on the substitution class obliges one to construe bound 'F' and 'p' as syntactically like singular terms; it will be observed that this strains the reading, since if 'F' is a singular term, 'Fx' must be read as 'x HAS F' to make a grammatical sentence. And the interpretation in terms of objects obliges one to regard second-order quantification as committing one to (abstract) objects. Not caring for such supposed objects as properties or propositions, but obliged by the objectual interpretation to allow that second-order quantification would commit him to their existence, Quine prefers not to indulge in second-order quantification at all, but to confine himself to first-order theories.

However, with the substitutional interpretation one is not restricted to singular terms as substituends; and while in the case of first-order quantification singular terms would be suitable, in the case of second-order quantification as in 2 and 3 predicates or formulae, respectively, would be the appropriate substituends. 2 will say that some substitution instance of '$...x$' is true, 3 that some substitution instance of '$... \rightarrow -...$' is true. Now it is no longer necessary to strain the reading of the bound variables to make them name-like, and of

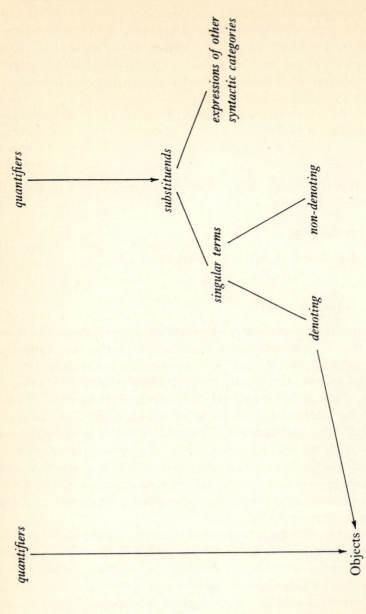

OBJECTUAL INTERPRETATION

quantifiers

Objects

SUBSTITUTIONAL INTERPRETATION

quantifiers

substituends

expressions of other syntactic categories

singular terms

denoting

non-denoting

Fig. 3   Quantifiers and ontology

course there is no commitment to intensional objects, since there is no commitment to objects (see fig. 3).

These thoughts have some relevance, I think, to metaphysical issues. Nominalists admit the existence only of particulars, whereas realists, or Platonists, also allow the reality of universals. C. S. Peirce thought that the influence of nominalism on the history of philosophy since Ockham had been so pervasive that nominalism and 'nominalistic Platonism', the view that universals are a sort of abstract particular, had come to seem the only alternatives; rejecting both, he urged a realism which, rather than assimilating them, allowed the difference between particulars and universals. Now if only names are substitutable for bound variables one is, as it were, obliged to choose between a kind of nominalism (allow only first-order quantification, with variables replaceable by names of particulars: Quine's position) and a kind of nominalistic Platonism (allow second-order quantification, with variables replaceable by names of abstract objects, properties or propositions: Church's position). Allowing substituends from other syntactical categories, however, gives a third option; which may well be, from a metaphysical point of view, appealing.

Other important issues also depend upon the provision of an acceptable interpretation of second-order quantifiers. One of these is the feasibility of the redundancy theory of truth; and the considerations of the present section will be highly pertinent when I come, in ch. 7 §7, to discuss that question in detail.

5

Singular terms

I Singular terms and their interpretation

Some formulations of the predicate calculus employ singular terms ('*a*', '*b*' ... etc.) as well as variables. If the quantifiers are to be interpreted substitutionally, of course, the presence of singular terms in the language to supply the appropriate substitution instances is essential. What, in informal argument, corresponds to singular terms in formal logic? Singular terms are usually thought of as the formal analogues of proper names in natural languages. (Where the variables range over numbers, the numerals would correspond to the singular terms.) The formal interpretation of singular terms assigns to each a specific individual in the domain over which the variables range; and, in natural languages, proper names are thought to work in a similar way, each standing for a particular person (or place or whatever).

So while in the case of the quantifiers the main controversy surrounds the question of the most suitable formal interpretation, in the case of singular terms the problems centre, rather, on the understanding of their natural language 'analogues'. The formal interpretation of singular terms in straightforward extensional languages is uncontroversial; however, rival views about how to understand proper names in natural languages have been used in support of alternative proposals about the formal interpretation of singular terms in less straightforward, e.g. modal, calculi. Among the disputed questions about how, exactly, proper names work are, for instance: just which expressions are *bona fide* proper names? For example, are 'names' for mythical or fictional entities ('Pegasus', 'Mr Pickwick') to count? And if so, what is one to say of the truth-value of sentences containing such 'non-denoting' names? Especially, how is one to explain the intuitive truth of negative existentials like 'Pegasus never existed'? If the role of names is purely and simply to denote an individual, how can a true identity statement (like 'Cicero = Tully') be informative, and how can substitution of one name for another denoting the same individual sometimes change the truth-value of a sentence (as, the presumably true 'One needs no knowledge of Roman history to know that Tully = Tully', and, the presumably false 'One needs no knowledge of Roman history to know that Tully = Cicero')? A central issue, and the one on which I'll concentrate, is whether proper names have meaning ('sense', 'connotation') as well as denotation, and if so, what meaning they have. Those who think that proper names do have meaning generally associate their meaning more or less closely with the meaning of co-designative definite descriptions. The first view, that names have denotation but no meaning, makes for a sharp differentiation between proper names ('Socrates', 'Bismarck' etc.) and descriptions ('The teacher of Plato', 'The Chancellor responsible for the unification of Germany'), whereas the second view sees names as rather like descriptions. This leads to a second key question: how do definite descriptions work?

2 Names

I'll take the first question first. The alternatives are sketched in table 1.

Some preliminary comments about the distinction between proper names and definite descriptions may be in order. Ordinarily the distinction isn't hard to draw, but there are some expressions which are tricky to classify; for example, although the Morning Star isn't a star, but a planet (Venus), it is still *called* 'the Morning Star', so that 'the Morning Star' seems to have become more like a name and less like a description than, perhaps, it was originally; the capital letters may be significant of this intermediate status. (The University of Warwick isn't at Warwick, either.) Furthermore, not all names are of the same kind; logicians are apt to take as their examples names of persons or, less commonly, places, but there are also titles of books, brand names, trade names...(and notice how trade names have a habit of turning into common nouns, and even verbs, e.g. 'hoover'). It is also worthy of attention that logicians are fondest of the names of famous people ('Aristotle', 'Napoleon' etc.); and salutary to recall that there are no doubt many Aristotles and Napoleons, and only a background of shared information to make us all think of the same one. Drawing

TABLE 1. *Do proper names have meaning as well as denotation?*

	Yes		No
Frege Russell (Quine)	proper names have the sense of some co-designative definite description known to the speaker	Mill Ziff	proper names have denotation but no connotation and are not part of the language
Wittgenstein Searle	proper names have the sense of some indeterminate sub-set of some open-ended set of co-designative descriptions	Kripke	proper names are 'rigid designators'; causal account of the correct use of names
Burge (Davidson)	proper names as predicates		

attention to the variety of kinds of proper name may induce some caution about assuming that there is such a thing as *the* way in which proper names work.

Names as purely denotative

One view is that proper names, by contrast with definite descriptions, are, so to speak, mere labels; they serve simply to stand for a person, place, or thing. I don't think that people who take this view mean, or need, to deny that in the case of personal names there are conventions about which names are given to males and which to females, for example, about a child's taking his father's surname, and so forth; nor that names have a 'sense' derived from their etymology, as, ''Peter' means 'a rock''. The name a person has may, in virtue of conventions of the kind mentioned, convey some information about him; what is being denied, rather, is that the name *describes* him.

According to Mill 1843, proper names have denotation but no connotation, that is, no meaning. Ziff 1960 subscribes to something like this view; proper names have no meaning, and, indeed, in some sense are not even part of the language. Another writer who denies that proper names have meaning is Kripke, who in 1972 sketches an account both of the semantic and of the pragmatic aspects of proper names. Proper names are 'rigid designators'; that is to say, they have the same reference in all possible worlds. For example, the name 'Aristotle' designates the very same individual in all possible worlds, whereas the definite description 'the greatest man who studied under Plato', though it designates Aristotle in the actual world, may designate other individuals in other possible worlds; for it is possible that Aristotle should not have studied under Plato. The idea is this: a proper name simply designates a specific individual, and since it doesn't describe that individual, it designates it, not in virtue of its being the individual which..., but simply *qua* that specific individual; and so, no matter how different the individual that the name designates were to be from the way it actually is, the proper name would still designate that individual – and this is what Kripke means by saying that it designates the same individual in all possible worlds. (Kripke would apparently identify an individual by virtue of its origin; in the case of persons, by their date of birth and parentage.)

Kripke doesn't deny that the *reference* of a name may be fixed by means of a definite description, that one might introduce a name to denote the referent, in the actual world, of some definite description, fixing the reference of 'Fido', say, as the first dog to go to sea. What he denies is that the definite description gives the *sense* of the name; Fido, presumably, might not have been the first dog to go to sea, but in a possible world in which he isn't, while 'the first dog to go to sea' designates a different dog, 'Fido' still designates *Fido*, i.e. the dog that, in the actual world, was the first to go to sea.

The semantic account is supplemented by a causal explanation of the pragmatics of naming; the object is to explain how a speaker can use a name correctly even though he is quite unable to give a description that applies uniquely to the individual named – who knows of Feynman, for instance, only that he is a physicist. According to Kripke, a speaker uses a name correctly if there is a suitable chain of communication linking *his* use of the name with the individual designated by the name in an initial 'baptism'. A baby is born, his parents name him, other people meet him, he becomes a physicist, writes papers which other people read and write about...and so forth; then a speaker uses the name 'Feynman' correctly, to refer to Feynman, if his use of this name is causally linked in an appropriate way to the chain of communication which goes back to Feynman himself. Of course, there needn't literally have been an initial baptism, and the chain of communication may be very long indeed, as in our use of 'Julius Caesar' for instance. As Kripke is aware, 'causally linked *in an appropriate way*' stands much in need of amplification; since he does not offer any further explanation, there is not yet a guarantee that the causal account won't turn out either trivial or false.

The connection between the pragmatic and semantic strands of Kripke's account is, presumably, that his criteria for correct use of a name make no appeal to the speaker's knowledge of or beliefs about the individual designated, but require only that his use of the name be appropriately connected, causally, with that individual; this is consonant with the insistence, in the semantic account, that a name only designates and does not describe. However, if the reference of a name may, as Kripke allows, be fixed by means of a definite description, a gap could open between the semantic and the pragmatic accounts; for if I fix the reference of a proper name by means of a definite description which, in fact, though I don't know it, designates nothing (e.g. if I decide to call the man who stole my suitcase 'Smith', when actually my suitcase hasn't been stolen, but only moved by a porter) there can't be an appropriate causal chain to the bearer of the name, since there is no bearer.

It follows from the thesis that proper names are rigid designators that all true identity statements of the form '$a = b$', where 'a' and 'b' are names, are necessary. If 'a' and 'b' are names, and '$a = b$' is true, so that 'a' and 'b' designate the same individual in the actual world, then, since both names, being rigid designators, designate the same individual in all possible worlds, '$a = b$' is true in all possible worlds, that is to say, it is necessarily true.

Names assimilated to descriptions

Now, it was precisely because of a problem about identity statements that Frege introduced (1892a) his distinction between sense (*Sinn*) and reference (*Bedeutung*), and argued that proper names have sense as well as reference. How, Frege asks, can:

(i) $a = b$

differ in 'cognitive value' from, i.e. be more informative than:

(ii) $a = a$

if *a is b*? His answer is that, while, if *a* is *b*, the reference of 'a' is the same as the reference of '*b*' (they stand for the same object), the sense of '*a*' is different from the sense of '*b*', and this difference accounts for the greater informativeness of (i) over (ii).[1]

Frege explains the informativeness of true statements of the form '*a* = *b*' as arising from the difference of sense of the names '*a*' and '*b*'. How would Kripke, who doesn't admit that names *have* senses, and according to whom all true identities are necessary, explain it? His explanation is that, though statements of the form '*a* = *b*' are necessary, not all necessary statements can be known *a priori*; that is, it may be a *discovery*, for all that it is necessary, that *a* is *b*. For instance, the name 'Hesperus' was given to a certain heavenly body seen in the evening, and the name 'Phosphorus' to a heavenly body seen in the morning; both are rigid designators, and designators, as it turns out, of the very same heavenly body (the planet Venus); but astronomers had to *discover*, and didn't know *a priori*, that they designate the same heavenly body. (Kripke comments that there is nothing especially remarkable about one's knowing of some proposition that it is necessary *if* it is true, and yet not knowing whether it *is* true; Goldbach's conjecture would be an example.)

Frege, however, regards proper names as having sense as well as reference. By 'proper name' Frege understands *both* ordinary names and definite descriptions (he says that a name is any expression that

---

[1] Although the distinction is originally introduced specifically for names, it is extended to apply to predicates, and then, on the principle that the sense (reference) of of a compound expression is to depend on the sense (reference) of its parts, to sentences. Thus:

expression	*sense*	*reference*
proper name	meaning of the name	object
predicate	meaning of the predicate expression	concept
sentence	proposition	truth-value

The reference of a sentence must be its truth-value, Frege argues, since if some component of a sentence is replaced by another with a different sense but the same reference (as 'The Morning Star is a planet'/'The Evening Star is a planet') it is the truth-value that remains unchanged. Always strongly anti-psychologistic, Frege stresses that the sense, or meaning, of an expression is to be distinguished from the idea that may happen to be associated with that expression; so when he says that the sense of a sentence is the 'thought' (*Gedanke*) it expresses, he means 'proposition' rather than 'idea'. In 'oblique' contexts, Frege adds (i.e. intensional contexts, e.g. indirect speech), sentences have, not their customary, but an 'indirect' reference, the direct reference being the customary sense, i.e. the proposition expressed. So in 'Tom said that Mary would come', the reference of 'Mary would come' is not its truth-value, but the proposition that Mary would come.

refs to a definite object, though in fact he also envisages the possibility of names, like 'Odysseus', that don't denote a real object).
And he equates the sense of an ordinary name with the sense of
a definite description which refers to the same object. *Which* co-
designative definite description? Apparently (1892a p. 58n, and cf.
1918 p. 517) one that the speaker has in mind, or happens to know.
Frege realises that this has the consequence that different people may
attach different meanings to a name, depending on what they know
about the person named; he comments that such variations of sense,
though they should be avoided in a perfect language, are tolerable so
long as the reference remains the same. In view of the fact that one of
the objections he frequently brings against identifying the sense of an
expression with the associated idea is that this would mean that the
sense varied from person to person, this tolerance is surprising.

Russell, like Frege, identifies the meaning of ordinary proper names
with the meaning of some relevant definite description (though, as will
appear below, he differs from Frege both in his view of meaning, and
in his view of how definite descriptions, in their turn, should be
explained). And, again like Frege, Russell saw that it followed that
names have a different meaning for different speakers.

Russell also distinguished, however, a special category of *logically
proper names*: these are expressions whose role is purely to denote
a simple object, and the meaning of which is the object denoted (so in
the case of logically proper names Russell *equates* meaning and
reference). In Russell's version of logical atomism, the 'simple objects'
are 'objects of acquaintance', so logically proper names denote
objects of acquaintance; according to Russell we are directly
acquainted not with ordinary objects, people, etc., but only with
sense-data. So the only expressions he allows to be logically proper
names are 'this', 'that' and (during the period in which he believed
in a directly introspectible ego) 'I'. No ordinary proper names are
logically proper names, for no ordinary proper names denote objects
of acquaintance. Russell sometimes uses 'acquaintance' in a more
commonsensical fashion, distinguishing between persons and places
one has actually met or visited and those one has only heard about,
and treats names of persons or places with which one is acquainted in
this sense as logically proper names. But it is clear that this is a loose
usage, and that the strict theory according to which no ordinary
names are logically proper names is the one to be taken seriously.

Identifying the meaning of a proper name with some co-designative description known to the speaker has, as Frege and Russell realised, the uncomfortable consequence that the meaning of the name is variable between speakers. This difficulty could be avoided by identifying the meaning of the name, instead, with the set of all descriptions true of the bearer. But this has the unhappy consequence that every true statement of the form '*a* is (was) the person who...', where '*a*' is a proper name, is analytic, and every false statement of that form, contradictory, for '*a*', on this view, just *means* 'the person who...' for all descriptions true of the bearer. This problem, in turn, could be deflected by loosening the connection between the meaning of the name and the set of descriptions of its bearer. An idea of this kind is found in the *Philosophical Investigations* (Wittgenstein 1953), where it is suggested that a name hasn't a fixed, unequivocal meaning, but is loosely associated with a set of descriptions; by 'Moses' one may mean the man who did most, or much, of what the Bible relates of Moses, but how much, or what part, of the story has to be false before one says that there was no such person as Moses, is not fixed (§79). Something like this is also proposed by Searle 1969: while no one of what are thought of as established facts about *a* need necessarily be true of him, nevertheless the disjunction of them must be (p. 138). It isn't analytic that Moses was found in the bullrushes, nor that he led the Israelites out of Egypt, nor...etc., but it is analytic, according to Searle, that either Moses was found in the bullrushes, or...etc. Like Wittgenstein, Searle stresses that how many of the disjuncts may be false before it is true to say that *a* never existed is indeterminate.

Thus far, then, there are these alternatives:

let $d_1 \ldots d_n$ be all the descriptions (supposedly) true of *a*

then either:

the meaning of '*a*' is some member(s) of the set

or:

the meaning of '*a*' is the conjunction d_1 & d_2 & ... d_n of all the members of the set

or:

the meaning of '*a*' is some subset of the set of descriptions, there being indeterminacy about which, and how many, of the d_i to include.

These proposals identify, or more loosely associate, the sense of a proper name with that of related definite descriptions. Another proposal, in somewhat similar spirit, is offered by Burge 1973 (and endorsed by Davidson); on this account, instead of a name's being regarded as abbreviating a definite description, it is held to be, itself, a predicate. Burge points out that proper names rarely, in fact, stand for a unique object, that they take plural endings ('there are three Jacks in the class') and the definite and indefinite articles ('the Jack who wrote this', 'there is a Mary in the class but no Jane'). Burge is concerned with literal, not with metaphorical, uses of names, with 'Callaghan is a James' rather than 'Callaghan is no Churchill'. 'Jack is tall', on Burge's account, is best regarded as a sort of open sentence, with 'Jack' as a predicate governed by a demonstrative, 'that Jack is tall' (like 'that book is green') the reference of which is fixed by the context. Regarded, thus, as a predicate, 'Jack' is, according to Burge, true of an object just in case that object *is a Jack*, that is to say, just in case that object has been given that name in an appropriate way. Burge's account has some affinities with a suggestion to be found in Kneale 1962a, that the meaning of the name '*a*' is 'person called '*a*''. Kripke objects to Kneale's proposal that it is viciously circular. Burge, however, points out that his treatment of proper names as predicates could be supplemented by a theory of naming, a theory which would fill in the conditions in which an object is a Jack, the conditions, that is, in which it is true to say that it 'has been given the name 'Jack' in an appropriate way'. There is no reason, of course, why the kind of causal relation that Kripke stresses shouldn't have a role to play at this level.

There is a tendency to think of proper names as, so to speak, the means by which language gets its most direct grip on the world; and perhaps for this reason there is strong motivation to give a neat and tidy picture of the way naming works. In the theories I have sketched, two kinds of picture emerge of the connection between names and the individuals named: the purely denotative, or 'harpoon', picture, and the descriptive, or 'net', picture. (I derive the useful metaphor from Fitzpatrick; but I've changed his 'arrow' to 'harpoon' to give a place to the role of the causal chain of naming in Kripke's account.) I've already suggested that ordinary proper names in natural languages are very various, and that they work against a background of shared, or partly shared, information, or misinformation. Some confirmation for my suspicion that there may not be only one way in which all names work may be found in the way that the two pictures, officially presented as rivals, seem actually to complement each other: the harpoon picture explains how we can manage to talk about someone even though we are ignorant, or misinformed, about him – he'd slip, as it were, through our net; the net picture how we can talk, without confusion, about one of several or many people of the same name.

The details of the net picture will depend, obviously, on what account is given of the descriptions that, on this view, are associated with a name. It is to this question that I turn next.

3 Descriptions

Though Frege and Russell both equate the meaning of (ordinary) proper names with that of corresponding definite descriptions, they give quite different explanations of the way these descriptions work.

According to Russell's *theory of descriptions* (Russell 1905) definite descriptions, such as 'the tallest mountain in the world', are 'incomplete symbols', that is to say, they are contextually eliminable. Russell gives, not an explicit definition enabling one to replace a definite description by an equivalent wherever it appears, but a *contextual definition*, which enables one to replace sentences containing definite descriptions by equivalent sentences not containing definite descriptions:

$$E! \, (\imath x) \, Fx = df. \quad (\exists x) \, (y) \, (Fy \equiv x = y)$$

i.e. 'the F exists' means 'there is exactly one F', and

$$G((\imath x) \, Fx) = df. \quad (\exists x) \, ((y) \, (Fy \equiv x = y) \, \& \, Gx)$$

i.e. 'the F is G' means 'there is exactly one F and whatever is F is G'. The latter will consequently have two 'negations':

$$-(\exists x) \, ((y) \, (Fy \equiv x = y) \, \& \, Gx)$$

i.e. 'It is not the case that (there is exactly one F and whatever is F is G)', and:

$$(\exists x) \, ((y) \, (Fy \equiv x = y) \, \& - Gx)$$

i.e. 'There is exactly one F and whatever is F is not G'.
Of these, only the first is the contradictory of 'The F is G'; the latter is its contrary. (In general, in fact, it has to be indicated what *scope* a definite description has when it is in a compound sentence.)

Russell remarks that the grammatical form of sentences like 'The tallest mountain in the world is in the Himalayas' is misleading as to their logical form; what he means is that, whereas the English sentence contains an expression, 'the tallest mountain in the world', which looks as if its role is to designate an object, its formal representative contains no singular terms at all, but only bound variables, predicates and identity. And this enables Russell to deal with the problem of definite descriptions, such as 'the present King of France', which aren't true of anything. The problem, as Russell sees it, is this: if 'The present King of France is bald' is, logically, as it is grammatically, a subject–predicate sentence, then its subject term, 'the present King of France' must be a logically proper name, the meaning of which is the object it denotes; but since there is no present King of France, either 'the present King of France' denotes an unreal object, or else it denotes nothing, and hence it, and consequently the entire sentence, is meaningless. Reluctant to accept either of these conclusions, Russell solves the problem by denying that 'The present King of France is bald' is, logically, of subject–predicate form at all; logically, it is an existential sentence. In the end, then, Russell denies that any ordinary proper names (or definite descriptions) are properly represented by the singular terms of his formal language; this privilege is restricted to logically proper names.

Russell regarded his theory of descriptions as ontologically liberating; for it freed him of the necessity to admit a domain of unreal entities as the denotation of apparently non-denoting names. (See his criticisms (1905) of Meinong, who did admit non-existent objects, and cf. §4 below.) After developing the theory, in fact, Russell quite severely pruned his ontological commitments. Early on, in revolt against Bradley's monism, he had admitted a luxuriantly pluralist ontology, believing, as he put it, in everything Bradley disbelieved in; but subsequently, influenced by Whitehead's advocacy of Ockham's razor, and equipped with the theory of descriptions which freed him of the need to admit an object as denotation to secure the meaningfulness of every apparent name, he dismissed not only Meinongian objects, but classes, properties, even physical objects, as 'fictions'. (Cf. Quine 1966b for details of the development of Russell's ontological views.)

Quine's proposal (discussed in ch. 4 §2) to eliminate singular terms in favour of co-designative definite descriptions is clearly in the spirit of Russell's approach to proper names; Quine does not acknowledge a special category of logically proper names, and neither would he accept the epistemological assumptions underlying Russell's doctrine of acquaintance, but he would, I think, sympathise with Russell's view of the theory of descriptions as an instrument of ontological restraint.

For Frege, who has no special category of logically proper names the meaning of which is identified with their denotation, the problem of non-denoting names looks somewhat different. Frege can allow that sentences containing non-denoting names or descriptions nevertheless have a perfectly good sense (express a *bona fide* proposition). However, given his principle that the reference of a compound expression depends on the reference of its components, he is obliged to admit that a sentence like 'The present King of France is bald', the subject of which has no reference, itself lacks reference, that is to say, it has no truth-value. So, whereas according to Russell's analysis 'The present King of France is bald' entails that there is a present King of France (for that there is, is part of what it says), according to Frege's account 'The present King of France is bald' *presupposes* that there is a present King of France; that is, it is neither true nor false unless 'The present King of France exists' is true. An adequate formal treatment of presupposition, pretty obviously, would require a non-bivalent logic, a logic in which truth-value gaps were allowed, i.e. in which some wffs are neither true nor false. However, Frege does not offer such a logic (but see Smiley 1960 and van Fraassen 1966 for formal reconstructions of Frege's idea); for he thinks of non-denoting singular terms as an imperfection of natural languages which ought not to be permitted in a logically perfect language, and so recommends that, in formal logic, all singular terms be guaranteed a denotation, if necessary by artificially supplying an object – he suggests the number 0 – as their referent. (The choice of the number 0 may be a little unfortunate, since it would presumably have the consequence that 'The greatest prime number is less than 1', for instance, was true.) Anyway, whereas on Russell's theory definite descriptions and ordinary proper names aren't genuinely singular terms, but are contextually eliminated, Frege treats ordinary names and descriptions as *bona fide* singular terms, each with a single referent, with 'rogue' terms like 'the greatest prime number' referring to 0. (A Fregean formal theory is to be found in Carnap 1942.)

In his influential critique of Russell's theory, Strawson 1950 (and cf. Nelson 1946 which anticipates some of Strawson's points) employs a notion of presupposition which is reminiscent of Frege's analysis. There are differences, though, to be sorted out first, deriving in large part from Strawson's stress on the distinction between sentences and statements. According to Strawson, while it is linguistic expressions which have meaning, it is uses of linguistic expressions which refer, and, in particular, uses of sentences – statements – which are true or false. So his diagnosis of the problem of non-denoting descriptions goes like this: though the expression 'the present King of France' is quite meaningful, a use of that expression fails to refer, and consequently a use of a sentence containing that expression fails to make a true or false statement. Strawson is ambiguous about whether his diagnosis is that a use of the sentence 'The present King of France is bald' fails to make a statement, or that such a use makes a statement, but a statement which is neither true nor false. (The ambiguity is set out clearly in Nerlich 1965.) There is also an ambiguity in Strawson's thesis that an utterance of 'The present King of France is bald' does not, as Russell thinks, entail, but presupposes, that there is a present King of France: some passages suggest that it is the speaker who presupposes that there is a present King of France, others, that presupposition is not this kind of epistemological relation, but a logical relation holding between the statement that the present King of France is bald, and the statement that there is a present King of France. In later papers (1954, 1964) Strawson settles for the second thesis: presupposing is a logical relation between statements, such that S_1 presupposes S_2 just in case S_1 is neither true nor false unless S_2 is true. Since logical relations only hold, according to Strawson, between statements, this also resolves the first ambiguity noted above – an utterance of 'The present King of France is bald' must be allowed to constitute a statement, but a statement that is neither true nor false. Notice, first, that, but for the insistence that it is a relation between statements, Strawson's account of presupposition is just like Frege's; and, second, that if an utterance of 'The present King of France is bald' does, after all, constitute a statement, Strawson's criticism that Russell's mistake was to fail to distinguish between sentences and statements cannot be sustained. (On this second point cf. Russell's (1959) reply to Strawson.)

I am doubtful whether the question, whether 'The present King of France is bald' should be accounted false or truth-valueless could, or even should, be settled by appeal to 'what we would ordinarily say'. The issue turns, rather, on whether one is prepared to tolerate some artificiality (either, in the case of Russell's theory of descriptions, in the translation from natural languages into the formalism, or, in the case of Frege's preferred theory, in the choice of referent for otherwise non-denoting expressions) in order to conserve bivalence, since the Fregean 'presupposition' theory advocated by Strawson would require a non-bivalent base logic. And, if, of course, one thought there were other reasons for doubting bivalence, this would be relevant to one's estimate of the relative costs and benefits. (The comments about rival strategies in formalisation in ch. 9 §1 are pertinent to this particular choice.)

Strawson is careful to say that it is uses of expressions which refer. But there is, again, some ambiguity about what he takes to be the conditions for successful reference. Some passages hint at a pragmatic account, according to which it is a sufficient condition for a use of an expression to succeed in referring to an object that the speaker have a certain object in mind, and his use of the expression bring that object to the hearer's attention – regardless, that is, of whether the expression used actually denotes that object (cf. Strawson 1959 ch. 1 and 1964). But generally Strawson prefers a semantic account, according to which it is necessary, for a use of an expression to succeed in referring to an object, that the expression denote that object.

Donnellan 1966 brings the pragmatic notion of reference to the fore. Donnellan distinguishes between *attributive* and *referential uses* of definite descriptions. (The same definite description can be put to either use.) A definite description is used attributively if the speaker wants to assert something about whoever or whatever fits the description; referentially if, rather, he wants to draw his audience's attention to some particular person or thing and assert something about that. Donnellan gives as example the use of the sentence 'The man who murdered Smith is insane', attributively, to convey that anyone who murdered Smith must be insane, or referentially, to convey that Jones (whom the speaker and the audience know to have been convicted of the murder – perhaps wrongly) is insane. And one can use a definite description referentially, in Donnellan's sense, even if it is not true of – and even if speaker and hearer know it is not true of – the person or thing referred to; for the criterion of successful referential use is simply that the speaker should manage to bring to the audience's attention the person or thing he has in mind. Strawson's account, Donnellan suggests, is applicable only to attributive and not to referential uses.

It is true – as I had already suggested earlier – that Strawson's theory is, in the end, more semantic and less pragmatic than his official stress on the use of expressions might have led one to expect. It might be a helpful artifice to distinguish between *reference* and *denotation* or *designation*, and to use the former for the pragmatic notion (what speakers do) and the latter for the semantic one (what expressions do); then one can, if one wishes to adopt Donellan's standards of successful reference, say that a speaker may refer to a person or thing by the use of an expression which doesn't denote that person or thing. One advantage of this is to make clear that one needn't regard Donellan's account of the 'referential use' of definite descriptions as a rival to Frege's or Russell's theory.

4 Non-denoting names: fiction

The issues here are complex and tangled, and I can't hope to comment on them all. Some – the relations between singular terms and bound variables, and the possibility of eliminating the former in favour of the latter – have been touched upon already (ch. 4 §2). Others will receive more attention in subsequent chapters – the role of singular terms in modal contexts and the consequences of rival theories of naming for problems about the identity of individuals across possible worlds in ch. 10, theories of presupposition in ch. 11. One – the question of non-denoting names – I'll tackle now.

It emerged in the above discussion that there are two kinds of discrepancy between proper names in natural languages and singular terms in formal languages: while singular terms are each assigned *just one* individual in the domain, proper names sometimes have *more than one* bearer, and sometimes *none*. It is not unknown for writers simply to dismiss these discrepancies, assuming 'for the sake of argument' that ordinary proper names reliably denote a unique individual (e.g. McDowell 1977); but some interesting questions are evaded if they are so lightly disregarded. I shan't discuss, here, the first discrepancy, that proper names ('John Smith') frequently have several, or many, bearers, though it is worth observing that, of the theories I have sketched, Burge's is the one that takes this possibility most seriously. For the present, I shall confine myself to some comments about the other discrepancy, the phenomenon of non-denoting names, and, relatedly, to some thoughts about fictional discourse.

The problems raised by non-denoting names can be thrown into relief by considering them from the point of view of Russell's theory. Take the name of a fictional character, 'Sherlock Holmes', for instance. According to Russell, the meaning of a *bona fide* ('logically') proper name is to be equated with its denotation, so, if 'Sherlock Holmes' were a *bona fide* name, it would, since it is non-denoting, be meaningless, and so, too, would all sentences about Sherlock Holmes, including some, like 'Sherlock Holmes never existed', which one takes, surely with some justification, to be straightforwardly true (the 'problem of negative existentials', cf. Cartwright 1960). Russell would avoid this difficulty by denying that 'Sherlock Holmes' is a genuine name; it is a disguised definite description, and sentences about Sherlock Holmes are disguisedly existential, perfectly meaningful, and either straightforwardly true or straightforwardly false: 'Sherlock Holmes never existed' is true, while other statements about Sherlock Holmes, like 'Sherlock Holmes was a detective' or 'Sherlock Holmes was a policeman', are false.

Russell's account provides an explanation of how it is possible for us to speak meaningfully about non-existents, and to say truly that they *are* non-existent, and at the same time a simple solution to the problem of the truth-values of such statements. But some have felt that the assignment of 'false' alike to, say, 'Sherlock Holmes was a detective' and 'Sherlock Holmes was a policeman', is too crude, and takes too little account of the intuition that the former is 'right' in some sense in which the latter is not.

Sherlock Holmes is a fictional character, and according to the works of fiction in which he features, he was a detective, and not a policeman. It has been suggested (cf. Routley 1963) that a formal language appropriate to represent discourse about Holmes might require a domain of fictional entities, so that the name 'Sherlock Holmes' does denote, only it denotes a fictional, not a real, object. (Such systems are known as 'free logics', free, that is, of existential commitment; see Schock 1968 and cf. remarks about alternative choices of domain in ch. 4 §1.) This approach, interestingly, is in the spirit of Meinong's theory of objects, which allows for meaningful discourse about non-existents by admitting not only real, spatiotemporal objects, such as physical objects and persons, and subsistent, non-spatiotemporal, objects such as numbers and properties, but also non-existent, non-subsistent, and even impossible objects as all, genuinely, objects (see Meinong 1904 and cf. Parsons 1974). Russell 1905 recognises, as we saw, that this offered an alternative to his own theory, but thought it ontologically objectionable, maybe because of its affinities with ontological extravagances in which he had himself once indulged (1903). The curious way in which free logics represent non-denoting terms as terms denoting unreal objects (somewhat as the third 'value' of some 3-valued logics is intended to represent a lack of truth-value) might be thought, similarly, to exhibit a certain ontological ambivalence.

Now although the story tells us a good deal about Holmes, there are also a good many statements about him the truth of which is *not* fixed by the story – whether he had an aunt in Leamington Spa, for instance. So there is some motivation not only to adjust the domain to allow fictional entities, but also to allow that while some statements about Holmes are true and others false, others, again, are neither. And this means that a suitable formal language might need to abandon the principle of bivalence, the principle that every statement is either true or false. In such a formal language there would be scope for the representation of the Fregean relation of presupposition, which, as I pointed out above, calls for a non-bivalent logic.

There is a question, of course, to what extent all talk of non-existents should be seen on the model of talk about fictional entities; though Sherlock Holmes and the greatest prime number are alike in not existing, it is debatable whether they are alike in all logically relevant respects. But for the present I shall confine myself to the consideration of fictional entities. It is clear, at any rate, that there is an important distinction between, on the one hand, discourse *about* fiction, and, on the other, discourse *in* fiction. (I don't mean to suggest, of course, that *all* discourse in or about fiction is discourse about fictional entities.) What I do when I talk about Sherlock Holmes is presumably not altogether on all fours with what Conan Doyle did in writing the Holmes stories. In particular, whereas in the former case one can see some grounds for the intuition that there is a sense in which what I say may be right or wrong, in the latter case it seems more appropriate to say that the question of *Doyle's* getting it right or wrong simply doesn't arise. The kind of response just considered, I think, looks more promising with respect to discourse about fiction than with respect to discourse in fiction.

What's unusual about discourse *in* fiction, I suspect, isn't semantic at all, but pragmatic. Uttering (or writing) sentences in the course of telling a story differs from uttering sentences in the course of reporting an actual event; one is not, in the former case, as one is in the latter, asserting, that is claiming the truth of, the sentences one utters (cf. Plantinga 1974 ch. 8 §4, Woods 1974, Searle 1975, Haack 1976b). Whereas one might feel the need for a free logic for discourse about fiction, one might reasonably hope to handle the distinctive features of discourse in fiction by means of a theory of pragmatics. For, if my hunch is right, the most significant difference between telling a story and making a report, so to speak, is not in the difference between the story and the report, but in the difference between the telling and the making.

Sometimes it is taken for granted that if the distinctive features of some kind of discourse are pragmatic, that necessarily puts it beyond the scope of formal logical methods. The ubiquitous importance of pragmatic aspects of all discourse in natural languages has been a recurring theme with critics, such as Schiller and Strawson, who regard formal methods as seriously inadequate to the subtleties of natural language. So perhaps I should stress that, in urging that the distinctive characteristics of discourse in fiction may be rather pragmatic than semantic, I do not take for granted that this necessarily excludes the possibility of formal treatment.

6

Sentences, statements, propositions

1 Three approaches

A recurrent issue in the philosophy of logic concerns the question, with what kind of item logic deals, or perhaps primarily deals. The alternatives offered are usually sentences, statements and propositions, or, more rarely these days, judgments or beliefs. I have put the question in a deliberately vague way, since more than one issue seems to be involved. Once again, as with the issue about the meanings of connectives, quantifiers, etc., the problem concerns the relation between formal and informal arguments: what in informal arguments corresponds to the well-formed formulae of formal languages? It may be useful to distinguish three approaches to the question:

(i) syntactic: what, in natural languages, is the analogue of the 'p', 'q' of formal logic?

In speaking thus far of 'sentence calculus', I did not mean to beg this question. Some prefer to speak of 'propositional calculus', 'propositional variables', 'propositional connectives'; and so far I have said nothing to justify my preference for the former usage.

(ii) semantic: what kind of item is capable of truth and falsity?

Since formal languages aim to represent those informal arguments which are valid extra-systematically, that is, which are truth-preserving, this will relate closely to the first issue.

(iii) pragmatic:[1] what kinds of item should one suppose

---

[1] I call this the pragmatic approach because pragmatics is concerned with relations between expressions and the users of those expressions ('syntax' and 'semantics' were explained in ch. 2). I derive this way of separating the issues from Gochet 1972.

to be the 'objects' of belief, knowledge, supposition, etc.?

('Know', 'believe', 'suppose', etc. are sometimes called the verbs of 'propositional attitude'.) Since one can know, believe or suppose either something true or something false, the third will relate quite closely to the second issue.

For the present, however, I shall not discuss (iii) (but cf. pp. 124–7 and ch. 12 § 3); I shall comment first, very briefly, on (i), and then, at greater length, on (ii).

2 Sentence, statement, proposition

A necessary preliminary, however, is to specify what I shall mean by 'sentence', 'statement' and 'proposition'; for one reason why discussion of these issues is often confusing is that there is scant uniformity of usage.

By a *sentence* I shall mean any grammatically correct and complete string of expressions of a natural language. For example, 'Snow is white', 'Shut the door', 'Is the door shut?' are sentences; 'Sat by in' and 'Is pink' are not. I hope this rough and ready account is sufficient to convey the idea I have in mind; it is, of course, imprecise to the extent that there is uncertainty about which strings of expressions are to count as grammatical. I shall need to distinguish between sentence *types* and sentence *tokens*. A sentence token is a physical object, a series of marks on paper or of sound waves, constituting an inscribed or spoken sentence. Sometimes, however, one thinks of two or more tokens as inscriptions or utterances of, in some sense, the same sentence; 'same sentence', here, means 'same sentence type'. For example, the two inscriptions:

All philosophers are slightly insane
All philosophers are slightly insane

are tokens of the same type. One could think of a sentence type either as a pattern which similar tokens exemplify, or as a class of similar tokens. The question of what to take as criteria of identity for sentence types is disputed; some would require typographical or auditory similarity (presumably one would also need to specify the conditions in which an utterance was of the same sentence type as an inscription), others would require sameness of meaning. I shall stick to the former criterion, and allow the possibility of ambiguous sentence types.

I need, again, to distinguish, among sentences, those which are inter-rogative or imperative, for example, from those which are 'declarative'. Sentences with their main verb in the indicative mood are declarative, but 'declarative' is meant to be rather broader than 'indicative', to include, for example, conditionals whose main verb is in the sub-junctive. Intuitively, one might say that declarative sentences are those eligible for truth and falsity, whereas non-declarative sentences are not; but to define 'declarative' thus, in the present context, would obviously be question-begging.

By a *statement* I shall mean what is said when a declarative sentence is uttered or inscribed. In its non-technical employment, 'statement' is ambiguous between the event of the utterance or inscription of a sentence, and the content of what is inscribed or uttered. Only the second sense is relevant to present concerns. The question now arises, whether every utterance or inscription of a declarative sentence will make a statement. Strawson seems to think that some uses of declara-tive sentences – his examples include utterances or inscriptions used in the course of acting a play or writing a novel – do *not* make state-ments. He also, as we saw in the previous chapter, seems to hint that utterances of sentences whose subject terms do not denote anything fail to make statements, though at other times he suggests, rather, that such utterances are statements, but statements which are neither true nor false. These questions will obviously be important to the issue about truth-bearers. When, now, do two utterances or inscrip-tions make the same statement? It is usually said that they do so just in case they 'say the same thing about the same thing'. This account works well enough in simple cases. For instance, the utterances:

> You are hot   (said by x to y)
> I am hot   (said by y)
> *J'ai chaud*   (said by y)

would, by these standards, make the same statement. Making the criterion precise, however, threatens to be difficult, for it may not always be easy to specify when two utterances are about the same thing, and it could be harder still to specify when they say the same thing about their subject, since this will require an appeal to the notoriously tricky notion of synonymy.

By a *proposition* I shall understand what is common to a set of synonymous declarative sentences. In this sense of 'proposition' two sentences will express the same proposition if they have the same meaning; so here again, as with statements, the problem of synonymy will have to be faced. Another account, popular since the advent of possible-worlds semantics for modal logics, identifies a proposition with the set of possible worlds in which it is true, or with a function from possible worlds into truth-values. It isn't clear, however, that this comes to anything very different from the account I gave before, since one distinguishes the possible world in which p from the possible world in which q by means of distinguishing p from q. (If 'Jack and Jill have one parent in common' expresses the same proposition as 'Jack and Jill are step-siblings', then all possible worlds in which the first holds are possible worlds in which the second holds, and if not, not.) Another account, which delimits a different idea, identifies the proposition with the common content of sentences in different moods. So:

> Tom shut the door.
> Tom, shut the door!
> Has Tom shut the door?

have as common content the proposition *Tom's shutting the door*. Propositions in this sense are unlikely candidates as truth-bearers, and for that reason I shall pay them rather little attention here. They do, however, have some relevance to the interpretation of e.g. imperative logic, on which I shall offer some brief comments below.

It is quite easy to check that sentences, statements and propositions, as characterised here, are distinct, that is, that one could have same sentence/different statement/different proposition, same statement/different sentence/different proposition, same proposition/different sentence/different statement (cf. Cartwright 1962).

One's attitude to statements or propositions may well be coloured by one's metaphysical views. Nominalists, who dislike abstract objects, or extensionalists, who suspect that meaning notions suffer from a crippling unclarity, are likely to be ill-disposed towards statements and propositions and better disposed towards sentences, while Platonists, admitting abstract objects, and intensionalists, comfortable with the theory of meaning, could admit statements or propositions with equanimity. (Compare Quine 1970 ch. 1 with Putnam 1971 chs. 2, 3, 5, for contrasting attitudes.) It is necessary to observe, however, that though sentence tokens are physical objects, sentence types are abstract; and that, while the identity criteria for both statements and propositions require appeal to synonymy, the identity criteria for sentence types require appeal to the not altogether unproblematic notion of similarity. (See Goodman 1970 for some of the problems which beset attempts to define similarity precisely.)

3   'Sentence letters', 'propositional variables', or what?

How one understands the 'p', 'q'...etc. of sentence logic will obviously depend upon whether one allows sentence letters to be treated as genuine variables to be bound by quantifiers, and, if one does, how one interprets those quantifiers.

The usual presentations of sentence logic do not use quantifiers. On the face of it, however, it seems reasonable to suppose that unquantified sentence calculus has an *implicit* generality which quantified sentence calculus merely makes *explicit*. A theorem like '$p \rightarrow (p \lor q)$' is usually understood to hold for all instances of 'p' and 'q', just as, in the usual, unquantified presentations of algebra, '$a+b = b+a$' is understood to hold whatever a and b may be. So the alternatives are either to regard the usual, unquantified formulation as simply an abbreviated version of quantified sentence logic, or else to find some other way of accounting for the implicit generality of the unextended calculus.

Quine, for reasons already touched upon in ch. 4 §3, prefers the second alternative. He proposes that 'p', 'q' etc. *not* be treated as genuine, bindable variables, but be construed, instead, as 'schematic letters'. A wff of sentence calculus, such as '$p \lor -p$', is to be thought of 'not as a sentence but as a schema or diagram such that all actual statements of the depicted form are true' (1953a p. 109).

If, however, one *does* treat sentence letters as genuine variables, one is then faced with the question of the interpretation of the quantifiers. If one adopts an objectual interpretation, one is next faced with the question of what kind of object the quantifiers are to range over: propositions are the most usual candidates, though Quine 1934 argued for a domain of sentences. (If one is concerned only with the usual, truth-functional sentence calculus, one might even construe such quantifiers as ranging over *truth-values*, that is to say, over the two values t and f; for in truth-functional sentence logic only the truth-values of the components are relevant to the truth-value of the compound. The addition of non-truth-functional sentence operators, 'necessarily', perhaps, or 's believes that', however, would rule out this alternative.) An adjustment to the usual reading is then needed:

in '$(p)(p \lor -p)$', if the quantifier is read 'for all propositions p', then '$p \lor -p$' must be construed as a singular term denoting a compound proposition ('the disjunction of a proposition with its own negation'), and an implicit predicate ('is true') has to be supplied to make the reading grammatical. If, on the other hand, one adopts a substitutional interpretation, '$(p)(p \lor -p)$' will be read 'All substitution instances of '$\ldots \lor - \ldots$' are true', where appropriate substitution instances result from putting the same sentence in each of the blanks. (It will not have escaped notice, I'm sure, that Quine's 'schematic letters' look much like bound variables of substitutional quantification with sentences as the substitution class.)

At this level, then, there seem to be several options. But what about the question of truth-bearers?

4 Truth-bearers

If an argument is valid, then if its premises are true, its conclusion must be true too; so presumably premises and conclusions need to be the kind of item capable of being true or false. So, many writers have considered it very important to decide whether it is sentences, statements or propositions which are properly called 'true' or 'false'. The issue has many ramifications; it has been suggested, for example, that confusion about truth-bearers underlies the semantic paradoxes (Bar-Hillel 1957, Kneale 1971), that it motivates the proposals for many-valued logics (Lewy 1946, Kneale and Kneale 1962, Kripke 1975 p. 700n), that it vitiates Russell's theory of descriptions (Strawson 1950). I have already commented (ch. 5 §3) on the last of these; I'll have something to say about the first in ch. 8, and about the second in ch. 11.

The dispute about truth-bearers usually proceeds along some such lines as the following: since truth is presumably a property, one should be able to identify the type of item which possesses it; it is usually taken for granted either that only one of the candidates can be the truth-bearer, or that one is primary and the others somehow derivative. The ensuing debate about which items are the, or the primary, truth-bearers, however, has been, to my mind, neither very conclusive nor very fruitful. You will shortly see what I mean.

Several writers (Strawson 1950, Pitcher introduction to 1964, Putnam 1971, for example) have claimed that it is improper, or even meaningless, to speak of sentences as being true or false. The arguments offered for this claim, however, seem pretty inconclusive. One is that if sentences were true or false some sentences would be sometimes true and sometimes false; another is that some sentences, non-declarative sentences, for instance, just aren't capable of truth or falsity, so not all sentences could be true or false. But a gate, after all, can quite properly be called red or green, though it may have one colour one year and another the next; and some glass, stained glass for instance, can properly have colour predicates ascribed to it, despite the fact that some glass is colourless (cf. Lemmon 1966, R. J. and S. Haack 1970).

Though these arguments certainly don't show that sentences cannot properly be called true or false, they may suggest an apparently more promising line of thought: that whatever items be chosen as truth-bearers, they should be such that (i) they can be relied upon not to change their truth-value, and (ii) all items of the relevant kind are either true or false. The acceptability of these *desiderata* will need investigation, of course. But even leaving that question aside for the present, it turns out that statements and propositions are scarcely more successful than sentences in these respects.

(i) Whether a statement can change its truth-value depends, obviously, on how exactly one understands 'saying the same thing about the same thing'. But on an intuitive understanding, at least, two utterances concerning the same Jones, half a minute apart, of 'Jones is wearing an overcoat' would presumably say the same thing about the same thing. Yet one utterance could be true and the other false, if Jones put on or took off his overcoat in the interval. Of course, one could guarantee against statements changing their truth-values by tightening up the criteria for statement identity so far that no non-simultaneous utterances count as making the same statement. But this would, in effect, correlate statements one–one with sentence tokens, and then one might justifiably wonder what the point was of introducing statements as distinct from sentences.

Since the sense of a sentence may remain stable over a considerable period, the proposition expressed by a sentence could also, presumably, change its truth-value; for instance, the proposition expressed by the sentence 'Louis XIV is dead' was once false and is now true. Some writers (Frege 1918, Moore 1953, Kneale 1971, for instance) have responded to this difficulty by tightening up the criteria of propositional identity so as to disallow change of truth-value; this seems to be vulnerable to a similar objection to that made, above, to a comparable manoeuvre to prevent statements changing their truth-values.

(ii) Since it is uncertain whether every utterance of a declarative sentence is supposed to make a statement, it is not clear, either, whether every statement must be either true or false. Strawson concedes, however, that it is not part of the definition of 'statement' that every statement is either true or false (1952 p. 69); and, as we saw, there are traces in 1950, and an explicit claim in 1964, that utterances of 'reference failure' sentences make statements which are neither true nor false. So some statements will lack truth-value.

In some cases where a sentence is neither true nor false, one could plausibly argue that there is no corresponding proposition, and to that extent propositions fare better than sentences at satisfying (ii). Among the sentences which are neither true nor false, there are, so it is often said, some which though grammatically correct are meaningless ('Virtue is triangular' for instance); being meaningless, such sentences express no proposition. Imperative and interrogative sentences also presumably fail to be true or false, and it could, again, be claimed that such sentences do not express propositions. However, it is doubtful whether one could specify which kinds of sentence do express propositions except by restricting oneself to declarative sentences (as in §2 above); so this argument does not show propositions to be better off with respect to (ii) than sentences. And some declarative sentences (vague sentences and future contingent sentences for instance) are thought by some writers to be neither true nor false, and yet, being meaningful, express propositions which are therefore themselves neither true nor false.

I am not suggesting, of course, that sentences fare better than statements or propositions with respect to (i) and (ii). I have already mentioned, above, several kinds of sentence which may fail to have any truth-value, so sentences don't meet (ii). As for (i): many sentence types obviously change their truth-value ('I am hungry', for instance, would be true in some mouths at some times, false in others and at others); even some sentence tokens can be shown capable of changing their truth-value. (A token of 'There is a person in this room', written on the blackboard in my office, would usually be true at 12 noon and false at 12 midnight.) Quine has pointed out that we can specify a class of sentence types which do not change their truth-value; it would include both sentences stating physical and mathematical laws, to which temporal considerations are, he argues,

4

irrelevant, and sentences completely specified as to time and place, with tensed verbs and indexicals like 'now' replaced by tenseless verbs, dates and times. Quine calls these stable types 'eternal sentences' (cf. ch. 9 §3).

Truth-bearers and theory of truth

One argument which might be offered in favour of allowing sentences as truth-bearers is this: some theories of truth, certain versions (Wittgenstein's but not Austin's, for example) of the correspondence theory, and, most notably, Tarski's semantic theory, exploit grammatical structure in the definition of truth (details in ch. 7). Sentences, of course, have grammatical structure; statements and propositions, however, being extra-linguistic, do not. And since the same statement may be made by uttering, and the same proposition expressed by, sentences in different languages with different grammatical structures, it will be hard for statements or propositions to 'borrow' a structure from the sentences which make or express them. However, while some would regard the plausibility of Tarski's theory as a reason for regarding sentences as truth-bearers, others, on the basis of their conviction that sentences cannot be truth-bearers, are disposed to reject Tarski's theory (see e.g. White 1970 pp. 94–9). Some, again, would argue that the fact that Tarski's definition of truth has to be language-relative, that he defines 'true-in-L' rather than 'true', is a point against it. And others propose modifying Tarski's theory in ways which would make it applicable to propositions (Popper 1972) or statements (Davidson 1967).

One can see, on reflection, that such requirements as (i) and (ii), which those who object to sentences implicitly impose on truth-bearers, themselves relate to assumptions – which turn out to be questionable – about the theory of truth: that a correct theory will be bivalent and will make truth timeless. I shan't discuss the question of truth's supposedly timeless character here, but simply refer the reader to Putnam 1957 and Haack 1974 pp. 69–70. One or two brief comments about bivalence may be in order. Undue weight placed on the idea that every item of a kind to have a truth-value should be either true or false often lies behind an undesirable kind of conservatism about deviant logics. For some writers react to the suggestion that certain sentences, being neither true nor false, perhaps call for a non-bivalent logic, by retorting that such sentences cannot make statements or cannot express propositions, and so, since it is with statements or propositions that logic is concerned, are outside its scope (see e.g. Lewy 1946, and cf. Kripke 1975 p. 700n; the 'no item' thesis is discussed in Haack 1974 pp. 47–53). This reaction is apt to trivialise serious issues.

Some theories of truth – the descendants of Ramsey's 'redundancy' theory – suggest a radical solution to the problem about truth-bearers. The question what truth is a property of arises on the – natural enough – assumption that truth is a property. But these theories (ch. 7 §7) deny that truth is a property, and hence bypass the question, what it's a property of. One could be excused for thinking that, in view of the unsatisfactory state of that question, it is a virtue of such theories to avoid it.

5 The problem reformulated

Arguments against sentences seem to impose requirements on truth-bearers which statements and propositions also fail, and which are themselves questionable anyhow; some argue in favour of sentences as truth-bearers that Tarski's truth theory requires them, others reject Tarski's theory because it requires sentences as truth-bearers... One begins to suspect that the formulation of the problem may be in need of improvement. I think the problem which underlies the debate *can* be reformulated in a way which makes it rather more manageable. I began, you may remember, by observing that the issues about sentences, statements, propositions and so forth arose, as philosophical problems in logic are apt to, from questions about the relations between formal and informal arguments. Now suppose one has a formal argument in sentence calculus such as:

$$p \lor -q$$
$$\underline{-p}$$
$$-q$$

and wants to know what informal arguments can properly be regarded as instances of it. Obviously this is something one needs to know if formal logic is to help one assess informal arguments. One question which needs to be answered now is what can stand, in an informal argument, for the 'p' and 'q'. Well, one wants to say, any sentence you like can correspond to 'p' and 'q', provided the same sentence corresponds to each occurrence. That's a start, but more constraints are needed: declarative sentences can correspond to 'p' and 'q', but not imperative or interrogative sentences; if the sentences corresponding to '*p*' and '*q*' are tensed, then the time reference should stay constant throughout the argument; if they contain indexicals like 'I', 'he', 'now', their reference should stay constant through the argument; and if they're ambiguous, they should be used in the same sense throughout the argument. Otherwise, though the formal argument is valid, its supposed analogue in informal argument is apt to be *in*valid; if, for instance, the last condition is not observed, one has a 'fallacy of equivocation'.

This way of putting the problem has the advantage of metaphysical neutrality, so that it raises neither nominalist nor Platonist hackles; and yet it seems to ask the right questions about how to apply formal logic to informal argument. And the fact that the constraints on what, in informal argument, can stand where '*p*' and '*q*' do in formal logic, reflect the identity conditions proposed for the various candidate truth-bearers is some confirmation of my claim to have reformulated the original problem rather than replace it by a different one. (But it turns out, interestingly, that in its reformulated version the problem arises even on the theories which do not regard truth as a property.)

The reformulated problem does not refer to 'truth-bearers' directly, but, rather, asks what vagaries of the sentences put for '*p*' and '*q*' may interfere with validity. In the case of classical sentence logic this amounts to asking what may prevent the same sentence's having the same truth-value at different occurrences within an argument; it is because an ambiguous sentence may be true in the premises and false in the conclusion that equivocation interferes with validity. But the greater generality of the reformulated problem should prompt another look at the relations between validity and truth.

Validity again

I observed earlier that to insist that logic deal only with items which are either true or false is to give uncharitably short shrift to non-bivalent logics. Furthermore, if such enterprises as imperative or erotetic logic (logic of questions) are to be feasible, it must be conceded that logic may deal with sentences incapable of truth and falsity. Now the extra-systematic account of validity that I gave in ch. 2 was in terms of truth-preservingness. If, however, one takes serious account of the possibility of logics which deal with non-truth-bearing items, one is likely to need an extended conception of validity. If, for example, one wants to handle imperative sentences, it may prove appropriate to define an analogue of truth (a 'designated value' if you like) which *is* applicable to them. Ross 1968 suggests: 'p!' is satisfied[1] iff 'p' is true. (E.g. 'Close the door!' is satisfied iff 'The door is closed' is true.) Validity, for imperative logic, would then be preservation of satisfaction rather than preservation of truth.

It should not be dismaying – nor even very surprising – that developments such as non-bivalent or imperative logic may call for changes or extensions of the intuitive conception of validity to which the standard logical apparatus gives formal expression. It is often enough by modification or extension of its key ideas that a science grows.

[1] This use of 'satisfaction' should be kept distinct from that to be introduced in the next chapter, in the discussion of Tarski's theory of truth.

7

Theories of truth

1 A summary sketch[1]

The object of this section is to sketch the main kinds of
theories of truth which have been proposed, and to indicate how they
relate to each other. (Subsequent sections will discuss some theories
in detail.)

Coherence theories take truth to consist in relations of coherence
among a set of beliefs. Coherence theories were proposed e.g. by
Bradley 1914, and also by some positivist opponents of idealism, such
as Neurath 1932; more recently, Rescher 1973 and Dauer 1974 have
defended this kind of approach. *Correspondence* theories take the
truth of a proposition to consist, not in its relations to other propositions, but in its relation to the world, its correspondence to the facts.
Theories of this kind were held by both Russell 1918 and Wittgenstein
1922, during the period of their adherence to logical atomism; Austin
defended a version of the correspondence theory in 1950. The *pragmatist* theory, developed in the works of Peirce (see e.g. 1877),
Dewey (see e.g. 1901) and James (see e.g. 1909) has affinities with
both coherence and correspondence theories, allowing that the truth
of a belief derives from its correspondence with reality, but stressing
also that it is manifested by the beliefs' survival of test by experience,
its coherence with other beliefs; the account of truth proposed in
Dummett 1959 has, in turn, quite strong affinities with the pragmatist
view.

[1] Proponents of the theories I shall discuss take different views about
what kinds of items are truth-bearers. In what follows I shall speak
variously – depending upon which theory I am discussing – of
'beliefs', 'sentences', 'propositions' etc. as true or false; only when
the difference makes a difference shall I draw attention to it.

time

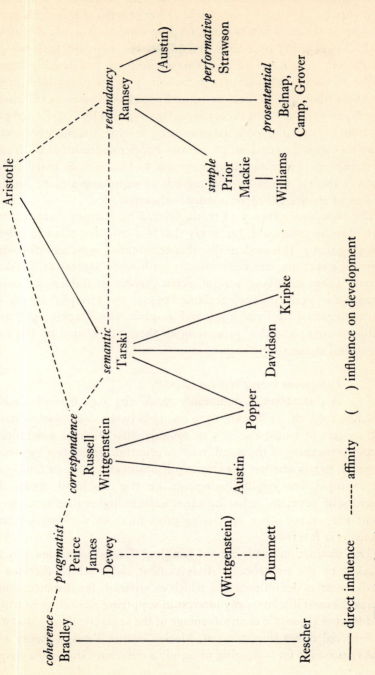

'to say of what is, that it is'...etc.
Aristotle

redundancy
Ramsey

(Austin)

performative
Strawson

prosentential
Belnap,
Camp, Grover

simple
Prior
Mackie

Williams

semantic
Tarski

Kripke

Davidson

Popper

correspondence
Russell
Wittgenstein

Austin

pragmatist
Peirce
James
Dewey

(Wittgenstein)

Dummett

coherence
Bradley

Rescher

—— direct influence   ----- affinity   ( ) influence on development

Fig. 4   Theories of truth

Aristotle had observed that 'to say of what is that it is not, or of what is not that it is, is false, while to say of what is that it is, or of what is not that it is not, is true'. In proposing his *semantic* theory of truth, Tarski 1931, 1944 aims to explicate the sense of 'true' which this dictum captures. Truth, in Tarski's account, is defined in terms of the semantic relation of satisfaction, a relation between open sentences (like '$x > y$') and non-linguistic objects (such as the numbers 6 and 5). The truth theory recently proposed by Kripke 1975 is a variant of Tarski's, modified essentially to cope in a more sophisticated way with the semantic paradoxes. Popper's account of truth and his theory of verisimilitude or nearness to the truth is based upon Tarski's theory, which Popper regards as supplying a more precise version of traditional correspondence theories.

The *redundancy* theory of truth, offered by Ramsey 1927, claims that 'true' is redundant, for to say that it is true that p is equivalent to saying that p. It is evident that this account has some affinities with Aristotle's dictum, and consequently with some aspects of Tarski's theory. There have been several recent variants of Ramsey's theory: Strawson's 'performative' account (1949); the 'simple' theory of truth suggested by Prior 1971 and amplified by Mackie 1973 and Williams 1976; and the 'prosentential' theory presented by Grover, Camp and Belnap 1975.

Definitions versus criteria of truth

A distinction is commonly made (by e.g. Russell 1908b, Rescher 1973 ch. 2, Mackie 1973 ch. 1) between *definitions* of truth and *criteria* of truth; the idea is, roughly, that whereas a definition gives the meaning of the word 'true', a criterion gives a test by means of which to tell whether a sentence (or whatever) is true or false – as, for example, one might distinguish, on the one hand, fixing the meaning of 'feverish' as having a temperature higher than some given point and, on the other, specifying procedures for deciding whether someone *is* feverish.

This distinction needs careful handling. One's suspicions may be aroused by the existence of disagreement about which theories of truth count as definitional and which as criterial: for instance, while Tarski himself disclaims any interest in supplying a criterion of truth, and Popper regards it as an advantage of the semantic theory that it is definitional rather than criterial, Mackie counts Tarski's theory as – and criticises it for – aspiring to supply a criterion. And one's suspicions should be confirmed by some clearly inappropriate uses of the distinction. For example, Russell accused the pragmatists of having confused the definition and the criterion of truth, when the pragmattists held that the meaning of a term is correctly given precisely by supplying criteria for its application. (It is not at all unusual, I'm afraid, for a philosopher who deliberately identifies As and Bs to find himself facing the criticism that he has 'confused' As and Bs.)

However, one cannot simply decide to refrain from using the distinction, problematic as it is, because of its importance to such questions as whether the coherence and correspondence theories need be regarded as rivals, between which one is obliged to choose, or as supplementing each other, correspondence supplying the definition and coherence the criterion. This question is at issue even between proponents of the coherence theory. Thus Bradley, conceding that 'Truth to be truth must be true of something, and this something itself is not truth' (1914 p. 325), seems to allow that an account of the meaning of truth may require appeal to something like correspondence, while coherence is rather a mark, a test, of truth. Blanshard, by contrast, insists that truth *consists in* coherence, which is a definition as well as a criterion. This insistence seems to be based on the conviction that there must be some intimate connection between a dependable criterion and what it is a criterion *of*. Coherence could not be the test, but correspondence the meaning, of truth, he argues, for then there is no explanation why coherent beliefs should be the ones that correspond to the facts; if coherence is to be a reliable test of truth, it must be because it is constitutive of the meaning of truth (see Blanshard 1939 p. 268).

Rescher proposes (1973 chs. 1 and 2) to deflect this argument by distinguishing between *guaranteeing* (infallible) and *authorising* (fallible) criteria, and arguing that only in the case of guaranteeing criteria need there be the connection with the definition that Blanshard thinks inevitable. This distinction illuminates some issues touched upon earlier. Rescher counts C as a guaranteeing criterion of x if:

necessarily (C iff x obtains)

But – as Rescher observes – in this sense, any definition of truth would also supply an infallible criterion of truth. For instance, if truth consists in correspondence to the facts, then, necessarily, if 'p' corresponds to the facts, 'p' is true, so correspondence is an infallible criterion.[1] (The idea that Tarski gives a criterion of truth may derive from this conception of criteria.)

So: if one has a definition, one thereby has a 'guaranteeing' criterion. The converse, however, is a bit less straightforward. It is a guaranteeing criterion of a number's being divisible by three, for example, that the sum of its digits be divisible by three, but this, I take it, is not what it means for a number to be divisible by three. Rather: if one has a guaranteeing criterion, then either it *is*, or else it is *a logical consequence of*, a definition.

An authorising criterion, however, is fallible: it is not necessarily the case that (*C* iff *x* obtains); so, either it is true, though not necessarily, that *C* iff *x* obtains, or perhaps it is not invariably true that *C* iff *x* obtains. (Rescher considers the second but not the first kind of case.) So an authorising criterion of *x* is distinct from a definition of *x* – it need not be logically related to the meaning of '*x*'.[2]

But now why, if any definition supplies a guaranteeing criterion, should one ever want an authorising criterion? The answer is rather clear, I think, but hard to put precisely: if one wants to find out whether *x* obtains, one would like, ideally, a reliable indicator of the presence of *x* which is *easier to discover to obtain* than *x* itself. A definition gives an indicator which is perfectly reliable, but exactly as difficult to discover to obtain as *x* itself; an authorising criterion gives an indicator which may be less than completely reliable, but which, by way of compensation, is easier to discover to obtain. For example, one might think of the characteristic spots as an authorising criterion of measles; not a foolproof test, since it is not logically necessary that one has the spots iff one has the measles, but much more easily discovered than, say, the presence of a given bacterium which is (or

---

[1] If one identifies meaning and criterion – as the pragmatists do – then one is obliged to hold the criterion to be guaranteeing. This will be pertinent to the discussion in §6 below of Popper's argument that the pragmatist theory of truth threatens fallibilism.

[2] Rescher does not explicitly amplify the 'necessarily' in his account of a guaranteeing criterion, but contextual clues indicate that he has in mind logical necessity, which is the interpretation I have used. If physically necessary tests were included, the previous and some subsequent paragraphs would have to be rewritten to allow criteria which are related to that of which they are a test by physical necessity, as well as criteria related by logical necessity, to count as guaranteeing. Of course, the distinction between logical and physical necessity – and indeed, the distinction between the necessary and the contingent – is not unproblematic.

so I shall suppose for the sake of argument) the guaranteeing criterion.

So far, then, Rescher's vindication of Bradley's view of coherence as a criterion (an authorising criterion, that is) but not a definition, of truth, against Blanshard's argument for an inevitable connection between definition and criterion, is successful. However, it is pertinent that a weaker version of Blanshard's idea seems to work even for authorising criteria. It seems plausible to argue that, if C is an authorising criterion (even in the least favourable case when its presence isn't invariably correlated with that of x), then there ought to be *some* kind of connection – not, indeed, a logical connection, but perhaps a causal connection, for example – between x and C. Consider, again, spots as an authorising criterion of measles; there is a causal connection between the spots and the disease of which they are the symptom. And, indeed, this is relevant to a feature of Bradley's account which Rescher neglects. It is plausible to think that Bradley believed there to be a connection between one's beliefs' being coherent, and their corresponding to reality (i.e. between the authorising criterion and the definition), for he holds that reality is coherent.

The concept of truth is as important to epistemology as to philosophy of logic. Some theories of truth have an important epistemological component, are concerned with the accessibility of truth; and the search for a criterion of truth is often a manifestation of this concern. It is noticeable that on the whole the theories on the left side of the sketch of truth-theories (fig. 4) take the epistemological dimension more seriously than those on the right, with the coherence and pragmatist theories epistemologically rich, but redundancy theories, at the other extreme, with virtually no epistemological 'meat' (as Mackie puts it) on them.

2 Correspondence theories

Both Russell and Wittgenstein, during their 'logical atomist' periods,[1] offered definitions of truth as the correspondence of a proposition to a fact.

Propositions, according to Wittgenstein, are verbal complexes; molecular propositions (such as '$Fa \lor Gb$') are composed truth-functionally out of atomic propositions (as, 'Fa'). The world consists

---

[1] Wittgenstein was the originator of logical atomism, but Russell's version appeared first, in his 1918 lectures, while Wittgenstein's was presented in 1922 in the *Tractatus*.

of simples, or logical atoms, in various complexes, or arrangements, which are facts. And in a perfectly perspicuous language the arrangement of words in a true, atomic proposition would mirror the arrangement of simples in the world; 'correspondence' consists in this structural isomorphism. The truth-conditions of molecular propositions can then be given; ' $-p$ ' will be true just in case ' p ' is not true, ' $p \lor q$ ' will be true just in case either ' p ' is true or ' q ' is true, and so forth.

Wittgenstein's version of logical atomism is austere; Russell augmented it with an epistemological theory according to which the logical simples about whose character Wittgenstein is agnostic are sense-data, which Russell took to be the objects of direct acquaintance, and the meaningfulness of a proposition is supposed to derive from its being composed of names of objects of acquaintance. These epistemological additions do not vitally affect the core of the account of truth; but some other differences between Russell's and Wittgenstein's versions are more relevant. Russell's account has the virtue of recognising the difficulties in regarding all molecular propositions, notably belief propositions and quantified propositions, as truth-functions of atomic propositions. Other features of Russell's version, however, seem to create unnecessary difficulties; for instance, he allows (though with less than complete confidence, because of the adverse reaction this thesis received at Harvard!) negative as well as positive facts, so that the truth of the negation of p can consist in its correspondence to the fact that not p, rather than p's failure to correspond to the facts; and the suggestion that there are two correspondence relations, one of which relates true propositions and the other false propositions to the facts, seems gratuitous, indeed, in view of the admission of negative facts, doubly so.

Numerous critics have observed that the trouble with the correspondence theory is that its key idea, correspondence, is just not made adequately clear. Even in the most favourable cases the required isomorphism between the structure of a proposition and that of the fact involves difficulties; consider:

The cat is to the left of the man   (the proposition)

(the corresponding fact)

even here (as Russell concedes, pp. 315–16) it looks as if the fact has two components, the proposition at least three; and of course the difficulties would be much severer in other cases (consider '*a* is red', '*a* is married to *b*', or for that matter 'the cat is to the right of the man'). The interpretation of correspondence as a structural iso-morphism is intimately connected with both the theory about the ultimate structure of the world and the ideal of a perfectly perspicuous language, characteristic theses of logical atomism. The question arises, therefore, whether the correspondence theory can be divorced from logical atomism, and, if it can, what account could then be given of the correspondence relation.

Austin 1950 supplies a new version of the correspondence theory, a study of which offers some answers. Austin's version does not rely either on an atomist metaphysics or on an ideal language; the corre-spondence relation is explicated, not in terms of a structural iso-morphism between proposition and fact, but in terms of purely conventional relations between the words and the world. Correspon-dence is explained via two kinds of 'correlation':

(i) 'descriptive conventions' correlating words with *types* of situation

and

(ii) 'demonstrative conventions' correlating words with *specific* situations

The idea is that in the case of a statement such as 'I am hurrying', uttered by *s* at *t*, the descriptive conventions correlate the words with situations in which someone is hurrying, and the demonstrative con-ventions correlate the words with the state of *s* at *t*, and that the state-ment is true if the specific situation correlated with the words by (ii) is of the type correlated with the words by (i). Austin stresses the con-ventional character of the correlations; *any* words could be correlated with *any* situation; the correlation in no way depends on isomorphism between words and world.

A difficulty with this account of correspondence, which essentially appeals to *both* kinds of correlation, is that it applies directly only to statements made by sentences which are indexical, since the demon-strative conventions would have no role to play in the case of sentences like 'Julius Caesar was bald' or 'All mules are sterile', which can't be used in statements referring to different situations. (Austin's com-ments on these cases, p. 23n, are none too reassuring.)

On the other hand, Austin's version, I think, makes an improvement on Russell's account of 'the facts'. The point is hard to put clearly, but it is significant enough to be worth putting even somewhat vaguely. Russell is apt to speak as if the truth of p consists *in its correspondence to the fact that p*; but the trouble with this is that the relation between 'p' and the fact that p is just *too* close, that 'p' couldn't fail to correspond to *that* fact. His evasiveness about the criteria of individuation of facts may indicate that he felt this discomfort. Austin's version, however, locates the truth of the statement that p not in its correspondence to the fact that p, but rather in *the facts'* being as 'p' says, or, as Austin puts it, in the demonstrative conventions' correlating 'p' with a situation which is of the kind with which the descriptive conventions correlate it. (Austin is aware of this difference; see 1950 p. 23; and cf. Davidson 1973 and O'Connor 1975.)

3   Coherence theories

A coherence theory of truth was held by the idealists (I shall discuss Bradley's account, but related views were held by his German philosophical ancestors Hegel and Lotze) and also by some of their logical positivist opponents. So the relation between coherence theories and idealism is rather like that between correspondence theories and logical atomism – in that in each case the theory of truth became divorced from the metaphysical outlook with which it was originally characteristically associated.

It will be useful – because this way some significant relations between coherence and correspondence theories can be highlighted – to begin in the middle, with Neurath's defence of a coherence view. A little history will not go amiss: the logical positivists, under the influence of Wittgenstein's *Tractatus*, originally subscribed to a correspondence view of the character of truth. They were, however, strongly motivated by epistemological concerns, and consequently desired a test (authorising criterion) of truth – a way to tell whether or not a sentence indeed corresponds to the facts. Carnap and Schlick tackled the problem in two parts; statements reporting immediate perceptual experience, they argued, are incorrigible, that is to say, we can directly verify that they correspond to the facts, and the truth of other statements can then be tested by means of their logical relations to these. Already a characteristic feature of the correspondence theory – that truth lies in a relation between beliefs and the world – is modified: the test of the truth of all but perceptual statements derives from their relations with other statements, the perceptual ones, which are supposed to be verified by direct confrontation with the facts. Neurath, however, raised doubts about the supposed incorrigibility of 'protocols', and having thus denied the possibility of a direct check of even perceptual beliefs' correspondence to the facts, held the only test of truth to consist of relations among beliefs themselves. Our search for knowledge requires a constant readjustment of beliefs, the aim of which is as comprehensive a belief set as consistency allows. (This is strongly reminiscent of the 'method of maxima and minima' in James' epistemology (James 1907); Quine's position in 'Two dogmas of empiricism' (1951), where he endorses Neurath's metaphor of the process of acquisition of knowledge as repairing a raft while afloat on it, is similar. Cf. Hempel 1935 for an excellent account of the development of the positivists' view of truth, and Scheffler 1967 ch. 5 for a lively 'blow by blow' report of the controversy between Schlick and Neurath.)

Neurath's final position has much in common with Bradley's account of the test of truth as 'system', which he explains as requiring both *consistency* and *comprehensiveness* of the belief set. And in Bradley as in Neurath the appeal to coherence is connected with the denial that our knowledge has any incorrigible basis in the judgments of perception. However, Bradley's theory has intimate connections with his absolute idealism. Briefly and roughly, reality, according to Bradley, is itself essentially a unified, coherent whole. (Russell's pluralistic logical atomist metaphysic was motivated by reaction against the idealists' monism.) And while Bradley conceded something to the idea of truth as correspondence to reality, he held that, strictly speaking, nothing short of the fully comprehensive, consistent belief set at which we aim is really true; at best, we achieve partial truth – *part* of the truth is not fully true. The point of these remarks is to bring out a point anticipated earlier (§1) – that the connections between Bradley's view of truth and his view of reality are close enough for it to be somewhat misleading simply to regard him as offering coherence as the test, while leaving correspondence as the definition, of truth; rather, the explanation of the success of coherence as the test derives from an account of reality as itself essentially coherent.

A persistent difficulty with the correspondence theory, as I observed above (§2) has been the difficulty of supplying a precise account of 'corresponds'. A similar problem dogs the coherence theory; it needs to be specified exactly what the appropriate relations between beliefs must be for them to be 'coherent' in the required sense. Unsympathetic critics of coherence theories – Russell, for example – have been apt to assume that simple consistency is sufficient; Bradley, however, was already insisting (as early as 1909, against criticism from Stout; see Bradley 1914) that comprehensiveness as well as consistency is required.

Rescher, who defends a coherentist epistemology (coherence as the test of truth) offers a detailed explication of the twin requirements of 'system': consistency and comprehensiveness. The problem facing the coherentist, as Rescher sees it, is to supply a procedure for selecting, from incoherent and possibly inconsistent data ('truth-candidates', not necessarily truths) a privileged set, the warranted beliefs, those one is warranted in holding true. A 'maximal consistent subset' (M.C.S.) of a set of beliefs is defined thus: S' is an M.C.S. of S if it is a non-empty subset of S which is consistent, and to which no member of S not already a member of S' can be added without generating an inconsistency. But the data-set is likely to have more than one M.C.S.; this is the basis of Russell's criticism that coherence cannot distinguish the truth from a consistent fairy tale. To avoid this difficulty Rescher proposes that the M.C.S.s of the data-set be 'filtered' by means of a plausibility index, dividing data into those which are, and those which are not, initially plausible, and thus reducing the number of eligible M.C.S.s. However, this may be insufficient to single out a unique M.C.S.; so Rescher recommends the adoption of the disjunction of those M.C.S.s permitted by the plausibility filter.

Though Rescher's work has contributed significantly to the detailed working-out of a coherentist epistemology, difficulties remain. An obvious problem is the specification and justification of the standards of plausibility (Schlick's appeal to the alleged incorrigibility of protocols could be seen as an alternative response to a related difficulty). A less obvious, but also important, difficulty is that the recommended procedure is, so to speak, static in character: it tells one how to select a privileged, 'warranted', subset from an initial set of data, but correspondingly underestimates the importance of seeking *new* data. (Bradley's insistence that only the most fully comprehensive belief set – the whole truth – is strictly speaking true could be seen as a response to this difficulty.) Coherence will surely form part, but not the whole, of a satisfactory epistemology.

Thus far, I have followed Rescher (with some qualifications in Bradley's case) in taking coherence to be intended as a test of truth, as playing an epistemological role, while allowing correspondence the metaphysical part. (Cf. the large role played by coherence in Quine's epistemology, from 1951 to 1970, with his adoption of the semantic definition of truth, 1970 ch. 3). The pragmatists, however, challenge this distinction with their characteristic criterial theory of meaning.

4 Pragmatic theories[1]

Peirce, James and Dewey offer characteristically 'pragmatic' accounts of truth, which combine coherence and correspondence elements.

According to the 'pragmatic maxim' the meaning of a concept is to be given by reference to the 'practical' or 'experimental' consequences of its application[2] – 'there can *be* no difference' as James put it (1907 p. 45) 'that *makes* no difference'. So the pragmatists' approach to truth was to ask what difference it makes whether a belief is true.

According to Peirce, truth is the end of inquiry, that opinion on which those who use the scientific method will, or perhaps would if they persisted long enough, agree. The significance of this thesis derives from Peirce's theory of inquiry. Very briefly: Peirce takes belief to be a disposition to action, and doubt to be the interruption of such a disposition by recalcitrance on the part of experience; inquiry is prompted by doubt, which is an unpleasant state which one tries to replace by a fixed belief. Peirce argues that some methods of acquiring beliefs – the method of tenacity, the method of authority, the *a priori* method – are inherently unstable, but the scientific method enables one to acquire (eventually) stable beliefs, beliefs which will not be thrown into doubt. For the scientific method, Peirce argues, alone among methods of inquiry, is constrained by a reality which is independent of what anyone believes, and this is why it can lead to consensus. So, since truth is the opinion on which the scientific method will eventually settle, and since the scientific method is constrained by reality, truth is correspondence with reality. It also follows that the truth is satisfactory to believe, in the sense that it is stable, safe from the disturbance of doubt.

[1] This section draws upon Haack 1976c.
[2] Peirce stressed the connection of 'pragmatic' with Kant's use of '*pragmatische*' for the empirically conditioned, James the connection with the Greek '*praxis*', action.

James' major contribution was an elaboration on this idea. The advantage of holding true beliefs, he argued, was that one was thereby guaranteed against recalcitrant experience, whereas false beliefs would eventually be caught out ('Experience...has ways of *boiling over*...', 1907 p. 145). James' account of the way one adjusts one's beliefs as new experience comes in, maximising the conservation of the old belief set while restoring consistency – strikingly like Quine's 1951 view of epistemology – introduces a coherence element. True beliefs, James comments, are those which are verifiable, i.e. those which are, in the long run, confirmed by experience.

Thus far, I have stressed the continuities between Peirce's and James' views, but there are some differences which should be mentioned. First, while Peirce was a realist, James was inclined towards nominalism (cf. Haack 1977d), and therefore embarrassed by the possible-but-not-yet-realised verifications to which the view of truth as verifiability committed him; consequently, although in principle he allows that beliefs are true (false) though no one has yet verified (falsified) them, in practice he is sufficiently persuaded of the pointlessness of dwelling on this that he slips into speaking, inconsistently, as if new truths come into existence when beliefs get verified. (The idea that truth is *made*, that it grows, was taken up by the English pragmatist, F. C. S. Schiller.) Second, James often speaks of the true as being the 'good', or the 'expedient' or the 'useful' belief (e.g. 1907 pp. 59, 145). Unsympathetic critics (e.g. Russell 1908b, Moore 1908) have taken James to be making a crass, not to say morally objectionable, identification of the true with the congenial belief. The comments which provoked this critical fury, when taken in context, can often be read, much more acceptably, as pointing to the superiority of true beliefs as *safe from falsification* (cf. James' own defence, 1909 p. 192 – 'Above all we find *consistency* satisfactory'). But James is also making another claim: that since at any given time the evidence available to us may be insufficient to decide between competing beliefs, our choice may depend upon such grounds as simplicity or elegance (1907 p. 142); a claim which does have connections with his 'will to believe' doctrine.

Dewey adopts Peirce's definition as 'the best definition of truth' (1938 p. 345n). He prefers the expression 'warranted assertibility' to 'truth', and adds the thesis that it is precisely warranted assertibility that characterises those beliefs to which we give the honorific title, knowledge (cf. Ayer 1958). Dummett's view of truth, the direct inspiration for which derives from the work of the later Wittgenstein and from Intuitionism in the philosophy of mathematics, resembles Dewey's in its stress on assertibility; see Dummett 1959.

The main theses of the pragmatic account can be summarised as follows:

truth is:

the end of inquiry
correspondence with reality ⎫
satisfactory (stable) belief ⎬ Peirce ⎫
coherence with experience – ⎭ ⎬ James ⎫
   verifiability ⎬ ⎬ Dewey
what entitles belief to be called ⎭ ⎭
   'knowledge'

5 The semantic theory

Tarski's has been, of late, probably the most influential and most widely accepted theory of truth. His theory falls into two parts: he provides, first, *adequacy conditions*, i.e. conditions which any acceptable definition of truth ought to fulfil; and then he provides a definition of truth (for a specified formal language) which he shows to be, by his own standards, adequate. Both parts of this programme will be examined. The detailed statement of the theory is to be found in Tarski 1931; 1944 is a good introduction.

It isn't hard to see why Tarski's theory should have been so influential. For one thing, his adequacy conditions on definitions of truth promise a kind of filter to discriminate, among the embarrassingly numerous theories of truth, those which meet minimal conditions of acceptability, which therefore have some prospect of success. Furthermore, the methods employed in Tarski's definition of truth can be applied to a large class of formal languages. But the very features of Tarski's theory which contribute most to its appeal also, as we shall see, create problems for it: can Tarski's adequacy conditions be given independent motivation? and: have his methods any interesting application to the problem of truth for natural languages?

Adequacy conditions on definitions of truth

The problem which Tarski sets himself is to give a definition of truth which is both *materially adequate* and *formally correct*; the first of these conditions sets limits on the possible content, the second on the possible form, of any acceptable definition.

Material adequacy

Tarski hopes that his definition will 'catch hold of the actual meaning of an old notion' (1944 p. 53). However, the 'old' notion of truth is, Tarski thinks, ambiguous, and even doubtfully coherent. So he restricts his concern to what he calls the 'classical Aristotelian conception of truth', as expressed in Aristotle's dictum:

> To say of what is that it is not, or of what is not that it is, is false, while to say of what is that it is, or of what is not that it is not, is true.

And he proposes, as material adequacy condition, that *any acceptable definition of truth should have as consequence* all instances of the (T) schema:

(T) S is true iff p

where 'p' can be replaced by any sentence of the language for which truth is being defined and 'S' is to be replaced by a name of the sentence which replaces 'p'. An instance of (T) would be, e.g.:

'Snow is white' is true iff snow is white

where the sentence on the right-hand side is referred to by its 'quotation-mark name' on the left-hand side.

Tarski emphasises that the (T) schema is *not a definition* of truth – though in spite of his insistence he has been misunderstood on this point. It is a *material adequacy condition*: all instances of it must be entailed by any definition of truth which is to count as 'materially adequate'. The *point* of the (T) schema is that, if it is accepted, it fixes not the intension or meaning but the *extension* of the term 'true'. For suppose one had two definitions of truth, D_1 and D_2, each of which was materially adequate. Then D_1 would entail all instances of:

S is true$_1$ iff p

and D_2 all instances of:

S is true$_2$ iff p

so that D_1 and D_2 are co-extensive. Or, to put essentially the same point in another way, the material adequacy condition would rule out certain definitions of truth, those, that is, which did *not* entail instances of the (T) schema.

But exactly what kinds of definition will the material adequacy condition rule out? In answering this question I shall use a weakened version of the criterion: not that all instances of the (T) schema *be deducible from* any acceptable truth definition (Tarski's version), but that the truth of all instances of the (T) schema *be consistent with* any acceptable truth-definition. The reason for this modification is simply that the weakened adequacy condition is much more readily applicable to non-formal definitions of truth. Now it is to be hoped – and perhaps even expected – that it will allow the sorts of definition which have been seriously proposed, and disallow what one might call 'bizarre' theories. But matters turn out rather oddly. Consider the following definition of truth, which seems to me definitely bizarre: a sentence is true iff it is asserted in the Bible. Now it might be supposed that this definition (I shall call it 'D_B' for short) does not entail all instances of the (T) schema, not, for instance:

> 'Warsaw was bombed in World War II' is true$_B$ iff
> Warsaw was bombed in World War II.

Now it is indeed the case that someone who did not accept D_B might deny:

> 'Warsaw was bombed in World War II' is asserted in
> the Bible iff Warsaw was bombed in World War II.

But further reflection makes it clear that a proponent of D_B could perfectly well maintain that his definition *does* entail all instances of (T); he may allow that 'Warsaw was bombed in World War II' is true, but insist that it *is* asserted in the Bible (in an obscure passage in Revelation, perhaps), or if he agrees that 'Warsaw was bombed in World War II' is not asserted in the Bible, he will also, if he is wise, maintain the falsity of the right-hand side of the above instance of the schema. So, rather surprisingly, Tarski's material adequacy condition cannot be relied upon to be especially effective in ruling out bizarre truth-definitions.

The material adequacy condition *does*, however, apparently rule out a certain important class of truth theories, those, that is, according to which some sentences (statements, propositions, wffs or whatever) are neither true nor false. For suppose 'p' to be neither true nor false; then the left-hand side of:

> 'p' is true iff p

will be, presumably, false, while the right-hand side will be neither true nor false. So the whole biconditional will be false, or at any rate untrue. (This argument could, however, be avoided if one were prepared to allow that metalinguistic assertions such as ''p' is true' might themselves be neither true nor false.) It is arguable that Tarski's material adequacy condition would rule out at least some versions of the coherence theory; arguably it would *not* rule out a pragmatist theory, since the pragmatist view of meaning would rule meaningless any sentences which are neither verifiable nor falsifiable, so that there could be no meaningful but truth-valueless sentences. It certainly seems rather extraordinary to rule non-bivalent theories of truth out of court.

The idea behind Tarski's material adequacy condition is, presumably, that the truth of the (T) schema is so certain and obvious that it is proper that one should feel confident in rejecting any theory of truth which is inconsistent with it. For myself, I find the initial certainty and obviousness of the (T) schema somewhat modified when it turns out that not only some of the seriously propounded theories of truth, but also some very bizarre theories, are consistent with it, while some other serious theories are inconsistent with it (but see Davidson 1973 for a defence of 'convention T').

Formal correctness

The formal requirement which Tarski lays down concerns the structure of the language in which the definition of truth should be given, the concepts which may be employed in the definition, and the formal rules to which the definition must conform.

It is notorious that semantic concepts, incautiously handled, are apt to give rise to paradoxes (e.g. the Liar – 'This sentence is false'; Grelling's paradox – ''not true of itself' is true of itself iff it is not true of itself', and so forth). Tarski investigates the Liar paradox in some detail, and argues that the antinomy arises from the assumptions:

(i) That the language used contains, in addition to its expressions, (*a*) the means of referring to those expressions and (*b*) such semantic predicates as 'true' and 'false'. Such a language Tarski calls 'semantically closed'.

(ii) That the usual logical laws hold.

Being unwilling to reject assumption (ii), Tarski concludes that a formally correct definition of truth should be expressed in a language which is not semantically closed.

Specifically, this means that the definition of truth-in-O, where O is the *object language* (the language *for* which truth is being defined), will have to be given in a *metalanguage*, M (the language *in* which truth-in-O is defined). The definition of truth will have to be, Tarski argues, relative to a language, for one and the same sentence may be true in one language, and false, or meaningless, in another. The danger of the semantic paradoxes can be avoided by resort to a metalanguage; the Liar sentence, for instance, will then become the harmless 'This sentence is false-in-O', which is, of course, a sentence of M, and consequently not paradoxical. The object/metalanguage distinction is, of course, a relative one, and a whole hierarchy of languages would be required to define truth at every level. Since all equivalences of the form (T) must, by the material adequacy condition, be implied by the definition of truth, M must contain O or translations of all sentences of O as part, plus the means to refer to expressions of O; for instances of (T) have, on the left-hand side, an expression denoting a sentence of O, and, on the right-hand side, a sentence of O or a translation of a sentence of O. Notice that, in specifying, in the meta-metalanguage, that the metalanguage, M, should contain either the object language, O, itself, or a translation of each sentence of O, semantic notions are employed (explicitly in the latter case, and implicitly in the former, since M must contain the same expressions of O with the same interpretations as they have in O).

It is also required that the structure of O and M should be 'formally specifiable'. For in order to define 'true-in-O' it will be essential to pick out the wffs of O, since these are the items to which 'true-in-O' applies. (This is one of the reasons which Tarski gives for feeling sceptical about the possibility of defining 'true-in-English' – or 'true' for *any* natural language; the sentences of natural languages are not, he thinks, formally specifiable. Later followers of Tarski, notably Davidson, feel more optimistic on this point. It is one I shall need to investigate more closely.)

Tarski also requires that 'the usual formal rules of definition are observed in the metalanguage' (1944 p. 61). These rules include:

(i) no free variable may occur in the *definiens* which does not also occur in the *definiendum*

ruling out e.g. '$Fx = \mathrm{df}(x + y = 0)$', and

(ii) no two occurrences of the same variable may occur in the *definiendum*

ruling out e.g. '*Fxx* = df *Gx*'. Condition (i) prevents definitions which could lead to contradiction; condition (ii) prevents definitions in which the *definiendum* is ineliminable (cf. Suppes 1957 ch. 8).

Any acceptable definition of truth must, then, according to Tarski, satisfy both the material adequacy and the formal correctness conditions. He gives a definition, and shows that it is, by these standards, acceptable.

Tarski's definition of truth

It might be thought that the (T) schema, though not itself a definition of truth, provides an obvious way of giving such a definition. Tarski himself points out that one could think of each instance of (T) as a *partial* definition of truth, in that each instance specifies the truth-conditions of some one specific sentence; so that a conjunction of *all* instances of the (T) schema, one for each sentence of O, would constitute a complete definition. Tarski, however, argues that it is *not* possible to give such a conjunctive definition, for the number of sentences of a language may be infinite, and in this case it is impossible actually to give all the required instances of the (T) schema.

Neither, Tarski argues, can the (T) schema be turned into a definition of truth by universal quantification. It might be supposed that, using on the left-hand side a quotation mark name of the sentence used on the right-hand side, one could straightforwardly generalise to obtain:

$$\text{(D) } (p) \text{ ('}p\text{' is true}_O \text{ iff } p)$$

which would apparently constitute a complete definition, and one, furthermore, guaranteed to be materially adequate, since all instances of (T) are instances of it. But Tarski rejects this suggestion because he believes that the result of quantifying into quotation marks is meaningless. For, according to Tarski (and also according to Quine), the expression obtained by writing quotation marks around an expression is an indivisible unit, analogous to a proper name, so that:

Snow is white

is no more part of:

'Snow is white'

than (to use Quine's example) 'rat' is of 'Socrates'. Tarski concedes that if it were feasible to regard quotation as a function, then (D) would be no less well-formed than e.g.:

$$(x) (x^2 = x.x)$$

He thinks, however, that there are overwhelming objections to treating quotation as a function, and, in consequence, that (D) is no more well-formed than e.g.:

$$(x) (\text{Texas is large})$$

So Tarski thinks that the (T) schema not only is not, but also cannot be turned into a definition of truth. So he constructs his own definition by a more roundabout route. He takes it as a *desideratum* that no semantic terms should be taken as primitive, so that any semantic notion in terms of which 'true' is defined should itself previously be defined. Since he is to define 'true' using the concept of satisfaction, which is a semantic one, this means that he must first define 'satisfies'.

Informal account

The procedure is as follows:

(a) specify the syntactic structure of the language, O, for which truth is to be defined

(b) specify the syntactic structure of the language, M, in which truth-in-O is to be defined; M is to contain
  (i) either the expressions of O, or translations of the expressions of O
  (ii) syntactical vocabulary, including the names of the primitive symbols of O, a concatenation sign (for forming 'structural descriptions' of compound expressions of O), and variables ranging over the expressions of O
  (iii) the usual logical apparatus

(c) define 'satisfies-in-O', and

(d) define 'true-in-O' in terms of 'satisfies-in-O'

Why does Tarski first define 'satisfies'? Well, first, because he considers it desirable to employ, in his definition of truth, no semantic primitives; for he considers that semantic notions are none of them, pre-theoretically, sufficiently clear to be safely employed. But why 'satisfies'? This is a suitable notion in terms of which to define 'true' because closed, compound sentences are formed out of *open* sentences, rather than closed, atomic sentences. For example, '$(\exists x)\ Fx \lor Gx$' is formed out of 'Fx' and 'Gx' by the operations of disjunction and existential quantification; and the open sentences 'Fx' and 'Gx' are not true or false, but satisfied, or not, by objects. The definition of satisfaction is *recursive* – that is, definitions are given first for the simplest open sentences, and then the conditions are stated in which compound open sentences are satisfied. (The definition could, however, be turned into an explicit one.) This procedure will provide a definition of truth applicable to all sentences of O.

'*Satisfies*': open sentences are not true or false, they are satisfied, or not, by certain things, pairs of things, triples of things, etc. For instance: 'x is a city' is satisfied by London; 'x is north of y' is satisfied by ⟨London, Exeter⟩; 'x is between y and z' is satisfied by ⟨London, Exeter, Edinburgh⟩...etc. ('⟨..., ...⟩' indicates the *ordered n-tuple* of the n items which appear between the pointed brackets.) The order of the items is obviously important, since ⟨London, Exeter⟩ satisfies 'x is north of y' but ⟨Exeter, London⟩ does not. Satisfaction is a relation between open sentences and ordered n-tuples of objects. To avoid the difficulties arising from the fact that open sentences may have 1, 2, ... or *any* number of free variables, Tarski defines satisfaction as a relation between open sentences and *infinite* sequences, under the convention that '$F(x_1 \ldots x_n)$' is to be satisfied by the sequence ⟨$O_1 \ldots O_n, O_{n+1} \ldots$⟩ just in case it is satisfied by the first n members of the sequence; subsequent members are ignored.

The negation of an open sentence S_1 will be satisfied by just those sequences which do not satisfy S_1; and the conjunction of S_1 and S_2 by just those sequences which satisfy S_1 *and* satisfy S_2. The existential quantification of an open sentence will be satisfied by a sequence of objects just in case there is some other sequence of objects, differing from the first in at most the ith place (where the ith is the variable bound by the quantifier) which satisfies the open sentence resulting from dropping the quantifier. For instance, the sequence ⟨England, London, Edinburgh...⟩ satisfies '$(\exists x)\ (x$ is a city between y and $z)$' because e.g. the sequence ⟨York, London, Edinburgh⟩ satisfies 'x is a city between y and z'.

'*True*': Closed sentences are special cases of open sentences, those, namely, with *no* free variables. The first member of a sequence, and all subsequent members, are irrelevant to whether or not the sequence satisfies a o-place open sentence, i.e. a *closed* sentence. So Tarski defines a sentence as *true just in case it is satisfied by all sequences*, and as *false just in case it is satisfied by none*. This procedure may be made less mysterious by considering an example. The 2-place open sentence 'x is north of y' is satisfied by e.g. all sequences ⟨Edinburgh London, ...⟩, whatever their third and subsequent members. The 1-place open sentence 'x is a city' is satisfied e.g. by all sequences, ⟨Edinburgh, ...⟩ whatever their second and subsequent members. And the (true) o-place open sentence '$(\exists x)$ (x is a city)' is satisfied by *all* sequences ⟨..., ..., ...⟩, whatever their first and subsequent members; for there is a sequence, ⟨Edinburgh, ...⟩ for instance, which differs from any arbitrary sequence in at most the first place, and which satisfies 'x is a city'. Any closed sentence will be satisfied by *all* sequences or by *none*, and can't be satisfied by some and not others. Consider a rather austere language: first-order predicate calculus without singular terms. In the simplest case, a closed sentence is formed by existential quantification of a 1-place open sentence. Such an existentially quantified sentence is satisfied by an arbitrary sequence only if there is another sequence, differing from it in the first place at most, which satisfies the 1-place open sentence which results from dropping the initial existential quantifier; and so, if the existential sentence is satisfied by *any* sequence, it will be satisfied by *every* sequence. So a closed existential sentence will be satisfied either by all sequences or by none. The negation of a closed existential sentence, by the negation clause of the satisfaction definition, will be satisfied by a sequence iff the negated sentence is not satisfied by that sequence and so, once again, will be satisfied either by all sequences or by none; and similarly for the conjunction of two closed existential sentences, which will be satisfied by a sequence iff both conjuncts are satisfied by that sequence, and so, also satisfied by all sequences or by none. But why is 'true' defined as 'satisfied by all sequences', and 'false' as 'satisfied by none'? Well, consider again the closed sentence '$(\exists x)$ (x is a city)': let X be an arbitrary sequence of objects. By the clause of the definition of satisfaction which covers existentially quantified sentences, X satisfies this sentence iff there is some sequence Y differing from X in at most the first place which satisfies 'x is a city'; now an object O satisfies 'x is a city' just in case O is a city, so there is such a sequence just in case there is some object which is a city. Thus '$(\exists x)$ (x is a city)' is satisfied by all sequences just in case some object is a city. (Consult Rogers 1963 for further informal discussion of Tarski's definition.)

Two features of Tarski's definition deserve explicit mention at this point. First, it imposes an *objectual interpretation* of the quantifiers; as the previous example indicates, '(∃x) *Fx*' is true iff some object is *F*. A substitutional interpretation would avoid the need for the detour via satisfaction, for it would permit truth of quantified sentences to be defined directly in terms of the truth of their substitution instances (cf. ch. 4 §1). Second, in his original paper, Tarski gives an *absolute* rather than a *model-theoretic* definition; 'satisfies', and hence 'true', is defined with respect to sequences of objects in the actual world, not with respect to sequences of objects in a model or 'possible world' (e.g. 'there is a city north of Birmingham' is true, absolutely, but false in a model in which the domain is, say, {London, Exeter, Birmingham, Southampton}; cf. pp. 115, 122 below).[1]

Formal account

Tarski gives his definition of truth for a class calculus (the object language), and uses a formalised metalanguage. I shall give, instead, a definition of truth for a more familiar object language, the first-order predicate calculus, and I shall use English plus the object language (cf. (b)(i), p. 105) as metalanguage. This truth-definition will, however, follow Tarski's in all essentials. (It follows Quine's account in 1970 ch. 3 rather closely.)

Syntax of O

The expressions of O are:

variables: x_1, x_2, x_3 ... etc.

predicate letters: *F, G* ... etc. (each taking a given number of arguments)

sentence connectives: − , &

quantifier: (∃ ...)

brackets: (,)

---

[1] In 1957 Tarski and Vaught give a model-theoretic definition. The significance attached to the difference between absolute and model-theoretic definitions will depend, in part, on one's attitude to possible worlds (see pp. 190 ff. below). Those who think of the actual world as just one possible world among others will think of the absolute definition as simply a special case of a model-theoretic definition. However, not all writers regard the two approaches in this tolerant way. There is a question whether a model-theoretic definition satisfies all the constraints Tarski used in his 1931 paper; and this seems to some (Davidson for example; see below) to be an important reason to prefer an absolute definition.

In terms of this austere primitive vocabulary, of course, the other truth-functions and the universal quantifier can be defined. I am also assuming that singular terms have been eliminated. The advantage of choosing such a minimal vocabulary is, as will become apparent, that it much reduces the work which has to go into the truth definition.

The atomic sentences of O are those strings of expressions which consist of an n-place predicate followed by n variables.

(i)   All atomic sentences are well-formed formulae (wffs)
(ii) If A is a wff, $-A$ is a wff
(iii) If A, B are wffs, $(A \,\&\, B)$ is a wff
(iv) If A is a wff, $(\exists x) A$ is a wff
(v)   nothing else is a wff

Definition of 'satisfies'

Let X, Y range over sequences of objects, A, B over sentences of O, and let X_i denote the ith thing in any sequence X.

Then satisfaction can be defined for atomic sentences, by giving a clause for each predicate of the language.

1. for 1-place predicates:
    for all i, X: X satisfies 'Fx_i' iff X_i is F
    For 2-place predicates:
    for all i, X: X satisfies '$Gx_i x_j$' iff X_i and
        X_j stand in the relation G

and so on for each predicate.

2. for all X, A: X satisfies '$-A$' iff X does not satisfy 'A'
3. for all X, A, B: X satisfies '$A \,\&\, B$' iff X satisfies A and X satisfies B
4. for all X, A, i: X satisfies '$(\exists x_i) A$' iff there is a sequence Y such that $X_j = Y_j$ for all $j \neq i$ and Y satisfies 'A'

(Notice how each clause of the definition of satisfaction corresponds to a clause in the definition of a wff. This is why it is so convenient to work with minimal vocabulary.) A closed sentence is a wff with no free variables; closed sentences will be satisfied either by all sequences or by none.

Definition of 'true': a closed sentence of O is true iff it is satisfied by all sequences.

Tarski shows that his definition is both materially adequate and formally correct. He also shows that it follows from his definition of truth that of each pair consisting of a closed sentence and its negation one, and only one, is true. This was to be expected in view of the fact, already observed, that the material adequacy condition rules out non-bivalent theories of truth.

6   Commentary on the semantic theory

Tarski's theory has the distinction of having been criticised both for saying too little:

> the neutrality of Tarski's definition[1] with respect to the competing philosophical theories of truth is sufficient to demonstrate its lack of philosophical relevance. (Black 1948 p. 260)

and for saying too much:

> The Tarskian theory...belongs to factual rather than conceptual analysis...Tarski's theory has plenty of meat to it, whereas a correct conceptual analysis of truth has very little. (Mackie 1973 p. 40)

The question of the philosophical significance of Tarski's theory is evidently a hard one; I shall tackle it in three stages: first by discussing Tarski's own estimate of his theory's significance, and then by discussing the use made of the theory by two writers – Popper and Davidson – who have more ambitious hopes of it than Tarski himself.

(a) *Tarski's own estimate*

Tarski expresses the hope (1944 pp. 53–4) that his definition will do justice to the Aristotelian conception of truth, but sees little point in the question whether that is the 'correct' concept, offering, indeed, to use the word 'frue' rather than 'true' should the decision go against him on that issue (p. 68).

Tarski is also modest about the epistemological pretensions of his theory; he doesn't really understand, he says, what the 'philosophical problem of truth' might be (p. 70), but anyway:

> we may accept the semantic conception[2] of truth without giving up any epistemological attitude we may have had,

---

[1] Here Black apparently confuses the material adequacy condition with the definition, though elsewhere in the same paper he makes the distinction clearly enough.

[2] The context suggests that Tarski is here concerned primarily with his material adequacy condition.

we may remain naive realists or idealists, empiricists or
metaphysicians... The semantic conception is completely neutral toward all these issues. (p. 71)

Field suggests (1972) that Tarski may have attached metaphysical
importance to the constraint on which he insisted (but cf. p. 108n),
that truth be defined without the use of semantic primitives: a constraint he justified (1931 pp. 152–3) by urging the superior clarity of
syntactic notions. A comment in another paper, 'The establishment
of scientific semantics', suggests that he may also have had a deeper
significance in mind; after repeating that the use of semantic
primitives would threaten clarity, he goes on:

> this method would arouse certain doubts from a general
> philosophical point of view. It seems to me that it would
> then be difficult to bring this method into harmony with
> the postulates of the unity of science and of physicalism
> (since the concepts of semantics would be neither logical
> nor physical concepts). (1936 p. 406)

Field's conjecture is that Tarski's intention was to bring semantics
into line with the demands of physicalism, the thesis that there is
nothing but physical bodies and their properties and relations; and
that this is to be achieved by *defining* such non-physical concepts as
truth and satisfaction. It is confirmed by a passage, 1944 pp. 72–4,
where Tarski defends the semantic conception of truth against the
criticism that semantics involves metaphysical elements, by stressing
that his definition uses as primitives only logical terms, expressions of
the object language, and names of those expressions. The further
question, whether Tarski's theory indeed has this significance, is
tricky. Field believes that Tarski does not really succeed in reducing
semantics to physicalistically acceptable primitives. Tarski defines
satisfaction for complex open sentences recursively, in terms of satisfaction for atomic open sentences, but he defines satisfaction for
atomic open sentences *enumeratively*, a clause for each primitive predicate of the object language (as it were, 'X satisfies 'x_i is a city' iff X_i
is a city, X satisfies 'x_i is north of x_j' iff X_i is north of X_j...' and
so forth). Since Field holds that a successful reduction requires more
than extensional equivalence of *definiens* and *definiendum*, which is all
Tarski's definition guarantees, he finds that Tarski does not, as he
hoped, vindicate physicalism. It seems worth observing that there is

a strong tendency for physicalists to be extensionalists, and some reason, therefore, to suppose that Tarski would have thought extensional equivalence a sufficient constraint. The question remains, of course, whether extensional equivalence really is a sufficient constraint upon reductions, or whether, as Field suggests, some stronger requirement is proper.

(b) *Popper's claims on behalf of Tarski's theory*
Popper welcomes Tarski's theory as having:

> rehabilitated the correspondence theory of absolute or objective truth... He vindicated the free use of the intuitive idea of truth as correspondence to the facts...
> (1960 p. 224)

and he uses Tarski's ideas in developing his own account of the role of truth as a regulative ideal of scientific inquiry.[1]

Is Tarski's a correspondence theory?
According to Popper, Tarski has supplied just what was lacking with the traditional correspondence theories – a precise sense for 'corresponds' (1960 p. 223, 1972 p. 320). Initially, at least, this is puzzling, for Tarski explicitly comments that the correspondence theory is unsatisfactory (1944 p. 54), and observes that he was 'by no means surprised' to learn that, in a survey carried out by Ness, only 15% agreed that truth is correspondence with reality, while 90% agreed that 'It is snowing' is true if and only if it is snowing (1944 p. 70; and see Ness 1938).

So what is it that leads Popper to think of Tarski as having vindicated the correspondence theory? Some comments (e.g. 1960 p. 224) suggest that what he specifically has in mind is Tarski's insistence on the need for a metalanguage in which one can both refer to expressions of the object language and say what the object language says. It is as if he thinks of the left-hand side of each instance of the (T) schema, such as:

> 'Snow is white' is true iff snow is white

as referring to the language, and the right-hand side to the facts. But this seems a pretty inadequate reason for taking Tarski's to be a correspondence theory, for the material adequacy condition, though

---

[1] This section amplifies and modifies some points from Haack 1976d; and cf. Sellars 1967 ch. 6 for some pertinent discussion.

its role is to rule out some definitions, certainly does not single out the correspondence theory as uniquely correct; presumably it permits, for instance, a redundancy definition such as Mackie's:

(p) (the statement that p is true iff p)

It is just for this reason that Tarski himself stresses the epistemological neutrality of the (T) schema.

However, though Popper does not explicitly refer to them, there are features of Tarski's *definition* of truth which are reminiscent of correspondence theories. A difficulty here is that it isn't very clear what is required for Tarski's to count as really a version of the correspondence theory; and it is aggravated by Popper's insistence that until Tarski there had been no genuine, no satisfactory, correspondence theory. Still, one can make some progress by comparing Tarski's definition first with the logical atomist version given by Russell and Wittgenstein, and then with Austin's version.

Tarski defines truth in terms of satisfaction, and satisfaction is a relation between open sentences and sequences of objects; the account of satisfaction bears some analogy to Wittgenstein's view of truth as consisting in the correspondence between the arrangement of names in a proposition and the arrangement of objects in the world. On the other hand, Tarski's definition of *truth* makes no appeal to specific sequences of objects, for true sentences are satisfied by all sequences, and false sentences by none. It is symptomatic that logical as well as factual truth is embraced by Tarski's definition; it is surely less plausible to suppose that logical truth consists in correspondence to the facts than that 'factual' truth does. Two historical observations seem called for here: first, that Wittgenstein thought that quantified wffs could be understood as conjunctions/disjunctions of atomic propositions, and that if this were indeed so, Tarski's detour through satisfaction would be unnecessary; and secondly, that Russell allowed 'logical facts'.

Tarski's exploitation of the structure of sentences in the recursive definition of satisfaction is, then, an analogy with Russell's and Wittgenstein's gloss on 'corresponds'. It is equally a *dis*analogy with Austin's account. Austin insists that statements, not sentences, are the primary truth-bearers. This has at least two relevant consequences: Tarski ignores problems raised by sentences containing indexicals such as 'I' and 'now', upon which Austin concentrates; and while Tarski's definition of satisfaction relies on the syntactic structure of open sentences, Austin's account of correspondence stresses its purely conventional, arbitrary character – in another language, the statement that nuts could, he says, be true in just the circumstance that the statement in English that the National Liberals are the people's choice is true.[1] There is, however, one point of analogy which deserves mention. Austin's account, I suggested earlier, avoids locating correspondence in the too intimate connection between the statement that p and the fact that p, explaining it rather as consisting in the situation to which the statement that p refers being of the kind which the statement says it is. Here one can see, without too severe a strain, a resemblance to Tarski's enumerative account of satisfaction for atomic open sentences: for example, X satisfies 'x_i is white' iff the ith thing in the sequence X is white.

So: Tarski does not regard himself as giving a version of the correspondence theory, and his material adequacy condition is neutral between correspondence and other definitions. However, Tarski's definition of satisfaction, if not of truth, bears some analogy to correspondence theories: the clauses for atomic open sentences to Austin's, the clauses for molecular open sentences to Russell's and Wittgenstein's version.

Is Tarski's theory 'absolute' and 'objective'?

Whether or not one considers the affinities strong enough for Tarski's to count as a version of the correspondence theory, it is worth asking whether the semantic definition of truth has, anyway, what Popper considers to be the major virtues of the correspondence theory, its 'absolute' and 'objective' character.

Tarski stresses that truth can be defined only *relatively to a language* – what he defines is not 'true' (period), but 'true-in-O'. This is for two reasons; that the definition must apply to sentences (which, unlike such extralinguistic items as propositions, have the syntactic structure which it exploits) and one and the same sentence can be true in one language and false, or meaningless, in another; and that only a hierarchy of object language, metalanguage, and meta-metalanguage can avoid the semantic paradoxes. In this sense, therefore, Tarski's is not an absolute, but a relative, truth definition.

---

[1] Here, then, is a case where the issue about truth-bearers acquires a real significance. (I shall not resist the temptation to draw attention to Austin's complaint (1950 p. 30), that his fellow-symposiast, Strawson, had failed to make the crucial distinction between sentence and statement.) I shall touch on the question, how Tarski's theory might be adapted to deal with indexical sentences, in the section on Davidson.

Popper, however, who is apt to take a somewhat cavalier attitude to the question of truth-bearers (1972 pp. 11, 45, 319n) is unconcerned with this sense of 'absolute'. He takes no interest, either, in the fact that Tarski's original definition is absolute rather than model-theoretic.

Popper seems, rather, to equate 'absolute' and 'objective', contrasting both with 'subjective', that is, 'relative to our knowledge or belief'. In this respect Popper believes the correspondence theory to be superior to

> the coherence theory...[which] mistakes consistency for
> truth, the evidence theory...[which] mistakes 'known to
> be true' for 'true', and the pragmatist or instrumentalist
> theory [which] mistakes usefulness for truth. (1960 p. 225)

I needn't comment, I think, on the accuracy of Popper's characterisation of the rival theories; anyhow, the core of his argument, fortunately, does not depend on these details. The rival theories, Popper argues, are founded on the 'widespread but mistaken dogma that a satisfactory theory should yield a criterion of true belief' (1960 p. 225). And a criterial theory of truth is subjective because it cannot allow the possibility of a proposition's being true even though no one believes it, or false even though everyone believes it.

What exactly does Popper find objectionable about criterial truth-theories? Popper doesn't make this very clear; but I think the problem can be focussed. The crucial difficulty lies, not in the attempt to supply a criterion of truth, in itself, but in the adoption of a criterial theory of the meaning of 'true'. (His attitude is perhaps clearest in the appendix to the 1961 edition of vol. 2 of *The Open Society and its Enemies*.) If one gives the meaning of 'true' in terms of our criteria of truth, one cannot leave room for the possibility that a proposition be false though it passes our tests of truth, or true though it fails them. This is a particular problem for the pragmatists, since it poses a threat to their official fallibilism; though there is still room for mistakes in the *application* even of infallible tests of truth. Infallibilism *in itself* is not subjectivist; but the further claim that to say that a proposition is true (false) *just means* that it passes (fails) our tests poses a threat to objectivism.

Tarski expressly disclaims the aspiration to supply a criterion of truth (1944 pp. 71–2); and his definition certainly makes no reference to our tests of truth. (Ironically, the passage in which Tarski draws attention to these features is intended as a rebuttal of the 'objection' that his is a kind of correspondence theory which involves logic in 'a most uncritical realism'!)

So Tarski's is an objective theory in Popper's sense. But why does Popper attach so much importance to this point? The explanation lies in the epistemological use to which he proposes to put the concept of truth.

Truth as a regulative ideal: verisimilitude

Popper describes himself as a 'fallibilistic absolutist': fallibilist because he denies that we have any guaranteed method of acquiring knowledge; absolutist because he insists that there is such a thing as an objective truth to which scientific inquiry aspires. Tarski's theory is to supply a suitably objective account of this 'regulative ideal' of science.

This requires, of course, that Tarski's theory be applicable to the languages – presumably, fragments, more or less completely regimented, of natural and mathematical languages – in which scientific theories are expressed. I shall not here discuss the questions raised by this requirement; partly because Tarski himself expresses (1944 p. 74) a cautious optimism about the applicability of his work to the empirical sciences, and partly because in the next section, when I discuss Davidson's use of Tarski's work, I shall have to consider the reasons Tarski gives for doubting whether his methods apply to 'colloquial' language.

According to Popper, the business of science is to devise and test conjectures; scientists can't be confident that their current conjectures are true, nor even that they will ever reach the truth or would know, if they did reach the truth, that they had. But if truth is to be not just an ideal, but a *guiding* or 'regulative' ideal, it should be possible to tell whether, as one theory replaces another, science is getting closer to the truth. So Popper's problem is to explain in what sense, of two theories both of which may be false, one can be closer to the truth than another. His solution is his extension of Tarski's ideas in the theory of 'verisimilitude', or truth-likeness.

Popper's account of verisimilitude goes:

> Assuming that the truth-content and the falsity-content of two theories t_1 and t_2 are comparable, we can say that t_2 is more closely similar to the truth...than t_1 if and only if either:

(a) *the truth-content but not the falsity-content of t_2 exceeds that of t_1*

[or]

(b) *the falsity-content of t_1 but not its truth-content exceeds that of t_2.* (1963 p. 233)

The truth- (falsity-) content of a theory is the class of all and only its true (false) consequences. The truth- or falsity-content of one theory can exceed the truth- or falsity-content of another only if its truth- or falsity-content set-theoretically includes the other's, so this account applies only to theories which overlap in this way. Popper also suggests (1963 pp. 393–6, 1972 pp. 51, 334) measures of truth- and falsity-contents in terms of logical probability, so that any two contents can be compared. But I shall concentrate on the former, 'qualitative', rather than the latter, 'quantitative' version.

The definition of verisimilitude cannot show that science does progress towards the truth: but Popper hopes (1972 p. 53) that it supports his falsificationist methodology, which recommends that one choose the more falsifiable conjecture, the one with more content, for a theory with more content will have greater verisimilitude, unless, Popper adds, it has more falsity-content as well as more truth-content.

However, it has been shown[1] that a theory t_2 has greater verisimilitude than another, t_1, in accordance with Popper's (a) and (b) only if t_2 is a *true* theory from which the truth-content of t_1 follows. This means that *Popper's definition of verisimilitude does not apply to comparisons between theories both of which are false*; but that, of course, was the principal objective of the theory, which therefore fails of its epistemological purpose. This failure is, I think, important to the question of the feasibility of fallibilistic absolutism (see Haack 1977b); and it should also, to my mind, support Tarski's rather modest, as against Popper's rather more ambitious, assessment of the epistemological significance of the semantic theory of truth.

[1] Miller 1974; and cf. Tichý 1974 and Harris 1974. Very briefly, Miller's strategy is first to show, if t_1 and t_2 are comparable by truth-content, how they are also comparable by falsity-content; and then to show that for t_2 to be nearer the truth than t_1, t_2 must be a true theory from which the truth-content of t_1 follows, since otherwise t_2 will exceed t_1 in falsity- as well as truth-content, so that their verisimilitudes will not be comparable.

(c) *Davidson's use of Tarski's theory*

Truth and meaning. Any adequate theory of meaning, Davidson thinks, must explain how the meanings of sentences depend upon the meanings of words (otherwise, he argues, the language would be unlearnable). A theory of meaning must be consistent with – or, he sometimes says, explain – 'semantic productivity': speakers' ability to produce, and understand, sentences they have never heard before. What this amounts to, he claims, is that the theory should yield all sentences of the form:

S means m

where 'S' is a structure-revealing description of a sentence of the language for which the theory is being given, and 'm' a term denoting the meaning of that sentence. But the appeal to meanings implicit here, he suggests, contributes nothing useful; and reformulating the requirement thus:

S means that p

where 'p' is a sentence that has the meaning that the sentence described by 'S' has, leaves a problem with the 'means that', which, therefore, Davidson reformulates as 'is T iff' where 'T' is any arbitrary predicate which, given the above conditions on 'S' and 'p', satisfies:

S is T iff p

But, of course, any predicate satisfying this condition will be, by Tarski's standards, a materially adequate *truth*-predicate. Davidson concludes that what is required by a theory of meaning is, precisely, a definition of such a truth-predicate (Davidson 1967).

Meaning as truth-conditions

Though the route by which Davidson reaches this conclusion is somewhat indirect, the terminus – that the meaning of a sentence can be given by specifying its truth-conditions – is not unfamiliar. What is novel in Davidson's version is the imposition of 'Tarskian' constraints upon the account of truth-conditions.[1]

---

[1] Dummett urges a theory of meaning in terms rather of assertibility-conditions than truth-conditions (again a comparison with the pragmatists, now with their criterial theory of meaning, suggests itself). For critical discussions see Haack 1974 pp. 103ff. and cf. Brandom 1976.

The appeal of a truth-condition theory of meaning may perhaps be appreciated by recalling Quine's classification of semantic notions into two groups, the extensional, which he takes to constitute the business of the 'theory of reference' and the intensional, which he takes to constitute the business of the 'theory of meaning', thus:

semantic ideas

theory of reference	*theory of meaning*
(extensional)	(intensional)
e.g. 'designates'	e.g. 'is significant'
'satisfies'	'is synonymous with'
'is true'	'analytic'
	'means'

Quine argued in 1953a that the theory of reference was in considerably better shape than the theory of meaning. An appealing feature of the truth-condition theory is that it promises an explanation of meaning (from the more problematic right-hand side) in terms of truth (from the less problematic left-hand side).

Theory of interpretation

Later (1974) Davidson appends some further theory, of interpretation of another's discourse, in another or even in the same language as one's own; essentially, this consists in an account of how to tell when '*p*' is a sentence that has the meaning that '*S*' describes. Briefly, the idea is that to test, empirically, whether a sentence of the form

'*Es regnet*' is true iff it is raining

is a T-sentence, that is, meets Tarski's specification that the sentence on the right translates the one named on the left, one tests whether speakers of the language concerned (here, German) hold true '*Es regnet*' iff it is raining. The point of the appeal to what native speakers *hold true* is to get at the meaning of their utterances by, so to speak, holding their beliefs constant. In consequence an assumption, the principle of charity, to the effect that speakers of other languages generally agree with us about what is the case, is required. The holist character of Davidson's account, the insistence that the 'unit of interpretation' is the entire language, may derive at least in part from epistemic holism, the Duhemian idea, also stressed by Quine, that beliefs are verified/falsified not alone but in a corporate body.

Though there are many important questions to be asked about this theory of interpretation, I shall concentrate, in what follows, on Davidson's account of meaning, since it is there that Tarski's theory of truth plays the crucial role.

If the task of a theory of meaning is indeed, as Davidson thinks, to define a Tarskian truth-predicate, what work over and above that already accomplished by Tarski would be needed? Davidson is seeking a theory of meaning *for natural languages*, such as English; Tarski, of course, is thoroughly sceptical about the applicability of his theory to natural languages. So a first task, if Davidson's programme is to be feasible, is to show that Tarski's methods *can* be extended. This is an important question even independently of Davidson's special ambitions for Tarski's methods, for the concept of truth is of philosophical significance in many contexts where 'true' must be allowed to apply to sentences of natural languages – in epistemology, for instance. Despite Tarski's official modesty on this score, it seems to me that the usefulness of his work would be sadly restricted if the concept he defines turns out to be quite different from the concept of truth in natural languages.

Is Tarski's theory applicable to natural languages?
According to Tarski:

> *The very possibility of a consistent use of the expression*
> *'true sentence' which is in harmony with the laws of logic and*
> *the spirit of everyday language seems to be very questionable,*
> *and consequently the same doubt attaches to the possibility*
> *of constructing a correct definition of this expression.*
> (1931 p. 165)

Tarski's pessimism has two main sources: his formal correctness condition rules out the possibility of an adequate definition of truth for languages which are neither (i) semantically open nor (ii) formally specifiable. Natural languages, Tarski argues, fail on both scores, so there is no prospect of an adequate definition of truth for them.

(i) Tarski suggests that natural languages contain their own meta-languages, so that truth cannot be defined without running into paradox; though sometimes he hints, rather, that because natural languages are not formally specifiable, the question of their semantical closure cannot be answered. Davidson has no very satisfactory answer to this problem, but urges that 'we are justified in carrying on without having disinfected this source of conceptual anxiety' (1967 p. 10). He seems to propose that work proceed on those semantically open fragments of natural languages where the danger of paradox does not arise. There is some difficulty in squaring Davidson's attitude to the paradoxes (don't worry too much about them, concentrate on the rest of the job) with his holism, the insistence that an adequate theory of meaning must be a theory for a whole language; though he also hints that he doubts whether natural languages really are universal.

(ii) There seems to be a whole family of difficulties here; the problem of giving a precise account of just what strings count as sentences of a natural language, aggravated by the fact that natural languages are not static, but growing; and the prevalence in natural languages of such phenomena as vagueness, ambiguity, indexicality. Tarski is gloomy:

> Whoever wishes, in spite of all difficulties, to pursue the semantics of colloquial language with the help of exact methods will be driven first to undertake the thankless task of a reform of this language... It may however be doubted whether the language of everyday life, after being 'rationalised' in this way, would still preserve its naturalness and whether it would not rather take on the characteristic features of the formalised languages.
> (1931 p. 267)

The core of Davidson's reply to this is that, though some 'tidying up' will be needed before Tarski's methods can be applied to a natural language, this need not be such as to transform it out of all recognition. He would hold, I think, that work in transformational grammar (see e.g. Chomsky 1957) promises to overcome the first problem; and he is optimistic that more fragments of natural languages can be brought within the scope of Tarskian methods, rather as Frege's work on '(x)' and '$(\exists x)$' has already suitably regimented 'all', 'none' and 'some'.[1]

What Tarski regards as a 'thankless task' Davidson undertakes gladly, observing that 'It's good to know we shan't run out of work'. His main task, in fact, is to supply a suitable analysis of those locutions

[1] It is not beyond dispute that Frege's account does properly regiment natural language quantifiers; recall (ch. 4 §1) that Montague and Hintikka, like the early Russell, stress their affinities with singular terms, whereas according to Frege they belong to an entirely different syntactic category.

of natural languages which are initially recalcitrant to Tarskian treatment. And it is on his success or failure at this task that one's assessment of Davidson's response to Tarski's scepticism must be based.
It is worth observing that Davidson insists on using the 'absolute'
rather than a model-theoretic concept of truth; and that some of these
problems (e.g. problems created by the introduction of new predicates
as a natural language grows) are harder on an absolute than they
would have been on a model-theoretic approach; cf. Field 1972.

Logical form

Davidson describes himself as seeking 'the logical form' of natural
language locutions. For example, recall (ch. 2 §4) that, according to
Davidson, adverbial constructions in natural language are best represented as involving quantification over events, with adverbs construed
as adjectives of event terms. The logical form of 'John buttered the
toast with a knife', Davidson claims, is something like 'There is an
event which is a buttering of the toast by John and which is performed
with a knife'. Davidson's confidence that each natural language construction has a unique logical form springs from the belief that a
formal representation to which Tarski's method of defining truth
applies represents essential structure in an ideally perspicuous fashion.
(The analogy with Russell's and Wittgenstein's project, in their
logical atomist periods, of devising an ideal language which would
represent the *real* form of natural languages, is striking.) Interestingly,
Cargile has asked (1970; and cf. Davidson's reply in the same volume)
why the connection between a predicate and its adverbially modified
form need necessarily be assumed to be a matter of form rather
than content. It isn't, he suggests, as obvious as Davidson seems to
suppose what one should count as skeleton, and what as flesh; he
urges, in fact, a more flexible conception of logical form, closer to the
one presented in ch. 2.

Davidson's programme

So Davidson regards it as the task of a theory of meaning to analyse
the structure of sentences, not to supply an account of the meaning
of individual words. (This isn't *quite* right, because some particles –
'un' for instance – have a structural character.) For example,
Davidson does not require a theory of meaning to give the meaning of
'good', but he does require it to analyse the structure of e.g. 'Bardot
is a good actress' in such a way as to explain why it is not equivalent

to 'Bardot is good and Bardot is an actress' as 'Bardot is a French actress' is to 'Bardot is French and Bardot is an actress' (cf. 'small elephant', and the ambiguous 'poor violinist'). The appeal of Tarski's method, which is to define satisfaction for complex open sentences in terms of satisfaction of simple open sentences, is its promise of an explanation of how the meanings of compound sentences depend on the meaning of their parts; the challenge is to analyse sentences like 'Bardot is a good actress' so that Tarski's method applies to them as well as to the less recalcitrant 'Bardot is a French actress'. Davidson admits that the task is considerable, that:

> a staggering list of difficulties and conundrums remains.
> (1967 p. 321)

He includes ('to name a few') counterfactuals, subjunctives, probability statements, causal statements, adverbs, attributive adjectives, mass terms, verbs of belief, perception, intention, action. Obviously my consideration of details of the programme will have to be selective.

Indexicals

Tarski's theory needs to be relativised to speakers and times, Davidson suggests, because natural languages contain indexicals. The revised (T) schema will call for the theory to entail sentences like:

> 'I am tired' (s, t) is true iff s is tired at t

Truth, Davidson says, is a predicate rather of utterances than sentences. (This suggestion is relevant to the claim, canvassed by Strawson and, before him, by Schiller, that formal methods are inherently inadequate to deal with the context-dependence of statements in natural languages.)

But Davidson's concern with indexicals is also directed towards the problems raised by the analysis of quotation and verbs of 'propositional attitude' ('says that', 'knows that' etc.); for he thinks that these constructions all involve concealed demonstratives. An analysis of these indexicals ('this', 'that') given by Weinstein 1974 has been endorsed by Davidson. In this account, 'That is a cat', say, is true just in case the object indicated by the speaker at the time of utterance satisfies '...is a cat'.

Oratio obliqua

While truth-functional compounds raise no problems, there will obviously be a difficulty about applying Tarski's methods to compound English sentences the truth-values of which do not depend in any obvious way upon the truth-values of their parts. *Oratio obliqua* sentences are of this problematic, intensional kind; for the truth-value of 'Galileo said that the earth moves', for instance, does not depend in any direct way on the truth-value of 'the earth moves'; and there is failure of substitutivity, for from 'Tom said that the moon is round' and 'The moon = the sole planet of the earth' one cannot safely infer 'Tom said that the sole planet of the earth is round'.

The first step in the right direction, Davidson urges, is to parse:

> Galileo said that the earth moves.

along the lines of:

> Galileo said that.
> The earth moves.

The 'that' is to be construed not as a relative pronoun, but as a demonstrative pronoun referring to an utterance – rather as I might say 'I wrote that', pointing to a message on the notice-board.[1] Of course, Galileo didn't utter the very utterance which the speaker produces; indeed, Galileo didn't speak English; so some more explanation is needed. Davidson amplifies his analysis thus:

> The earth moves.
> $(\exists x)$ (Galileo's utterance x and my last utterance make us samesayers)

Galileo and I are samesayers, we are told, just in case he uttered a

---

[1] Two points of comparison are worth making. I have already mentioned the affinities between Tarski's definition of satisfaction and Wittgenstein's *Tractatus* account of truth; the verbs of propositional attitude, which present a problem to Wittgenstein's as to Davidson's approach, are discussed at 5.542. Wittgenstein's analysis is, however, notoriously obscure. Alun Jones has pointed out to me that Davidson's list of 'difficulties and conundrums' for *his* enterprise, and Anscombe's list (1959) of the problems for Wittgenstein's, are very similar. An analysis of indirect discourse strikingly like Davidson's was suggested by Kotarbiński (1955). Kotarbiński's aim was to support the thesis that only material bodies exist ('pansomatism') by analysing away apparent references to such abstract objects as propositions; this, in view of the conjecture that Tarski was motivated by sympathy with materialism, may be significant.

sentence which meant in his mouth what some utterance of mine meant in my mouth.

The application of Tarski's methods, as extended by Weinstein to cope with indexicals, gives a result along the lines of:

> 'Galileo said that the earth moves' (*s*, *t*) means that⎱
> $\qquad\qquad\qquad\qquad\qquad\qquad\qquad$ is true iff⎰
> Galileo uttered at *t'* (*t'* earlier than *t*) a sentence which meant in his mouth what the utterance demonstrated by *s* at *t''* (*t''* just after *t*) meant in *s*'s mouth, where the demonstrated utterance is of 'The earth moves'.

It may be useful to pause briefly to contrast Davidson's with some alternative accounts of the (so-called) 'propositional' attitudes. Frege, for instance, would regard 'that *p*' in '*s* said (believes) that *p*' as referring to a proposition (see ch. 5 §2). Carnap would analyse '*s* said (believes) that *p*' as '*s* uttered (is disposed to assent to) some sentence intensionally isomorphic to '*p*' in English' (see 1947). Scheffler treats 'that *p*' rather as an adjective than a noun: '*s* said (believes) that *p*' amounts to '*s* uttered (believes) a that-*p* utterance' where there is a separate predicate corresponding to each sentence '*p*' (see 1954); Quine goes yet further in the same direction, treating the whole of 'said (believes)-that-*p*' as a predicate of *s* (see 1960a §44).

Davidson believes his account to have the advantages that: unlike analyses which treat 'that *p*' as referring to a proposition, it doesn't require appeal to intensional entities; unlike Carnap's analysis, it does not require explicit reference to a language; and unlike analyses which treat 'says (believes)-that-*p*' as a single predicate, it allows that what follows the 'that' is a sentence with 'significant structure', structure a theory of meaning can exploit.

His account, Davidson argues, allows, as seems proper, that '*s* said that *p*' entails '*s* said something', for the analysis goes '*s* uttered a sentence which...'. At the same time, it explains, as is also required, why '*s* said that *p*' does not entail '*p*', for what seemed to be a sentence ('*p*') within a sentential operator ('*s* said that') becomes a single sentence ('*s* said that') containing a demonstrative ('that') which refers to an utterance of another sentence ('*p*'). And just as, although cats scratch, the sentence, 'that is a cat', which refers to a cat, doesn't scratch, so, although '*p*' entails '*p*', the sentence '*s* said that *p*', which refers to an utterance of '*p*', doesn't entail '*p*'.

Of course, as the last example brings out, in the regular cases considered by Weinstein, what 'that' refers to is a non-linguistic item, a cat, for instance. When the account is extended to 'that's in indirect speech, the referents will be utterances of sentences. And these sentences have significant structure (among the instances of '*s* said that *p*' would be e.g. '*s* said that *q* and *r*' and '*s* said that *s'* said that *q*') in virtue of which their meaning would be given.

Some comments are in order, here, about how Davidson's differs from Carnap's analysis. On Davidson's account '*s* said that *p*' involves reference to an utterance of the speaker's related to some utterance of *s*'s by *samesaying*; in Carnap's, reference to a sentence related to a sentence of English by *intensional isomorphism*. An utterance (here, Davidson makes it clear that he means a speech act, the event of uttering a sentence) is an utterance of some sentence in some specific language with some specific context; and so the need to specify the relevant language is avoided.[1]

This gives Davidson's account an unexpected character – for the concept of utterance (speech act) belongs rather to pragmatics than to semantics. Equally surprising, and methodologically also disquieting, is that Davidson's account, like Carnap's, requires a semantic primitive (respectively, samesaying and intensional isomorphism) in the metalanguage. *s* and *s'* are samesayers, Davidson explains, just in case some utterance of *s*'s *means the same as* some utterance of *s''*s. Now, Davidson insists that the truth-conditions be given in terms of an absolute definition of truth, a definition, that is, which uses no semantic primitives. And he avoids '*S* means *m*' and the formula '*S* means that *p*' because of their intensional character. Davidson apparently regards the appeal to samesaying as admissible because *local*; the general account of meaning appeals only to Tarskian truth-conditions, though the specific account of 'says that' requires samesaying as semantic primitive. It is questionable, though, whether the appeal *is* local in the relevant sense; for surely 'says that' counts as structure rather than vocabulary in the sense in which the dependence of the meaning of 'good' on the meaning of 'actress' in 'Bardot is a

---

[1] Davidson sometimes speaks as if it is the reference to an utterance (rather than a sentence) that prevents '*s* said that *p*' entailing '*p*'. But this is surely sufficiently explained by appeal to the fact that (an utterance of) '*p*' is *referred to by*, and not *contained in* '*r* said that *p*'. The sense of 'utterance' in which, according to Davidson, truth is a property of utterances, has, presumably, to be the 'content', and not, as in this context, the 'act' sense.

good actress' is structural (Davidson objects to the Fregean account *of indirect discourse* because it requires intensional objects). The problem is what exactly the constraints should be on Davidson's enterprise: what apparatus should he be permitted to use, and where? It is pertinent that the appeal of his enterprise derives in large part from the austerity of method it appears, at the outset, to promise.

Since the enterprise was launched, Davidson and his followers have tackled, with various degrees of success, many of the 'difficulties and conundrums' pointed out in 1967. By 1973 Davidson speaks of 'fairly impressive progress', pointing to work on propositional attitudes, adverbs, quotation (Davidson 1967, 1968a, b), proper names (Burge 1973), 'ought' (Harman 1975), mass terms and comparatives (Wallace 1970, 1972).

The success of Davidson's programme would vindicate, in large measure, the applicability of Tarski's theory to natural languages; but the assessment of his programme obviously depends on the detailed study of the specific analyses offered. And as I have suggested with reference to the analysis of *oratio obliqua*, this study in its turn raises some methodological questions which are at any rate tricky enough that one cannot say with any confidence that Davidson *has* shown that Tarski's theory applies to English.

7 The redundancy theory
Ramsey

The redundancy theory (though suggested earlier by some remarks of Frege in 1918) derives primarily from the work of F. P. Ramsey in 1927. Ramsey offers his sketch of a theory in a very brief passage (pp. 142–3) in the course of a discussion of the proper analysis of belief and judgment; the context is significant of Ramsey's estimate of the importance of the issue: 'there is' he thinks, 'really no separate problem of truth, but merely a linguistic muddle'.

Briefly, his idea is that the predicates 'true' and 'false' are redundant in the sense that they can be eliminated from all contexts *without semantic loss*;[1] he allows that they have a pragmatic role, for 'emphasis or stylistic reasons'. Ramsey considers two kinds of case where 'true' and 'false' typically occur. The cases he uses to introduce the theory are of the more straightforward kind, where the

---

[1] There is an allusion here to Russell's doctrine of 'incomplete symbols', symbols, that is, which are contextually eliminable. Cf. ch. 5 § 3 for a discussion of this doctrine with reference to Russell's theory of descriptions.

proposition to which truth or falsity is ascribed is explicitly given: 'it is true that p', Ramsey argues, *means the same as* 'p', and 'It is false that p' *means the same as* 'not p'. Cases where the relevant proposition is not actually supplied but only described present rather more initial difficulty, for, as Ramsey realises, one cannot simply eliminate 'is true' from, for instance, 'what he says is always true'; this difficulty he proposes to overcome by using the apparatus of propositional quantification, to give, in the case mentioned, something along the lines of 'For all p, if he asserts p, then p'.[1]

Whether the second-order quantifiers which Ramsey needs can be suitably explicated is a key question, as it turns out, for the feasibility of the redundancy theory; but I shall begin by pointing out some of the advantages of the theory before turning to its problems.

Truth-bearers

In view of the embarrassments caused by the trappings – facts and propositions – of the correspondence theory the austerity of the redundancy theory is appealing. Ramsey understandably regards it as a virtue of his theory that it avoids the questions raised by a correspondence account about the nature and individuation of facts. 'It is a fact that...', he urges, has the same semantic redundancy, and the same emphatic use, as 'It is true that...'.

Again, since the effect of Ramsey-style theories is to deny that in 'It is true that p', '...is true...' is to be thought of as a predicate ascribing a *bona fide* property to whatever 'p' stands for, the question of the truth-bearers is similarly bypassed; if truth isn't a property, one needn't ask what it's a property *of*. I observe, however, that what I argued (ch. 6 §5) to be the real issue lying behind disputes about truth-bearers – the question of the appropriate constraints on instances of sentence letters, i.e. what one can put for 'p' – does still arise. (Ramsey's preference for the locution 'It is true that p', rather than ''p' is true' is of some significance in this regard.) I should count it an advantage of my diagnosis of the issue about truth-bearers that it is applicable even to redundancy theories, and an advantage

---

[1] Tarski writes (1944 pp. 68–9) as if Ramsey's theory simply has no way to handle this kind of case; Ramsey would presumably analyse the two problematic cases Tarski gives – 'The first sentence written by Plato is true' and 'All consequences of true sentences are true' – as '(p) (if the first thing Plato wrote was that p, then p)' and '(p) (q) (if p, and if p then q, then q)'.

of the redundancy theory that there the issue arises in its fundamental form.

Of course, this will be a genuine economy only if it is certain that
one doesn't need propositions (or whatever) for other purposes
besides truth-bearing. Those who believe that we need propositions
as objects of belief, for instance, are liable to be less impressed by the
redundancy theory's ability to do without them as bearers of truth.
It is significant, therefore, that Prior, who accepts Ramsey's theory,
urges (1971 ch. 9) an account of belief according to which '*s* believes
that...' in '*s* believes that *p*' is a sentence-forming operator on
sentences like 'It is not the case that...', rather than 'believes' being
a relation symbol with arguments '*s*' and 'that *p*', the latter denoting
a proposition. Again, one might suppose that propositions (or whatever) may be required as bearers of *other* properties, and that the
redundancy theory is therefore in danger of sacrificing the analogy
between '...is true', and, say, '...is surprising' or '...is exag-
gerated' without, in the end, any compensation by way of genuine
ontological economy. And it is significant, in this regard, that Grover
et al., in a paper (1975) urging the claims of a redundancy-style
theory, argue that it is only a misleading appearance that '...is true'
and '...is surprising' are ascriptions to the very same thing.

The object language/metalanguage distinction

The redundancy theorist denies that 'It is true that *p*' is about
the sentence '*p*': 'It is true that lions are timid', like 'It is not the case
that lions are timid', is in his view about lions, not about the sentence
'Lions are timid'. This means that he sees no need for insistence on
the distinction between object language and metalanguage which is so
vital to Tarskian semantics (Prior shows most awareness of this point;
e.g. 1971 ch. 7). This raises some questions about the redundancy
theory's capacity to handle problems where the object language/meta-
language distinction apparently plays an important role.

The idea that truth is a metalinguistic predicate seems, for example,
to contribute to the usual explanations of the semantics of the sentence connectives, as: "'$-p$' is true iff 'p' is false', '$p \lor q$' is true iff
'p' is true or 'q' is true'. How adequate an alternative theory can the
redundancy theory offer? Since that theory equates both 'It is false
that *p*' and 'It is true that $-p$' with '$-p$', all that remains of the
'explanation' of negation seems to be '$-p$ iff $-p$'. The redundancy
theorist might urge that there is indeed less than meets the eye to the

usual explanations of negation, for there is, according to him, less than meets the eye to the usual explanations of truth. (Cf. Dummett 1958, and Grover *et al.*'s acknowledgment that 'It is not the case that...' may not be eliminable.)

Another, related, difficulty is that the redundancy theorist seems to be unable to allow an apparently genuine distinction between the law of excluded middle ('$p \vee -p$') and the metalinguistic principle of bivalence ('for all p, 'p' is either true or else false'). For if ''p' is true' means the same as 'p', and ''p' is false' means the same as '$-p$', then ''p' is either true or else false' means '$p \vee -p$'. Once again, the redundancy theorist might accept the consequence, that this is a 'distinction' without a difference; but since it is a distinction with, apparently, some explanatory power, this leaves him with some explaining to do. (For instance, would he insist that van Fraassen's 'supervaluational' languages, where '$p \vee -p$' is a theorem but the semantics allow truth-value gaps, must be confused? Cf. Haack 1974 pp. 66 ff. and ch. 11 §4 below.)

I pointed out above (pp. 101–2) that the (T) schema seems to require bivalence, and this raises the question whether a redundancy theory isn't also committed to the thesis that 'p' must be either true or else false. But this consequence is avoidable, for the redundancy theorist may deny that, if it is neither true nor false that p, it is false that it is true that p; after all, since his theory is that 'it is true that p' means the same as 'p', he could reasonably insist that, if it is neither true nor false that p, it is also neither true nor false that it is true that p. So he isn't obliged to deny the possibility of truth-value gaps and hence, the previous argument doesn't entail that he is obliged to insist on the law of excluded middle.

In Tarski's work, of course, the most important role of the object language/metalanguage distinction was to secure formal adequacy, specifically, to avoid the semantic paradoxes. So its capacity to deal with the paradoxes will be a pretty crucial question for one's assessment of the feasibility of the redundancy theory. This question must wait till ch. 8; but some of the considerations about propositional quantifiers, to which I now turn, will be relevant to it.

The quantifiers: '(p) (*if he asserts that p, p*)'

Ramsey proposes to eliminate 'true', where what is said to be true is not explicitly supplied but only obliquely referred to, by means of second-order quantification: 'What he says is always true', for instance, is to be explained as meaning 'For all p, if he asserts p, then p'. He admits that there is some awkwardness in this analysis, for, he thinks, English idiom seems to call for a final 'is true' (as: '(p) (if he asserts p, then p is true)' to make the final 'p' into a *bona fide* sentence; but this apparent obstacle to elimination is overcome, he argues, if one remembers that 'p' is itself a sentence, and already contains a verb. Supposing that all propositions had the logical form '$a R b$', he suggests, one could observe the grammatical proprieties by writing 'For all a, R, b, if he asserts $a R b$, then $a R b$'. But of course, as Ramsey is well aware, all propositions are *not* of the form '$a R b$', and neither is there much prospect of giving a finite disjunction of all possible forms of proposition, so this scarcely solves the problem.

Ramsey's discomfort is understandable, for the problem is real. If, in his formula:

$$(p) \text{ (if he asserts } p, \text{ then } p)$$

the quantifier is interpreted in the standard, objectual style, one has:

For all objects (propositions?) p, if he asserts p, then p

Here the bound 'p's are syntactically like singular terms, and the final 'p' has, therefore, to be understood elliptically, as implicitly containing a predicate, to turn it into something of the category of a sentence, capable of standing to the right of 'then', along the lines of:

For all propositions p, if he asserts p, then p *is true*

But if the analysis turns out to contain the predicate 'is true', truth hasn't, after all, been eliminated, and it isn't, after all, redundant. (This is the difficulty Ramsey sees; it is stated rather clearly, with reference to Carnap's version of the redundancy theory, in Heidelberger 1968.) If, on the other hand, the quantifier is interpreted substitutionally, one has:

All substitution instances of 'If he asserts...then...'
are true

and once again 'true' appears in the analysis, and so, hasn't really been eliminated.

So this much is clear: if Ramsey's theory is to work, some *other* explication of the second-order quantifiers will be needed, since on either of the usual interpretations, 'true' seems not to be eliminated.

Prior sees the difficulty as the result of a deficiency in English, which lacks suitable colloquial locutions for reading second-order quantifiers, and obliges one to resort to such misleadingly nominal-sounding locutions as 'Every*thing* he says...'. He therefore suggests (1971 p. 37) 'anywhether' and 'somewhether' as readings of '(p)' and '$(\exists p)$', and reads '$(p)(p \to p)$', for instance, as 'If anywhether, then thether'.

Grover also thinks that the quantifiers can be supplied with suitable readings, and offers some further grammatical apparatus to this purpose. The difficulty of giving an appropriate reading arises, as Prior suggests, from the lack of words and phrases to stand in for sentences in the way that *pronouns* stand in for names and descriptions; what is needed, as Grover puts it, is *prosentences*.

Pronouns and prosentences are two kinds of *proform*; cf. proverbs like 'do', and proadjectives like 'such'. A proform must be capable of being used anaphorically, for cross-reference, either like pronouns of laziness (Geach 1967) as in '*Mary* meant to come to the party, but *she* was ill', or like 'quantificational' pronouns, as in 'If *any car* overheats, don't buy *it*'. Prosentences are like pronouns in occupying positions that sentences could occupy, as pronouns occupy positions that nouns could occupy, and fulfil a similar anaphoric role. Grover's proposal is that one read '(p) (if he asserts that p, then p)' as:

For all propositions, if he asserts that thatt, then thatt

where 'thatt' is a prosentence. Notice that what is proposed is a novel *reading*; it is, Grover argues, compatible with either an objectual or a substitutional account at the level of formal interpretation.

This ingenious proposal raises a number of questions, to which I can offer only tentative answers. First, remember that the problem with which I began was whether it is possible to give a reading of Ramsey's propositional quantifiers which is grammatical, and which doesn't re-introduce the predicate 'true'. Does Grover's reading meet these requirements? Well, it would be somewhat odd to ask whether her reading is grammatical, since it isn't, of course, English; it expressly calls for an *addition* to English. It would be more appropriate to ask whether there are sufficiently strong grammatical analogies to justify her innovation; but this, in view of the 'sufficiently strong', is none too precise a question. English, as Grover allows, doesn't have any atomic prosentences – though it does, I think, have compound expressions that play such a role: 'It is', for instance, which one might describe as a prosentence composed of a pronoun and a proverb. And the second part of the question, whether Grover's reading genuinely eliminates 'true', is equally tricky. In fact, there are two points to be raised here. The first is that even if a suitable *reading* is supplied, this leaves open a question about whether there isn't still an implicit appeal to truth at the level of formal interpretation. (And what exactly must one eliminate 'true' *from* to show that it is redundant?) The second question is whether one's understanding of 'thatt' implicitly requires the notion of truth.

The 'prosentential theory of truth'

Some light may be shed on this problem by Grover's own application of her account of propositional quantification to the theory of truth. Grover *et al.* 1975 propose a modified version of the redundancy theory according to which 'that is true' is explained as being itself a prosentence. Truth-ascriptions, on their account, are eliminable in favour of 'It is true' *as an atomic prosentence*, i.e. one in which 'true' is not a separable predicate.[1]

What does this show about whether the 'prosentential' theory really eliminates 'true'? 'True', one is told, is eliminable; not from English, to be sure, but from English + 'thatt'. But how are we to understand 'thatt'? Well, there's nothing *exactly* like it in English, but it works like 'That's true', except for being atomic rather than compound. . . .

It is open to doubt, I think, whether Ramsey's hope of eliminating talk of truth altogether has been vindicated. Nevertheless, there is something important to be learned from the discussion of the prosentential theory: that the truth-predicate plays a crucial role in enabling us to talk *generally*, to talk, that is, about propositions which

---

[1] Ramsey thought that all truth talk is eliminable; Grover *et al.* admit that there is a residue. In some cases the elimination of 'true' calls for modification of the contained sentence, as 'It used to be true that Rome was the centre of the known world'/'Rome used to be the centre of the known world' or, 'It might be true that there is life on Mars'/'There might be life on Mars'. And where this phenomenon is combined with quantification, as in 'Some sentences used to be true but are true no longer', they are obliged to introduce new connectives, as '($\exists p$) (it-used-to-be-the-case-that p but it-is-no-longer-the-case-that p)', which they admit to be, in effect, truth-locutions. Their comments about 'It might be true that', on the other hand, suggest an interesting alternative to the idea that necessary truth, like truth, is a property of sentences or propositions.

we don't actually exhibit, but only refer to indirectly, a role it shares with the apparatus of second-order ('propositional' or 'sentential') quantifiers. This similarity of function will turn out to be relevant to the diagnosis of the semantic paradoxes.

8

Paradoxes

1 The Liar and related paradoxes

The importance of the Liar paradox to the theory of truth has already become apparent; for Tarski's formal adequacy conditions on definitions of truth are motivated, in large part, by the need to avoid it. It is time, now, to give the Liar and related paradoxes some direct attention on their own account.

Why the 'Liar paradox'? Well, the Liar sentence, together with apparently obvious principles about truth, leads, by apparently valid reasoning, to contradiction; that is why it is called a paradox (from the Greek, '*para*' and '*doxa*', 'beyond belief').[1]

The Liar comes in several variants; the classic version concerns the sentence:

(*S*) This sentence is false

Suppose *S* is true; then what it says is the case; so it is false. Suppose, on the other hand, that *S* is false; then what it says is not the case, so it is true. So *S* is true iff *S* is false. Variants include indirectly self-referential sentences, such as:

The next sentence is false. The previous sentence is true.

and the 'postcard paradox', when one supposes that on one side of a postcard is written:

The sentence on the other side of this postcard is false

and on the other:

The sentence on the other side of this postcard is true.

---

[1] The 'paradoxes' of material and strict implication – discussed at length in ch. 11 – are, at worst, counter-intuitive, and not, like the Liar, contradictory; hence the scare quotes.

Another variant, the 'Epimenides' paradox, concerns a Cretan called Epimenides, who is supposed to have said that all Cretans are always liars. If a liar is someone who always says what is false, then if what Epimenides said is true, it is false. The Epimenides is, however, somewhat *less* paradoxical than the Liar, since it can be consistently supposed to be false, though not to be true (cf. Anderson 1970). There are also 'truth-teller' ('This sentence is true') and imperative ('Disobey this order') variants.

Other paradoxes involve 'true (false) of ...' rather than 'true (false)'. 'Heterological' means 'not true of itself'; so e.g. 'German', 'long', 'italicised' are heterological, while 'English', 'short', 'printed' are autological, true of themselves. Now, is 'heterological' heterological? Well, if heterological *is* heterological, it is not true of itself; so, it is not heterological. If, however, it is *not* heterological, it is true of itself; so, it is heterological. So 'heterological' is heterological iff 'heterological' is not heterological (Grelling's paradox).

Others again involve 'definable' or 'specifiable'. The number ten is specifiable by a name of one syllable, the number seven by a name of two syllables, the number seventeen by a name of three syllables. Consider, then, the least number not specifiable in fewer than twenty syllables. That number is specifiable in nineteen syllables, by 'the least number not specifiable in fewer than twenty syllables' (Berry's paradox). Let E be the class of decimals definable in a finite number of words, and let its members be ordered as the first, second, third ... etc. Now let N be the number such that if the nth figure in the nth decimal in E is m, then the nth figure in N is $m+1$, or o if $m = 9$. Then N differs from every member of E, and yet has been defined in a finite number of words (Richard's paradox).

Other paradoxes involve the concept of set. Some sets are members of themselves, while others are not (e.g. the set of abstract objects, being itself an abstract object, is a member of itself; the set of cows, not being itself a cow, is not). Now consider the set of sets which are not members of themselves. Is it a member of itself or not? If it *is* a member of itself, then it has the property which all its members have, that is, it is *not* a member of itself; if, on the other hand, it is *not* a member of itself, then it has the property which qualifies a set for membership in itself, so it *is* a member of itself. So the set of all sets which are not member of themselves is a member of itself iff it is not a member of itself (Russell's paradox). Other set-theoretical paradoxes include Cantor's paradox: no set can be larger than the set of all sets, but, for any set, there is another, the set of all its subsets, which is larger than it is; and Burali-Forti's: the series of all ordinal numbers has an ordinal number, Ω, say, but the series of all ordinals up to and including any given ordinal exceeds that ordinal by one, so the series of all ordinals up to and including Ω has the ordinal number $\Omega + 1$.

This by no means exhausts the range of paradoxes to be found in the literature (cf. Russell 1908a, Mackie 1973 appendix, for more examples). I hope, however, that my list is sufficiently representative to illustrate the kind of problems with which a solution to the paradoxes must deal; the point of considering a number of variants is to enable one to check whether proposed solutions are sufficiently broad in scope.

'*Set-theoretical*' versus '*semantic*' paradoxes?

Though some of these paradoxes had been known long before, they began to be of serious philosophical concern after Russell's discovery of his paradox. Frege had reduced arithmetic to sentence calculus, predicate calculus, and set theory. Russell, however, showed that his paradox was actually a theorem of Frege's system, which was, therefore, inconsistent. (Since Frege had hoped to supply foundations for arithmetic by reducing it to self-evident principles, the fact that his 'self-evident' logic axioms turned out to be contradictory was, naturally, a pretty severe epistemological shock; cf. ch. 1 §2.) The paradoxes cannot be dismissed as mere tricks or puzzles, for they follow from intuitively obvious set-theoretical principles and thus threaten the very foundations of set theory. In view of the fact that anything whatever is derivable from a contradiction, the consequences of paradoxes for a theory in which they are derivable are quite intolerable (but cf. ch. 11 §6 for further thoughts about '$p \ \& \ -p \vdash q$'). Russell's paradox operates as a key constraint on attempts to devise consistent set theories; the Liar paradox, similarly, operates as a key constraint on attempts to devise consistent semantic theories.

But this raises an important, though difficult, question. As the comment about the analogy between the role of Russell's paradox in set theory and the role of the Liar paradox in semantic theory suggests, it is possible to classify the paradoxes in two distinct groups, those which essentially involve set-theoretical concepts, such as '$\in$' and 'ordinal number', and those which essentially involve semantic concepts, such as 'false', 'false of ...', and 'definable'. In fact, it is commonplace to distinguish the *set-theoretical* and the *semantic* paradoxes (the distinction goes back to Peano; its currency derives from Ramsey's championship in 1925):

set-theoretical	*semantic*
paradoxes	*paradoxes*
(Ramsey: '*logical*')	(Ramsey: '*epistemological*')
Russell's paradox	Liar paradox and variants
Cantor's paradox	Grelling's paradox
Burali-Forti's paradox	Berry's, Richard's paradoxes
(Essentially involve	(Essentially involve
'set', '∈', 'ordinal number')	'false', 'false of', 'definable')

The second group is the one which is of immediate concern for semantic theory.

Russell himself, however, didn't think of the paradoxes as falling into two distinct groups, *because he thought that they all arose as the result of one fallacy*, from violations of the 'vicious circle principle'. If one supposes that some paradoxes arise because of some peculiarity of set-theoretical concepts, and others because of some peculiarity of semantic concepts, the classification into two groups will be acceptable; but if, like Russell, one thinks that the trouble lies in something deeper, common to all the paradoxes, one will find it misleading. It is hard to deny, I think, that all the paradoxes sketched do have a *prima facie* affinity with each other and that a solution to them all would surely be more satisfying than a solution to only some; and in view of this, the safest course seems to be *not* to beg, by concentrating exclusively on the 'semantic' paradoxes, questions which could be left open.

2   'Solutions' to the paradoxes
Requirements on a solution

Before attempting to assess the solutions which have been offered, it is wise, I think, to try to get a bit clearer just what would constitute a 'solution'. Well, what exactly is the problem? – that contradictory conclusions follow by apparently unexceptionable reasoning from apparently unexceptionable premises. This suggests two requirements on a solution; that it should give a consistent formal theory (of semantics or set theory as the case may be) – in other words, indicate which apparently unexceptionable premises or principle of inference must be disallowed (the *formal* solution); and that it should, in addition, supply some explanation of *why* that premise or principle is, despite appearances, exceptionable (the *philosophical* solution). It is hard to make precise just what is required of such an explanation, but roughly what is intended is that it should be shown that the rejected premise or principle is of a kind to which there are independent objections – objections independent of its leading to paradox, that is. It is important, though difficult, to avoid supposed 'solutions' which simply *label* the offending sentences in a way that seems, but isn't really, explanatory. Further requirements concern the scope of a solution; it should not be so broad as to cripple reasoning we want to keep (the 'don't cut off your nose to spite your face' principle); but it should be broad enough to block all relevant paradoxical arguments (the 'don't jump out of the frying pan into the fire' principle); the 'relevant', of course, glosses over some problems. At the formal level, the latter principle urges simply that the solution be such as to restore consistency. Frege's response to the inconsistency found by Russell in his set-theory was a formal restriction which avoids Russell's paradox but still allows closely related paradoxes, and thus breaches this requirement (see Frege 1903, Quine 1955, Geach 1956). At the philosophical level, the 'frying pan and fire' principle urges that the explanation offered go as deep as possible; this, of course, is what underlies my hunch that a solution to *both* 'semantic' and 'set-theoretic' paradoxes, if it were possible, would be preferable to a solution local to one group.

The force of these requirements may perhaps be appreciated by looking briefly at some proposed solutions which fail to meet them.

It is sometimes suggested that the paradoxes be resolved by banning self-reference; but this suggestion is at once too broad and too narrow. It falls foul of the 'don't cut off your nose to spite your face' principle: for not only are many perfectly harmless sentences ('This sentence is in English', 'This sentence is in red ink') self-referential (cf. Popper 1954, Smullyan 1957), but also some mathematical argument, including Gödel's proof of the incompleteness of arithmetic, makes essential use of self-referential sentences (cf. Nagel and Newman 1959 and Anderson 1970); so that the consequences of a ban on self-reference would be very serious. And yet, since not all the variants of the Liar are straightforwardly self-referential (neither sentence in 'The next sentence is false. The previous sentence is true' refers to itself) this proposal is, at the same time, too narrow.

The argument to a contradiction from the Liar sentence uses the assumption that 'This sentence is false' is either true or false; and so, unsurprisingly, it has often been suggested that the way to block the argument is to deny this assumption. Bochvar proposed (1939) to deal with the Liar by adopting a 3-valued logic in which the third value, 'paradoxical', is to be taken by the recalcitrant sentences. (See also Skyrms 1970a, 1970b, and ch. 11 §3.) This proposal, too, is in danger of being both too broad and too narrow: too broad, because it requires a change in elementary (sentence calculus) logical principles; and yet still too narrow, for it leaves problems with the 'Strengthened Liar' paradox – the sentence:

This sentence is either false or paradoxical

which is false or paradoxical if true, true if false, and true if paradoxical.

Another approach also denies that the Liar sentence is true or false, without, however, suggesting that it has a third truth-value, by arguing that it is not an item of the appropriate kind to have a truth-value. Only statements, it is argued, are true or false, and an utterance of the Liar sentence wouldn't constitute a statement. (See Bar-Hillel 1957, Prior 1958, Garver 1970; and cf. – *mutatis mutandis* with 'proposition' for 'statement' – Kneale 1971.) This kind of approach suffers, I think, from inadequate explanatoriness – it doesn't supply a suitable rationale for denying the offending sentences a truth-value. Even granted for the sake of argument that only statements or propositions can be either true or false (but granted *only* for the sake of argument – cf. ch. 6) one would need an argument why in the case of the Liar one does not have an item of the appropriate kind. After all, the Liar sentence suffers from no obvious deficiency of grammar or vocabulary. The minimum requirements would be, first, a clear account of the conditions under which an utterance of a sentence constitutes a statement; second, an argument why no utterance of the Liar could fulfil these conditions; third, an argument why only statements can be true or false. Otherwise, one is entitled to complain that the solution is insufficiently explanatory.

*Russell's solution: the theory of types, the vicious circle
principle*

Russell offers (1908a) both a formal solution, the theory of
types, and a philosophical solution, the vicious circle principle.

Nowadays, it is customary to distinguish in Russell's formal
solution the simple and the ramified theory of types. *The simple
theory of types* divides the universe of discourse into a hierarchy:
individuals (type 0), sets of individuals (type 1), sets of sets of individuals (type 2), ... etc., and correspondingly subscripts variables
with a type index, so that x_0 ranges over type 0, x_1 over type 1...etc.
Then the formation rules are restricted in such a way that a formula
of the form '$x \in y$' is well-formed only if the type index of y is one
higher than that of x. So, in particular, '$x_n \in x_n$' is ill-formed, and
the property of not being a member of itself, essential to Russell's
paradox, cannot be expressed. *The ramified theory of types* imposes a
hierarchy of orders of 'propositions' (closed sentences) and 'propositional functions' (open sentences), and the restriction that no
proposition (propositional function) can be 'about', i.e. contain a
quantifier ranging over, propositions (propositional functions) of the
same or higher order as itself. 'True' and 'false' are also to be sub-
scripted, depending on the order of the proposition to which they are
applied; a proposition of order n will be true (false) $n + 1$. The Liar
sentence, which says of itself that it is true, thus becomes inex-
pressible, just as the property of not being a member of itself did in the
simple theory. (I have simplified considerably; see Copi 1971 for a
more detailed account.)

Russell himself, however, did not see the paradoxes as falling into
two distinct groups; he believed that *all* the paradoxes arose from one
and the same fallacy, from violations of what he, following Poincaré,
called 'the vicious circle principle' (V.C.P.):

> 'Whatever involves *all* of a collection must not be one of
> the collection'; or, conversely, 'If, provided a certain
> collection had a total, it would have members only
> definable in terms of that total, then the said collection
> has no total'. [Footnote: I mean that statements about *all*
> its members are nonsense.] (1908a p. 63)

He states the V.C.P. in several, not obviously equivalent, ways: e.g. a
collection mustn't 'involve', or, 'be definable only in terms of'
itself. The V.C.P. motivates the type/order restrictions imposed upon

the formal theory, by showing that what the formulae ruled ill-formed say is demonstrably meaningless. It is important that the very same philosophical rationale is given for both the simple and the ramified theories. Indeed, since Russell held that sets are really logical constructions out of propositional functions, he saw the restrictions of the simple theory as a special case of those of the ramified theory (cf. Chihara 1972, 1973).

At both the formal and the philosophical levels, Russell's account runs into difficulty. Formally, there is some danger that Russell has cut off his nose to spite his face; the restrictions avoid the paradoxes, but also block certain desired inferences. Remember that Russell was trying to complete the programme, begun by Frege, of reducing arithmetic to 'logic', i.e. to sentence calculus, first-order predicate calculus, and set theory. However, the type restrictions block the proof of the infinity of the natural numbers, and the order restrictions block the proof of certain bound theorems. In *Principia Mathematica* these proofs are saved by the introduction of new axioms, respectively, the axiom of infinity and the axiom of reducibility; this ensures the derivability of the Peano postulates for arithmetic; but the *ad hoc* character of these axioms lessens the plausibility of the claim that arithmetic has been reduced to a *purely logical* basis. Still, it could be thought that these difficulties, though they cast doubt on the feasibility of Russell's logicism, don't necessarily show his solution to the paradoxes to be misguided.

But one's suspicions are confirmed by difficulties at the philosophical level. In the first place, the V.C.P. certainly isn't stated with all the precision that might be desired; and it is correspondingly difficult to see what, exactly, is wrong with violations of it. Ramsey commented that he could see nothing objectionable about specifying a man as the one with, say, the highest batting average of his team – a specification apparently in violation of the V.C.P. Not *all* the circles ruled out by the V.C.P., he urged, are truly vicious (notice the analogy to the difficulties in the proposal to ban all self-referential sentences).

However, despite these difficulties, Russell's diagnosis and solution have continued to be influential; later, in §3, I shall argue that Russell's approach is, indeed, in certain respects, on the right lines. But my immediate concern is with other solutions which resemble Russell's in interesting ways. His diagnosis is echoed in Ryle's approach. Ryle 1952 argues that 'The current statement is false' must be unpacked as 'The current statement (namely, that the current statement...[namely, that the current statement...{namely ...etc.}]) is false', and no completely specified statement is ever reached. Like Russell, Ryle thinks that the 'self-dependence' of the Liar sentence somehow robs it of sense. Mackie 1973 agrees with Russell and Ryle that the problem lies in the Liar's 'vicious self-dependence', but prefers to say, for the good reason that the Liar sentence is apparently correctly constructed from *bona fide* components, that the upshot is not meaninglessness but 'lack of content'. However, since he is careful to distinguish 'lack of content' from lack of meaning *and* from lack of truth-value, one is left somewhat at a loss to understand just what lack of content is lack *of*. And Tarski's approach to the semantic paradoxes, to which I turn next, has some significant similarities (observed by Russell 1956; and cf. Church 1976) to the Russellian hierarchy of orders of propositions.

Tarski's solution: the hierarchy of languages

Tarski diagnoses the semantic paradoxes (to which his attention is restricted) as resulting from the two assumptions:

(i) that the language is semantically closed, i.e. contains (a) the means to refer to its own expression, and (b) the predicates 'true' and 'false'
(ii) that the usual logical laws hold

and, being reluctant to deny (ii) (but cf. the comments, above, on Bochvar's proposal) denies (i), proposing as a formal adequacy condition that truth be defined for *semantically open* languages. So Tarski proposes a *hierarchy of languages*:

> the object language, O,
> the metalanguage, M,
> which contains (a) means of referring to expressions of O and (b) the predicates 'true-in-O' and 'false-in-O',
> the meta-metalanguage, M',
> which contains (a) means of referring to expressions of M and (b) the predicates 'true-in-M', and 'false-in-M',
> etc.

Since, in this hierarchy of languages, truth for a given level is always expressed by a predicate of the next level, the Liar sentence can appear only in the harmless form 'This sentence is false-in-O', which must itself be a sentence of M, and hence cannot be true-in-O, and is simply false instead of paradoxical.

Though the appeal of Tarski's theory of truth has won this proposal a good deal of support, there have also been criticisms of its 'artificiality'. The language hierarchy and the relativisation of 'true' and 'false' avoid the semantic paradoxes, but they seem to lack intuitive justification independent of their usefulness in this regard. In other words, Tarski's approach seems to give a formal, but not a philosophical, solution. The reason Tarski gives for requiring semantic openness, is, simply, that semantic closure leads to paradox. There *is* an independent rationale for the relativisation of 'true' and 'false' to a language – that Tarski is defining 'truth' for sentences (wffs), and one and the same sentence (wff) can have a different meaning, and hence a different truth-value, in different languages; but this rationale does not supply any independent justification for insisting that 'true-in-L' always be a predicate, not of L, but of the metalanguage of L.

Intuitively, one does not think of 'true' as systematically ambiguous in the way Tarski suggests it must be. Perhaps this counter-intuitiveness would not, by itself, be an overwhelming consideration. But Kripke (1975) points out that ordinary ascriptions of truth and falsity cannot even be assigned *implicit* levels. Suppose, for instance, that Jones says:

All of Nixon's utterances about Watergate are false.

This would have to be assigned to the next level above the highest level of any of Nixon's utterances about Watergate; but not only will we ordinarily have no way of determining the levels of Nixon's utterances about Watergate, but also in unfavourable circumstances it may actually be impossible to assign levels consistently – suppose that among Nixon's utterances about Watergate is:

All of Jones' utterances about Watergate are false

then Jones' utterance has to be at a level one higher than all of Nixon's, and Nixon's at a level one higher than all of Jones'.

Tarski's approach, Kripke argues, fails to take adequate account of the 'risky' character of truth-ascriptions. Quite ordinary assertions about truth and falsity, he points out, are apt to turn out paradoxical if the empirical facts are unfavourable. Suppose e.g. that Nixon had said that all of Jones' utterances about Watergate are true; then

Jones' assertion that all of Nixon's assertions about Watergate are false would be false if true and true if false (cf. the 'postcard paradox' in §1). The moral, he suggests, is that one can scarcely expect the recalcitrant sentences to be distinguished by any syntactic or semantic feature, but must seek a rationale which allows that paradox may arise with respect to any truth-ascription if the facts turn out badly.[1]

Kripke's solution: groundedness

Kripke seeks to supply an explanation of the source of paradox which is more satisfactory in this respect, and then to build a formal theory on this basis. (My hunch is that this is the right way round to go about it.) His proposal depends upon the rejection of the idea – taken for granted by Tarski – that the truth-predicate must be totally defined, that is to say, that every suitably well-formed sentence must be either true or false. It thus has affinities both with Bochvar's proposal of a 3-valued logic, and with the no-item proposals discussed above. But Kripke stresses that his idea is *not* that paradoxical sentences have some non-classical truth-value, but that they have *no* truth-value.

The key idea in the explanation of how ordinary sentences are assigned truth-values – and how extraordinary sentences fail to get a value – is the concept of *groundedness*, first introduced by Herzberger 1970. Kripke explains the idea as follows:

Suppose one is trying to explain the word 'true' to someone who doesn't understand it. It could be introduced by means of the principle that one may assert that a sentence is true just when one is entitled to assert that sentence, and one may assert that a sentence is not true just when one is entitled to deny it. Now given that the learner is entitled to assert that:

Snow is white

this explanation tells him that he is entitled to assert that:

'Snow is white' is true.

Now he can extend his use of 'true' to other sentences, e.g. as 'Snow

---

[1] Kripke also makes the technical objection that Tarski's hierarchy has not been extended to transfinite levels, and that, furthermore, there are difficulties about so extending it.

is white' occurs in Tarski 1944, the explanation allows him to assert
that:

> Some sentence in 'The semantic conception of truth' is
> true.

And he can also extend his use of 'true' to sentences which already
contain 'true', e.g. to assert that:

> ''Snow is white' is true' is true

or:

> 'Some sentence in 'The semantic conception of truth' is
> true' is true.

The intuitive idea of *groundedness* is that a sentence is grounded just
in case it will eventually get a truth-value in this process. Not all
sentences *will* get a truth-value in this way; among the 'ungrounded'
sentences that won't are:

> This sentence is true

and:

> This sentence is false.

This idea has affinities with the notion – expressed in Russell's
V.C.P. and by Ryle and Mackie – that what's wrong with paradoxical
sentences is a kind of vicious self-dependence. However, ungrounded
sentences are allowed to be meaningful, whereas Russell's idea is that
violation of the V.C.P. results in meaninglessness.

Formally, this idea is represented (I simplify considerably) in a
hierarchy of interpreted languages where at any level the truth-
predicate is the truth-predicate for the next lowest level. At the
lowest level, the predicate 'T' is completely undefined. (This corresponds to the initial stage in the intuitive account.) At the next
level, the predicate 'T' is assigned to wffs which don't themselves
contain 'T'. It is assumed that this assignment will be in accordance
with Kleene's rules giving the assignment of values to compound
wffs given the assignment – or lack of assignment – to their components: '$-p$' is true (false) if 'p' is false (true), undefined if 'p' is
undefined; '$p \vee q$' is true if at least one disjunct is true (whether the
other is true, false, or undefined), false if both disjuncts are false,
otherwise undefined; '$(\exists x) Fx$' is true (false) if 'Fx' is true for some
(false for every) assignment to x, otherwise undefined. (This corresponds to the first stage, in which the learner assigns 'true' to a

sentence if he is entitled to assert the sentence.) At each level the wffs assigned '*T*' and '*F*' at a previous level retain those values, but new wffs, for which '*T*' was previously undefined, are assigned values – '*T*' gets *more defined* as the process goes on. But the process doesn't go on indefinitely with new sentences getting values at each level; eventually – at a 'fixed point' – the process stops. Now the intuitive idea of groundedness can be formally defined: a wff is grounded if it has a truth-value at the smallest fixed point, otherwise ungrounded. The smallest or 'minimal' fixed point is the first point at which the set of true (false) sentences is the same as the set of true (false) sentences at the previous level. All paradoxical sentences are ungrounded, but not all ungrounded sentences are paradoxical; a paradoxical sentence is one that cannot consistently be assigned a truth-value at *any* fixed point. This supplies some explanation of why 'This sentence is true' seems to share some of the oddity of 'This sentence is false', and yet, unlike the Liar sentence, is consistent. A truth-value *can* be given to 'this sentence is true', but only *arbitrarily*; a truth-value *cannot* consistently be given to 'This sentence is false'. The picture also allows for the 'riskiness' of truth-ascriptions: for the paradoxical character of a sentence may be either intrinsic (as it would be with 'This sentence is false') or empirical (as it would be with 'The sentence quoted on p. 147 ll. 22–3 is false').

I observed above that the relaxation of the requirement that 'true' be fully defined, the admission of truth-value gaps, gave Kripke's idea some analogy, also, to proposals, like Bochvar's, that the semantic paradoxes be avoided by resort to a 3-valued logic. This raises the question, how Kripke avoids the criticisms made earlier of Bochvar's solution. Kripke himself stresses that he does not regard his use of Kleene's '3-valued' valuation rules as a challenge to classical logic. Whether the use of 3-valued matrices necessarily carries such a challenge, is a difficult question, on which I shall have more to say in ch. 11 §3; for the present I shall allow Kripke's claim that his proposals are compatible with logical conservatism. What, though, of the Strengthened Liar?

Kripke doesn't tackle this issue directly, but it is possible to work out what he would say about it. The notions of 'groundedness' and 'paradoxicality', he says, unlike the concept of truth, don't belong in his hierarchy of language levels. (Consider again the intuitive picture of a learner having the concept of truth explained to him. His instructions give him no way to assign a truth-value to an ungrounded sentence like 'This sentence is true'; but he cannot conclude that 'This sentence is true' is not true, for his instructions do tell him that he may deny that a sentence is true only if he is entitled to deny that sentence.) Now if 'paradoxical' belongs, not in the hierarchy of language levels, but in the metalanguage of that hierarchy, then Kripke can draw the teeth of the Strengthened Liar, 'This sentence is either false or paradoxical' in much the way that Tarski draws the teeth of the Liar. But this may occasion some dissatisfaction; for it *is* a little disappointing to find that the novelty of Kripke's approach to the Liar must be compromised by a neo-Tarskian dismissal of the Strengthened Liar. (*Is* it indifferent whether one is hung for a sheep or a lamb?)

It will be worthwhile to summarise the main points of comparison and contrast between Kripke's approach, Russell's theory of types, and Tarski's language hierarchy:

RUSSELL	TARSKI	KRIPKE
formal solution		
hierarchy of orders of propositions	hierarchy of languages (problems with transfinite levels)	hierarchy of language levels (with limit levels)
systematic ambiguity of 'true' and 'false'	distinct truth and falsity predicates at each level	single, univocal truth-predicate, with application extended up to minimal fixed point
'true' and 'false' completely defined	'true' and 'false' completely defined	'true' and 'false' only partially defined
'This sentence is false' meaningless	'This sentence is false-in-O' false-in-M	'This sentence is false' neither true nor false.
rationale		
V.C.P.	(language-relativisation of 'true')	groundedness

3 Paradox without 'false'; some remarks about the redundancy theory of truth; and the V.C.P. again

I shan't, I'm afraid, be able to offer, in conclusion, a novel solution to the paradoxes. The purpose of the present section is rather more modest: to redeem the promise (pp. 130, 134) to comment upon the consequences for the paradoxes of the redundancy theory of truth, with its resistance to the idea of truth as a metalinguistic predicate; a consequence of considerations which this investigation brings to light, however, will be some support for a proposal which, as I shall argue, has affinities with the V.C.P.

One of Tarski's reasons for refusing to countenance the treatment of quotation as a function, and hence, for denying that truth could be defined by generalising the (T) schema, to obtain '(p) ('p' is true iff p)', was, if you recall (p. 104 above) that with quotation functions paradox would ensue even without the use of the predicates 'true' and 'false'. (And Tarski's semantic openness requirement, of course, would be powerless to cope with paradox generated without semantic predicates.) Tarski's argument goes as follows:

Let 'c' abbreviate 'the sentence numbered 1'.
Now, consider the sentence:
1. $(p) (c = \text{'}p\text{'} \to -p)$
It can be established empirically that:
2. $c = \text{'}(p) (c = \text{'}p\text{'} \to -p)\text{'}$
and so, assuming that:
3. $(p) (q) (\text{'}p\text{'} = \text{'}q\text{'} \to p \equiv q)$

'by means of elementary logical laws we easily derive a contradiction' (1931 p. 162).[1] Notice that here one has a paradox that arises, not intrinsically in the nature of a single statement, but extrinsically, due, as Kripke would put it, to the facts' turning out badly. Tarski's diagnosis is that quotation functions are the root of the trouble, and must not be allowed. Some writers have, in response, suggested that, rather than quotation functions being disallowed altogether, certain restrictions should be imposed upon them; Binkley, for instance,

---

[1] Tarski does not give the derivation, but it would presumably go along the following lines. From 1, if $c = \text{'}(p) (c = \text{'}p\text{'} \to -p)\text{'}$, then $-(p) (c = \text{'}p\text{'} \to -p)$, so, given 2, $-(p) (c = \text{'}p\text{'} \to -p)$; hence by RAA, -1. If -1, then $(\exists p) (c = \text{'}p\text{'} \& p)$. Suppose for instance that $c = \text{'}q\text{'} \& q$; then '$q$' $= \text{'}(p) (c = \text{'}p\text{'} \to -p)\text{'}$ since both $= c$, hence, by 3, $q \equiv (p) (c = \text{'}p\text{'} \to -p)$. But q; so $(p) (c = \text{'}p\text{'} \to -p)$, i.e. 1. Hence, 1 & -1.

suggests (1970) a 'no-mixing' rule, which prevents one and the same quantifier from binding both variables inside, and variables outside, quotation marks, and hence disallows 1 above. But neither Tarski's diagnosis, nor this kind of response, can be quite right; for an analogous paradox can be derived without the use of quotation marks:

> Let '§' be an operator forming a term from a sentence; it could be read e.g. 'the statement that...'
> Let 'c' abbreviate 'the statement made by sentence numbered 1'.

Now, consider the sentence:

1. $(p) (c = \S p \to -p)$

It can be established empirically that:

2. $c = \S (p) (c = \S p \to -p)$

and a contradiction follows as before.[1] Now one might try, again, to impose restrictions on term-forming operators like '§'; for instance, following the example of Harman 1971, one might rule that if 'p' belongs to L, '$\S p$' must belong, not to L, but to the metalanguage of L. But this kind of manoeuvre – quite apart from its disagreeably *ad hoc* character – again seems not to go to the heart of the problem; for an analogous paradox can be derived without the use of '§'; if one could let 'c' abbreviate the sentence numbered 1 (instead of 'the sentence numbered 1'; 'c' now abbreviates a sentence, not a term):

1. $(p) ((c \equiv p) \to -p)$

so that, in virtue of the abbreviation,

2. $(c \equiv (p) ((c \equiv p) \to -p))$

and once again a contradiction would be derivable.

[1] Some comments are called for about the moral to be drawn about quotation marks. Tarski holds (and Quine agrees) that the result of enclosing an expression in quotation marks is an expression denoting the enclosed expression, but *of which the enclosed expression is not genuinely a part*. The idea that quotation forms a sort of 'logical block', that 'dog' isn't part of ''dog'', leads to very curious consequences, and is quite counter-intuitive (cf. Anscombe 1957). So it is a relief to find that the failure of Tarski's diagnosis of the paradox leaves one free to treat quotation as a function; cf. Belnap and Grover 1973, Haack 1975 for more detailed discussion.

This shouldn't be too surprising. For the effect of a truth-predicate can, as investigation of the redundancy theory (pp. 130–4 above) showed, be achieved by using second-order (propositional) quantifiers; and adding negation gives the effect of 'false'. So the fact that a Liar-type paradox is derivable without explicit use of semantic predicates, provided propositional quantifiers and negation are available, was to have been expected.

But how are paradoxes of this kind to be avoided? Suppose the propositional quantifiers are interpreted – as I recommended in ch. 4 §3 – substitutionally. On a substitutional interpretation, a quantified formula, A, of the form $(v)\,\Phi\,(v)$, is true just in case all its substitution instances, $\Phi(s)$, are true. Since in the case under consideration the quantifier binds sentence letters, the substituends for v will be wffs, and may, therefore, themselves contain quantifiers. Now, the usual conditions of definitional adequacy require that only substituends which contain fewer quantifiers than A itself be allowed; otherwise ineliminability would result (see Marcus 1972, and cf. Grover 1973). This restriction is in no way *ad hoc*, since it is only a special case of quite ordinary conditions on definitions; but at the same time it is sufficient to block the paradoxical argument where the wff substituted for 'p' in '$(p)\,((c \equiv p) \to -p)$' is '$(p)\,((c \equiv p) \to -p)$'.

It wouldn't be altogether fanciful, I think, to see affinities between this idea and the theory of types, with its hierarchy of propositions ordered according to what propositional quantifiers occur in them; nor to see affinities between the motivation for the restriction on substituends for sentential variables, and the V.C.P. Russell's argument why a proposition 'about all propositions' can't itself be a member of that totality is that it 'creates' a new proposition not previously belonging to that totality, which is unconvincing since it assumes, what it is intended to prove, that the proposition about all propositions isn't already a member of that totality; Ryle and Mackie, however, urge, in favour of the V.C.P., that violations of it lead to a 'vicious self-dependence' which *results in ineliminability*. And, finally, the fact that paradoxes can be generated without semantic predicates might be thought to suggest that there might, after all, be *something* in Russell's hunch that the paradoxes weren't to be handled in distinct groups according as semantic or set-theoretic predicates occurred essentially in them, but were to be handled together, as all the result of one fallacy.

9

Logic and logics

...since one never knows what will be the line of advance, it is always most rash to condemn what is not quite in the fashion of the moment.
Russell 1906, cited in Rescher 1974

1 'Classical' and 'non-classical' logics

There are a great many formal logical systems. In fact, ever since the 'classical' logical apparatus was formulated, there have been those who urged that it should be improved, modified or replaced. An instructive example can be taken from the history of the material conditional; anticipated by the Stoics, 'material implication' was formalised by Frege 1879 and Russell and Whitehead 1910 and supplied with a suitable semantics by Post 1921 and Wittgenstein 1922. As early as 1880, however, MacColl had urged the claims of a stricter conditional; 'strict implication' was formalised by Lewis 1918; and after that dissatisfaction with its claims to represent entailment led to the introduction of 'relevant implication' (see ch. 10 §7).

My present object is to get some perspective on the great variety of logical systems, to approach such questions as how they relate to each other, whether one must choose between them, and, if so, how. My strategy will be to consider the various ways in which the standard logical apparatus has been modified, and the various pressures in response to which such modifications have been made. An initial note of caution should, however, be sounded: this strategy, of looking at 'non-standard' by contrast with the 'standard' logical apparatus, carries the danger of inducing an overly conservative attitude to logical innovations. (Wolf 1977 puts the point well by reminding one that 'possession is nine-tenths of the law'.) Awareness of this danger may, I hope, of itself help to some degree in avoiding it. And it will also be salutary to bear in mind that today's 'classical logic' was once itself a 'logical innovation'. Kant, after all, urged (1800) that logic was a completed science, finished, in all essentials, in the work of

Aristotle; the next century, however, saw the development, with the work of Boole, Peirce, Frege and Russell, of new, stronger and more rigorous logical techniques. Recall, too, that Frege confidently supposed that the principles of his logical system were self-evident, until Russell showed that they were inconsistent!

2 Responses to pressure to change the standard formalism

The pressures to change the standard 2-valued sentence calculus and first-order predicate calculus have come from worries about the apparent inadequacy of the standard apparatus to represent various kinds of informal argument, and about the interpretation and application of that apparatus. The reactions to such pressures have been very varied; I shall first sketch, and then illustrate, some of the commonest responses:

1. Informal arguments to which the standard apparatus does not comfortably apply may be ruled outside the scope of logic. For instance, pressure for a 'logic of meaninglessness' may be resisted on the grounds that meaningless sentences are simply outside the proper sphere of logical formalisation. I'll call this the *delimitation of the scope of logic* response.

2. Problematic informal arguments may be admitted as within the scope of logic, and the standard apparatus retained; but adjustments made in the way that the awkward informal arguments are represented in the formalism. For instance, Russell's theory of descriptions proposes that sentences containing definite descriptions be represented not in the obvious way, as '*Fa*', but as existentially quantified formulae. I'll call this the *novel paraphrase* strategy. (Since Russell comments that the grammatical form of such sentences conceals their logical form, in 1974 I called it the *misleading form* strategy. But I'd prefer not to seem to subscribe to his view that each argument has a unique 'logical form.')

3. A third response, like the second, admits the problematic arguments as within the scope of logic, and retains the standard apparatus without any change at the level of syntax; however, the interpretation of that apparatus is modified, in such a way that initially recalcitrant informal

locutions are after all adequately represented. For example, concern about the apparent ontological commitments of the predicate calculus may be met by the proposal that the quantifiers be interpreted substitutionally, and empty terms allowed as *bona fide* substituends, so that ontological neutrality is secured. I'll call this the *semantic innovation* response.

4. The standard apparatus may be extended to obtain a formalism applicable to informal arguments which were previously inaccessible to formal treatment. For example, new operators may be added – tense operators or modal operators for instance – and axioms/rules governing them; or the standard operations may be extended to cover novel items – imperative or interrogative sentences, for instance. I'll call this the *extended logic* response.

5. Alternatively, the standard apparatus may be restricted, in that, while its vocabulary remains the same, its axioms/rules of inference are restricted in such a way that classical theorems/inferences cease to be valid. For example, concern to avoid anomalies in quantum mechanics has led to proposals in which certain 'classical' principles, the distributive law for instance, no longer obtain. I'll call this the *restricted logic* response; its upshot is a 'deviant logic' (Haack 1974).

Sometimes novel formulations are proposed which at once extend and restrict classical logic – they add new operators and new principles governing them, but at the same time restrict the principles governing old operators. 'Relevance logics' which introduce a new conditional, while at the same time rejecting some classical laws, such as *modus ponens* for the material conditional, would be an example.

I distinguished 4 and 5 from 2 and 3 because the former involve modifications at the level of syntax, while the latter leave the standard syntax untouched. But, of course, an extension or a restriction of the standard syntax would, in turn, require semantic modification, so that an interpretation is supplied which verifies the extended or restricted set of theorems/inferences. Indeed, restrictions of logic have quite often been motivated by semantic considerations – as, for example, challenges to the assumption that every sentence within the scope of logic must be either true or false led to the development of many-valued logics, which characteristically lack classical theorems such as '$p \lor -p$'.

As one would expect, extensions are most usually proposed in response to a supposed *inadequacy*, restrictions in response to a supposed *incorrectness*, in the standard formalism.

6. Innovations in the logical formalism are sometimes accompanied by – and sometimes motivated by – innovations at the level of metalogical concepts. For example, the Intuitionists (who propose a restriction of the standard apparatus) do so in part because they challenge the concept of truth presupposed in classical logic; the relevance logicians challenge the classical conception of validity. I'll call this the *challenge to classical metaconcepts*.

7. Finally – and as, so to speak, the converse of the first response – there are challenges to the standard conception of the scope and aspirations of logic. These are often enough associated with challenges to classical metaconcepts, as in 6. For example, the Intuitionists not only restrict classical sentence calculus so that '$p \lor -p$', for instance, is no longer a theorem, and not only offer an alternative to the classical conception of truth; they also take a radically different view from most classical logicians of the role of logic, which they regard as secondary to mathematics, rather than as underlying reasoning about all subject-matters whatever. I'll call this the *revision of the scope of logic* response. (An Intuitionist, however, would see the classical logician as revising the scope of logic.)

Roughly speaking, I suppose, it would be right to think of these responses as increasingly radical. But *only* roughly speaking. For instance, although it is usually thought that a reinterpretation of the standard apparatus is more conservative than an extension of it, there is surely a sense in which the conservatism of 3 is *nominal* – I mean, that the system only *looks* the same, but, since it's been reinterpreted, the upshot is little different from the introduction of new symbolism. It is worth observing, for instance, that some urge, in the interests of clarity, that we use a different notation for substitutional than for objectual quantifiers. And I have drawn attention to the way that quite deep challenges to classical metaconcepts or to classical conceptions of the aim of formalisation may often underlie proposals for extending or restricting the classical formalism; in view of this, it is not altogether surprising that, as we shall see, such systems have sometimes been held, by conservatives, not to be really *logics* at all.

Later (ch. 12) I shall be using the distinctions drawn here to try to understand the epistemological issues raised by the existence of a plurality of logics. For the present, though, my concern is mainly to supply some kind of framework for looking at that plurality. Strategies 1–7 are not exclusive (nor, probably, exhaustive); it is of some interest to notice that some problems, the problems raised by the possibility of non-denoting singular terms, for example, have provoked several of them: Strawson proposes to rule sentences containing such terms outside the scope of logic, Russell to supply a novel translation that reveals their real logical form, Hintikka to devise a restricted logic.

Since I can't possibly consider all the issues raised by the choice between these strategies, I shall, instead, take a closer look at two examples which illustrate some of the issues very well. I begin with the problem of how to handle *tense* formally.

3   First case-study: the logic of temporal discourse

The pioneers of modern formal logic were primarily motivated by the desire to represent mathematical arguments in a rigorous way. Consequently, because of the irrelevance of considerations of tense to the (in)validity of mathematical arguments, they were able largely to ignore the fact that, in informal argument on non-mathematical subjects, tense is sometimes crucial.

While this problem is often enough dismissed – along with related problems about indexical expressions – with the comment that one must take care, in representing informal arguments in symbolic form, that tense remains constant throughout the argument (a sort of casual version of the no-item response), some writers have made more serious attempts to allow for tense. And two quite distinct strategies have been proposed: Quine urges that temporal discourse be represented within the standard apparatus by interpreting the variables of the predicate calculus as ranging, not over enduring spatiotemporal individuals, but over 'epochs'; Prior urges that temporal discourse be accommodated by an extension of the standard apparatus by the addition of tense operators.

So, on the one hand, Quine proposes to deal with the problem by means of a semantic innovation, while, on the other, Prior proposes an extended logic. Another difference between the two strategies is important: though both are attempts to accommodate considerations of time, Prior's approach does this by taking tense seriously, while Quine's approach tries to achieve the same end in an untensed formalism. And a consequence of this is that Quine needs to make adjustments in the way informal tensed discourse is represented formally, as well as in the way the formalism is adjusted. That is to say, his approach combines semantic innovation with the novel paraphrase strategy.

Quine's approach (1960a §36; his ideas have been developed in more detail in Lacey 1971, on which I'll also rely) is to represent what is logically relevant in the tensed discourse of informal arguments within the standard logical formalism. Although Quine admits the relevance of tense to the validity of informal arguments, he regards it as really inessential, a reflection of the bias of ordinary language towards the temporal perspective of the speaker. So he proposes to replace tensed by tenseless verbs with 'temporal qualifiers' such as 'now', 'then', 'before t', 'at t' and 'after t'. The variables 't', 'u' ... etc. are construed as ranging over what Quine calls 'epochs', which are stretches of space-time of any chosen duration, an hour, say, or a day. An epoch, Quine explains, is a 'slice of the four-dimensional material world, exhaustive spatially and perpendicular to the time axis' (1960a p. 172). Reference to ordinary spatiotemporal individuals, such as persons, is to be replaced by reference to 'time-slices' of individuals, such as a person through a given time. So ordinary tensed sentences get rewritten along these lines:

Mary is a widow	Mary at now *is* a widow
George married Mary	$(\exists t)$ (t *is* before now and George at t *marries* Mary at t)
George will marry Mary	$(\exists t)$ (t *is* after now and George at t *marries* Mary at t)

The notational conventions are that tenseless verbs are to be written in the present tense form, but italicised; the variable 't' is to range over epochs; 'George at t' and 'Mary at t' refer to time-slices of the spatiotemporal individuals George and Mary.

'Now', of course, retains the indexical character of ordinary language; but eventually Quine will eliminate this too, by means of singular terms denoting epochs. So 'now' will be replaced by the appropriate date, and the last trace of tensed discourse eliminated, as:

Mary is a widow   Mary at 12 March 1977 *is* a widow

The result is that tensed sentences the truth-value of which varies over time are superseded by what Quine calls *eternal sentences*, the truth-value of which remains constant. (Eternal sentences are, of course, Quine's answer to the supposed need for propositions, which, in view of their intensional character, he will not admit.)

It should be clear by now that Quine's proposal calls for considerable departures from ordinary language locutions as well as for considerable innovations in the interpretation of the variables, singular terms, and predicates of the predicate calculus. Nevertheless, Quine would regard his proposal as, in an important sense, a *conservative* one; because its point is to allow the representation of tensed discourse within an *extensional* formalism. This is why Quine – who regards extensionality as a touchstone of intelligibility – attaches so much importance to retaining the standard syntax.

However, Quine sees his proposal as having, besides, another virtue: its consonance with modern physics. For while ordinary tensed discourse *singles out* time, Quine's representations treat the temporal dimension quite on a par with the three spatial dimensions. The temporal parts of a thing are treated in the same way as its spatial parts (a point which Quine exploits (p. 171) in arguing how his approach illuminates the problem of personal identity: why should one expect a person's temporal parts to be alike, since his spatial parts, e.g. his head and his feet, are not?). Einstein's discoveries, Quine comments, leave 'no reasonable alternative to treating time as spacelike' (p. 172).

Prior's approach (see 1957, 1967, 1968) is interestingly different. He accommodates temporal considerations not by adjusting the tensed locutions of ordinary language to fit within a tenseless, extensional symbolism, but by extending the standard symbolism to accommodate tensed locutions. Prior begins from a regular sentence calculus, in which, however, the sentence letters are to be understood as standing for sentences uniformly in the present tense. (And hence for items vulnerable to change of truth-value, by contrast with Quine's tenseless eternal sentences.) He then enriches the symbolism with tense operators '*F*' and '*P*', which are sentence-forming operators on sentences, the former turning a present tense sentence into a future tense sentence, the latter turning a present tense sentence into a past tense sentence. Prior reads '*F*' as 'It will be the case that...' and '*P*' as 'It used to be the case that...' Compound tenses are built up by iterating these operators. For instance, if '*p*' is 'George is marrying Mary', one has:

George married Mary	Pp
George will marry Mary	Fp
George will have married Mary	FPp

The tense operators are not extensional; the truth-value of '*Fp*' or '*Pp*' does not depend solely upon the truth-value of '*p*'.

Axioms are supplied governing the new operators. In fact, Prior offers alternative axiom sets, each suitable, he suggests, to rival metaphysical views about time, such as whether time has a beginning and/or end, whether it is linear or circular, whether determinism is true, and so forth (see Prior 1968).

Prior observes that tense operators, instead of being taken as primitive, might be defined in terms of quantification over instants of time; 'It will be the case that *p*', for instance, would be 'For some time *t* later than now, *p* at *t*'.[1] This would perhaps lessen the contrast with Quine's approach to some degree. But 'instants' are temporal, not, like Quine's 'epochs', spatiotemporal. And Prior says, anyway (1968 p. 118) that he prefers to think of tense operators as primitive, and of instants of time as 'mere logical constructions out of tensed facts.'

Thus, Prior's approach achieves simplicity of paraphrase of informal arguments into formal symbolism, but at the same time increases the complexity of the formalism, requiring, in particular, the loss of extensionality. And it also contrasts with Quine's approach at the metaphysical level; for, though one is offered alternative axiom sets between which to choose on the basis of one's view of time, the very

[1] Prior's tense logics are closely modelled on C. I. Lewis' modal systems (cf. ch. 10); and the definability of tense operators via quantifiers over instants corresponds to the account, in the usual semantics for those modal logics, of necessity (possibility) as truth in all (some) possible worlds.

TABLE 2

Quine's approach	Prior's approach
semantic innovation, novel paraphrase strategies	extended logic
eliminates tense	introduces tense operators
eternal sentences, no change of truth-value	tensed sentences, change of truth-value
extensional formalism	intensional formalism
substantial 'regimentation' of informal arguments	conformity to ordinary language
consonant with relativity theory	Newtonian in spirit
ontology of 4-dimensional space-time world	ontology of objects occupying space and enduring through time

syntax of the system conforms to a 'Newtonian' conception of time as quite unlike space. The major points of contrast between the two approaches are summarised in table 2.

Prior's treatment is most consonant, I have suggested, with a view of time as categorically different from space, Quine's with a view of time as space-like. Not surprisingly, then, it has sometimes been suggested that there are metaphysical reasons for preferring one or other approach.[1] Quine, as I have already reported, thinks that modern science 'leaves no reasonable alternative' to his approach. Geach, on the other hand, argues (1965) that Quine's ontology of epochs and four-dimensional spatiotemporal objects is defective because it entails that there is no such thing as change. But this is

[1] Cf. MacTaggart 1908 where a distinction is drawn between the 'A-series', in which events are ordered according as they are past, present, or future and the 'B-series', in which they are ordered as earlier than, simultaneous with, later than each other. Prior's approach emphasises the former, Quine's the latter. See also Strawson 1959 for a defence of the former, and Whitehead 1919 for a defence of the latter metaphysical stance.

false; Quine's approach allows change, all right, it is just that it represents what one would ordinarily call change in an enduring object over time as a difference between the earlier and later time-slices of that object – as, for instance, my hair's turning grey would be represented by a difference in the hair colour of my earlier and later time-slices.

My present concern, though, is not with these metaphysical questions, but with some methodological issues raised by the choice of strategies.

In general, as in the present case, it seems reasonable to expect that the price of sticking (like Quine) to an austere symbolism will be a loss of naturalness of paraphrase of informal arguments. (To put it in Russellian terms: the fewer logical forms available, the more grammatical forms will have to be diagnosed as 'misleading'.) If one attaches great significance to some degree of austerity – in Quine's case, to extensionality – in one's formalism, one will have to accept a divergence from natural language. If one attaches great significance to conformity with natural language forms – as Geach does – one will need a richer formalism. For myself, I concede the desirability both of austerity of symbolism (after all, part of the point of formalising at all is to systematise, to have relatively few rules to cover relatively many cases) and of simplicity of paraphrase (for another part of the point of formalisation is to supply a technique for evaluating informal arguments); I fear that it is just a fact of logical life that these are competing *desiderata*.

A factor that may sometimes help one to decide such a competition is that a sacrifice either of austerity of formalism or of simplicity of paraphrase will be better justified the broader the scope of the advantage to be gained by it. For example, one would hope that a formalism equipped to cope with temporal discourse might also be able to represent discourse about action and discourse about causation – and clearly, if only one approach succeeded here, that would be reason to prefer it. (See Lacey 1971 for relevant discussion; and cf. Davidson 1968a where it is argued that to represent action and causal statements one needs to quantify over events. Recall (p. 124) that Davidson, like Quine, is committed to restricting himself to an extensional formalism.)

Quine appeals to the character of current physical theories to support his approach; Geach, on Prior's behalf, urges that it is quite improper to adjust logic to suit science. The issues here are tangled.

Geach's attitude derives, in part, from the fact that he apparently regards relativity theory as incoherent, since it involves denying what he takes to be a 'difference of category' between space and time. And his conviction that there *is* such a difference of category derives in turn from our ordinary concepts of space and time, as embodied in our ordinary, tensed discourse. Those who, like myself, allow that developments in physics may well lead to conceptual revision, will resist this facile diagnosis of relativity theory as 'conceptually confused.'

But, quite apart from the question of the coherence or otherwise of relativistic physics, there is a deeper point at issue. Quine expressly aims, in his choice of logical formalism, for a 'language adequate for science', and regards logic as, so to speak, continuous with science; Geach regards logic as autonomous of, indeed prior to, science. The history of logic offers some support for the former view; for example, the logic devised by Frege and Russell, unlike Aristotle's syllogistic, can express relations as well as properties; and it is just because of this superiority of expressive power that modern logic is capable – as Aristotelian logic was not – of representing the sorts of argument essential to modern mathematics. One needs, though, to distinguish the question of the expressive power of logic from the question of its doctrinal content; I mean, that while it seems unexceptionable to modify the expressive power of one's formalism to enable it to express styles of argument characteristic of science, it is a more serious matter to give up a supposed law of logic (as the quantum logicians, for instance, urge that one give up the distributive law) because of developments in science. This suggests that extensions of logic are less radical, epistemologically speaking, than restrictions of it; a point to which I shall return in ch. 12.

4   Second case-study: precisification versus 'fuzzy logic'

A good deal of informal discourse is, in some degree, vague. And so the question arises whether, and if so, how, logicians should take account of this fact.

A first point to make is that an important reason for constructing formal systems of logic is to supply *precise* canons of validity – a major advantage of formal logic over unregimented informal argument is its much greater rigour and exactness. In view of this it is not surprising that Frege and Russell should have regarded vagueness as a defect of natural languages, to be banished from an acceptable formal language. (And no doubt it is also relevant here, as to their neglect of tense considerations, that they were primarily concerned with the formalisation of mathematical argument.)

This perhaps suggests that it would be appropriate simply to exclude vague sentences as ineligible for logical treatment. But this strategy is too crude, I think, because it is clear that vague sentences can occur in informal arguments without threatening their validity. There is a significant contrast, here, with the case of meaningless sentences. An argument must be composed of meaningful sentences: a meaningless string of symbols wouldn't *be* an argument, and a sequence of meaningful sentences with a meaningless string interposed would, if regarded as an argument at all, be valid or invalid independently of the meaningless string. So it's entirely reasonable to exclude meaningless sentences from the scope of logic; 'logics of meaninglessness' (e.g. Halldén 1949, Routley 1966, 1969) are, to my mind, neither necessary nor desirable.[1] But a vague sentence *can* play a genuine role in an argument ('John likes capable girls; Mary is capable and intelligent; so John will like Mary'); and so logicians must take vagueness more seriously.

However, vague sentences do seem to present certain difficulties for the application of the standard logical apparatus. Formal logical systems are supposed to be relevant to the assessment of informal arguments; but the classical logical systems, in which every wff is either true or else false, seem inappropriate for the assessment of informal arguments with premises and/or conclusions which, because of their vagueness, one hesitates to call either definitely true or definitely false. Once the problem has been put in this way, there seem to be two natural approaches to its solution: to tidy up the vague informal arguments before submitting them to assessment by the standards of classical, 2-valued logic, or, to devise some alternative formal logical system which will apply to them more directly.

The first approach calls for informal arguments to be regimented so that the standard logical apparatus can be used. (The procedure would be quite analogous to the accommodations regularly made to take account of the discrepancies between the truth-functional connectives and their English readings.) Carnap proposes (1950

---

[1] I don't mean to deny that there may be some interesting philosophical issues about the character and sources of meaninglessness (consider the role played by the alleged meaninglessness generated by 'category mistakes' in Ryle 1949, for example).

ch. 1) what he calls a programme of precisification: before formalisation vague should be replaced by precise, e.g. qualitative by comparative or quantitative, predicates, in such a way that (usually but not invariably) the precise terms correspond in extension, in all clear, central cases, with the vague ones they replace, but also have well-defined application in cases which were borderline for the vague terms. This proposal involves elements of both the first and the third strategies distinguished in §2: informal arguments are tidied up before receiving formal representation (strategy 2), but in such a way that the regimented arguments always avoid the vagueness of the originals (hints of strategy 1).

Some writers (e.g. Russell 1923, Black 1937) have urged that natural languages are wholly vague; and if this were so, of course, Carnap's programme couldn't be carried out. However, no very convincing arguments have been offered why precision is impossible in principle (cf. Haack 1974 ch. 6), and I shall proceed on the assumption that precisification is feasible.

But granted that it is possible, is it desirable? Some support for a different strategy – of altering classical logic to fit informal argument, rather than informal argument to fit classical logic – has derived from the belief that the sort of successive refinement of scientific concepts urged by Carnap may result in restricted applicability and unmanageable complexity. Indeed, it is significant that the writer responsible for the most influential proposals for a revised logic of vagueness is an electrical engineer whose earlier work (Zadeh 1963, 1964) had been devoted to refining such concepts as 'static' and 'adaptive', but who eventually concluded (Zadeh 1972) that ''fuzzy thinking' may not be deplorable, after all, if it makes possible the solution of problems which are much too complex for precise analysis'. The idea that increase of precision may not be an unmixed blessing is not new; Duhem pointed out (1904 pp. 178–9) that the statements of theoretical physics, just because they are more precise, are less certain, harder to confirm, than the vaguer statements of common sense. Popper (1961, 1976) has also suggested that precision may be a 'false ideal'.

What is the alternative to precisification? Well, if informal arguments are not to be regimented so that classical logical apparatus can be applied, perhaps the logical apparatus can be modified in such a way that it can be applied to unregimented informal arguments. It has been suggested, for example, that a 3-valued logic would be more suitable than classical 2-valued logic (Körner 1966); the idea is that the trouble with vague predicates like 'tall' is that there are border-line cases, i.e. cases of which the predicate is neither straightforwardly true nor straightforwardly false, and that this problem may be solved by allowing a third category, distinct from 'true' and 'false', to accommodate borderline cases. But this doesn't solve the problem at all satisfactorily; for it requires a sharp line to be drawn between border-line cases and central, true or false, cases. Yet surely to insist that at a given height a man ceases to be a borderline case and becomes definitely tall, no less than to insist that at a given height a man ceases to be not tall and becomes definitely tall, imposes an artificial precision.

Zadeh also recommends that a non-standard logic be adopted, but his 'fuzzy logic' represents a much more radical departure from the classical. I'll first briefly sketch the salient formal features of fuzzy logic. (For fuller details the reader is referred to Zadeh 1975, and Gaines' survey, 1976.) Zadeh's non-standard logic is devised on the basis of a non-standard set theory, 'fuzzy' set theory. Whereas in classical set theory an object either is or is not a member of a given set, in fuzzy set theory membership is a matter of degree; the degree of membership of an object in a fuzzy set is represented by some real number between 0 and 1, with 0 denoting *no* membership and 1 *full* membership. (A fuzzy set will thus consist of all those objects which belong to it in any degree, and two fuzzy sets will be identical if the same objects belong to them in the same degree.) Now fuzzy set theory can be used to characterise, semantically, a non-standard logic; as values of sentence letters, instead of the two classical values, one has the indenumerably many values of the interval [0, 1], and sentence connectives can be associated with set-theoretic operations in the usual way (e.g. negation with set complementation, implication with set inclusion, etc.). The upshot is an indenumerably many-valued logic. The exact character of this logic will depend upon the characterisation of the fuzzy set-theoretical operations; one quite natural set of assumptions yields the indenumerably many-valued extension of Łukasiewicz's 3-valued logic (p. 206). Fuzzy logic is constructed on the basis of one or another indenumerably many-valued logic. There is thus a family of fuzzy logics, each with its own base logic. The indenumerably many truth-values of the base logic are superseded by denumerably many fuzzy truth-values, which are fuzzy subsets of the set of values of the base logic, characterised as:

true, false, not true, very true, not very true, more or less
true, rather true, not very true and not very false...
(Zadeh 1975 p. 410)

True is defined as a specified fuzzy subset of the set of values of the base logic, and the other linguistic truth-values are then defined; *very true*, for instance, is *true²*; if degree of truth 0·8 belongs to *true* to degree 0·7, it belongs to *very true* to degree 0·49.

What this amounts to, at an intuitive level, is something of the following kind. A vague predicate is taken to determine, not a classical set, but a fuzzy set; for example, a person *a* may be tall to some degree. If, say, *a* belongs to degree 0·3 to the set of tall people, then the sentence '*a* is tall' would receive, in the base logic, the value 0·3 ('*x* is tall' is true to degree *n* iff *x* ∈ *tall* to degree *n*). But according to Zadeh 'true' itself is vague, and so it receives analogous treatment; the degree of truth which '*p*' has may be quite low, rather high, not very high...etc. The linguistic truth-values of fuzzy logic can be thought of as corresponding to rather low ('*not very true*'), rather high ('*very true*'), not very high ('*more or less true*') degrees of truth in the base logic. So, to return to the example, if *a* ∈ *tall* to degree 0·3, so that '*a* is tall' has value 0·3 in the base logic, it will have, say, the value *not very true* in fuzzy logic, since its degree of truth is rather low.

In brief, one could think of fuzzy logic as the result of two stages of 'fuzzification': the move from 2-valued to indenumerably many-valued logic as a result of allowing degrees of membership to sets denoted by object language predicates, and the move to countably many fuzzy truth-values as a result of treating the metalinguistic predicate 'true' as itself vague. The term 'fuzzy logic' is sometimes also used of the non-standard base logics; but I have followed Zadeh's own, more restricted, usage, in which 'fuzzy logic' denotes a family of systems with fuzzy truth-values. And, according to Zadeh, the second stage of 'fuzzification' has radical consequences. Among the most notable – not to say alarming – are these. It turns out that the set of truth-values of fuzzy logic is not closed under the operations of negation, conjunction, disjunction and implication: for example, the conjunction of two sentences each of which has a linguistic truth-value in that set may not itself have such a value. So fuzzy logic has 'fuzzy truth-values...imprecise truth-tables...and...rules of inference whose validity is approximate rather than exact' (1975 p. 407).

Consequently, Zadeh claims, in fuzzy logic such traditional concerns as axiomatisation, proof procedures, consistency, and completeness are only 'peripheral' (Zadeh and Bellman 1976 p. 151). Fuzzy logic, in brief, is not just a logic for handling arguments in which vague terms occur essentially; it is *itself* imprecise. It is for this reason that I said that Zadeh's proposal is much more radical than anything previously discussed; for it challenges deeply entrenched ideas about the characteristic objectives and methods of logic. For the pioneers of formal logic a large part of the point of formalisation was that only thus could one hope to have *precise* canons of valid reasoning. Zadeh proposes that logic compromise with vagueness.

One is faced, here, with a striking example of strategy 7, a radical challenge to the traditional conception of the scope and aims of formal logic. In fact, we have seen that responses to vagueness have ranged all the way from the most conservative (attempts to exclude vague sentences altogether from the scope of logic) through the moderately innovative (proposals for a 3-valued logic of vagueness) to the most radical (the proposal that logic abandon its aspirations to precision).

Precision is certainly too central and important a *desideratum* of formalisation to be lightly surrendered. And in the present instance I think one is justified in asking whether the benefits can be expected to outweigh the costs. Obviously, the adoption of a fuzzy logic would result in a pretty serious loss in terms of simplicity (Zadeh himself admits that fuzzy logic is in some ways much less simple even than its non-standard base logic); and if one recalls that the reason Zadeh gives for preferring to make logic imprecise rather than to make informal arguments precise is that the latter is apt to introduce un-manageable complexity one is likely to feel even more doubtful whether the game is worth the candle. For another thing, it isn't even clear that fuzzy logic avoids the artificial imposition of precision. In the base logic, though one isn't obliged to insist that (say) Jack must be either definitely tall or definitely not tall, nor that he must be either definitely tall or definitely not tall or definitely borderline, one will be obliged to insist that he be tall to degree o·7 or tall to degree o·8, or...etc.; and in the resulting fuzzy logic one will be obliged to insist that, if 'Jack is tall' is true to degree o·8, it should count as *very true*, or only as *true but not very true*, or...etc. Zadeh proposes to define *true* as:

$$true = 0{\cdot}3/0{\cdot}6 + 0{\cdot}5/0{\cdot}7 + 0{\cdot}7/0{\cdot}8 + 0{\cdot}9/0{\cdot}9 + 1/1$$

i.e., as the fuzzy set to which degree of truth o·6 belongs to degree o·3, o·7 to degree o·5, o·8 to degree o·7, o·9 to degree o·9, and 1 to degree 1 (1975 p. 411); is not this an artificial imposition of precision? It is hard to avoid the suspicion that Zadeh's programme brings only doubtful benefits, and at excessive cost.

Postscript: degrees of truth

Zadeh's second stage of fuzzification – the extension of fuzzy set theory to 'true' and 'false' – is based on the idea that truth is a matter of degree, and is reflected in his list of linguistic truth-values, where adverbial modifiers such as 'not very' and 'more or less' (which he calls 'hedges') are attached to 'true' and 'false'. But Zadeh's list of linguistic truth-values is extremely odd: for example, though 'very true' and 'more or less true' sound acceptable, 'rather true', 'slightly true', and, for that matter, 'not very true' seem to me quite bizarre. This prompts me to look a little more closely at the linguistic evidence.

Among the adverbial modifiers which *do* apply to 'true' one has 'quite' and 'very'. Now 'quite' and 'very' apply to predicates of degree, i.e. predicates which denote properties which come in degrees (quite tall, heavy, intelligent..., very tall, heavy, intelligent...) where they indicate possession of the property in, respectively, modest or considerable degree. And Zadeh apparently thinks that, analogously, 'quite true' indicates the possession of a modest degree of truth, and 'very true' the possession of a high degree of truth. But whereas 'quite tall (heavy, intelligent)' can be roughly equated with 'rather (fairly) tall (heavy, intelligent)', 'quite true' certainly doesn't mean anything like 'rather true' or 'fairly true'. For 'rather' and 'fairly', like other adverbs which typically modify adjectives of degree, just don't apply to 'true' (I follow linguists' practice of starring unacceptable locutions):

* rather true
* fairly true
* somewhat true
* slightly true
* extremely true

In fact, 'quite true' can be roughly equated with 'perfectly true' or 'absolutely true', and (so far from contrasting with it) 'very true'. Again, when 'quite' (or 'rather' or 'fairly') is attached to a predicate of degree, as in 'quite (rather, fairly) tall (heavy, intelligent)' it cannot be preceded by 'not' ('not quite tall' is unacceptable); whereas when it is attached to an absolute predicate, as in 'quite ready', it can ('not quite ready'). The behaviour of 'quite' and 'very' with 'true', so far from supporting the hypothesis that 'true' is a predicate of degree, indicates that it is an absolute predicate.

But what about other adverbial modifiers which apply to 'true', such as 'wholly', 'completely', 'substantially', 'largely', 'partially', 'more or less', 'approximately', 'essentially', 'not strictly', 'not exactly'... and so forth? I conjecture that it may be possible to explain such locutions without treating truth as a matter of degree; roughly, one might expect something along the lines of ''p' is wholly true iff the whole of 'p' is true', ''p' is partially true iff part of 'p' is true', ''p' is approximately true iff 'approximately p' is true'...etc. These issues will receive further attention in ch. 11 §3.

IO

Modal logic

I Necessary truth

Modal logic is intended to represent arguments involving essentially the concepts of necessity and possibility. Some preliminary comments about the idea of necessity, therefore, won't go amiss. There is a long philosophical tradition of distinguishing between *necessary* and *contingent* truths. The distinction is often explained along the following lines: a necessary truth is one which could not be otherwise, a contingent truth one which could; or, the negation of a necessary truth is impossible or contradictory, the negation of a contingent truth possible or consistent; or, a necessary truth is true in all possible worlds (pp. 188ff. below), a contingent truth is true in the actual but not in all possible worlds. Evidently, such accounts aren't fully explanatory, in view of their 'could (not) be otherwise', '(im)possible', 'possible world'. So the distinction is sometimes introduced, rather, by means of examples: in a recent book (Plantinga 1974 p. 1) '$7 + 5 = 12$', 'If all men are mortal and Socrates is a man, then Socrates is mortal' and 'If a thing is red, it is coloured' are offered as examples of necessary truths, and 'The average rainfall in Los Angeles is about 12 inches' as an example of a contingent truth.

The distinction between necessary and contingent truths is a *metaphysical* one; it should be distinguished from the *epistemological* distinction between *a priori* and *a posteriori* truths. An *a priori* truth is one which can be known independently of experience, an *a posteriori* truth one which cannot. These – the metaphysical and the epistemological – are certainly different distinctions. But it is controversial whether they coincide in extension, whether, that is, all and only necessary truths are *a priori* and all and only contingent truths *a posteriori*. Opinion on this question has fluctuated: Kant thought there were contingent *a priori* truths; the logical positivists insisted on the coextensiveness of the necessary and the *a priori*, and the contingent and the *a posteriori*; Kripke has recently (1972) urged that there are, after all, contingent *a priori* (and necessary *a posteriori*) truths. I shan't enter into this question here, where necessary truth is the main preoccupation; it will have some relevance when I come, in ch. 12 §3, to the question of the epistemological status of logic.

Among necessary truths, it is also traditional to distinguish *physically* necessary truths (truths which physically could not be otherwise, the negations of which are physically impossible, true in all physically possible worlds) and *logically* necessary truths (truths which logically could not be otherwise, the negations of which are logically impossible, true in all logically possible worlds). Sometimes physical necessity is explained by means of logical necessity, as logical compatibility with the laws of nature. Or, again, one may resort to examples: 'Any two material bodies attract each other with a force proportional to their mass' can serve as an example of a physically necessary truth, 'If any two material bodies attract each other with a force proportional to their mass, then any two material bodies attract each other with a force proportional to their mass' as an example of a logically necessary truth. Some philosophers are sceptical about this distinction; see e.g. Kneale 1962a, Molnar 1969, and cf. Quine, 'Necessity', in 1966a. And of course the question whether there *are* any physically necessary truths raises important issues in the philosophy of science. But modal logics were designed, primarily, with the object of representing logical rather than physical necessity and possibility, which is why I only mention, and do not answer, the intriguing questions raised by the idea of physical necessity.

The distinction between logically necessary and logically contingent truths has sometimes been thought to rest, in turn, on that between *analytic* and *synthetic* truths. 'Analytic' and its opposite 'synthetic' have been variously defined: Kant defined an analytic truth as one the concept of whose predicate is included in the concept of its subject or – arguably not equivalently – as one the negation of which is contradictory; Frege defined an analytic truth as either a truth of logic, or a truth reducible to a logical truth by means of definitions in purely logical terms (thus, logicism is the thesis that the truths of arithmetic are, in this sense, analytic). More recently, analytic truths have been characterised as 'true solely in virtue of their meaning', synthetic truths as 'true in virtue of facts'; with truths of logic being thought of as a subclass, true in virtue of the meaning of the logical constants, of the larger class of truths in virtue of meaning. (Hintikka 1973 is informative on the history of 'analytic'. Notice the characteristic shift from Kant's quasi-psychological account, in terms of the *concepts* involved in *judgments* to more recent linguistic characterisations in terms of the *meanings* of the component words of *sentences*.)

Analyticity is thought to explain the *grounds* of necessary truth, what makes a necessary truth necessarily true. So the necessary/ contingent and analytic/synthetic distinctions are supposed to coincide, the idea being that an analytic truth, being true solely in virtue of its meaning, couldn't be otherwise than true, and so, is necessary.[1]

Now Quine is sceptical of the analytic/synthetic distinction;[2] and his scepticism is, as we shall see, one of the reasons for his distaste for modal logic.

The critique of analyticity in 'Two dogmas' is directed, primarily, at the second disjunct of a roughly 'Fregean' account of analyticity, as:

[1] But words can change their meaning; and if they do, may not previously analytic sentences become synthetic or false? The supporters of analyticity might reply that though one and the same sentence may at one time express an analytic truth, and at another time a synthetic truth, or perhaps a falsehood, the *proposition* originally expressed by the sentence remains analytic though the sentence ceases to express it.

[2] Historical note: Quine didn't always reject the analytic/synthetic distinction; in 1947 he used the concept of analyticity, though he comments in a footnote that Goodman had been urging scepticism about it. And before 'Two dogmas' appeared Morton White (1950) had already attacked the analytic/synthetic distinction as an 'untenable dualism'. It was Quine's attack, however, that proved the most influential. By 1960a Quine's scepticism about synonymy was buttressed by his thesis of the *indeterminacy of translation*: the thesis that meaning notions are not just, as he urged earlier, obscure and of doubtful empirical content, but demonstrably indeterminate. In 1973, however, though remaining officially sceptical about meaning, Quine offered his own *ersatz* conception of analyticity: a statement is analytic, in this sense, if everyone in the linguistic community learns that it is true by learning to understand it; notice that this conception is, characteristically, both genetic and social. For the present I shall be concerned only with Quine's straightforwardly sceptical views, with the period between 1951 and 1973; the reader is referred to Haack 1977c, where I have argued that his new conception of analyticity is apt to collapse into the traditional conception of truth-in-virtue-of-meaning.

A is analytic iff either:
(i) *A* is a logical truth

or

(ii) *A* is reducible to a logical truth by substitution of synonyms for synonyms

It will be convenient to call the class of statements falling under (i) or (ii) *broadly analytic*, and those which qualify under (ii) *narrowly analytic*; broad analyticity, in this terminology, is logical truth plus narrow analyticity. The picture Quine rejects is portrayed in fig. 5; his critique is aimed at the concept of narrow analyticity.

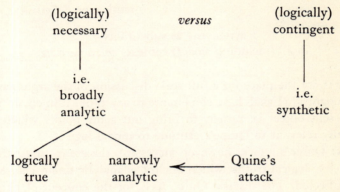

Fig. 5

Specifically, Quine's strategy is to argue that no satisfactory explanation can be given of the second clause, or of the conception of synonymy on which it relies. The explanations which have been offered, he claims, either fail correctly to characterise all the supposed analytic truths (for instance, Carnap's account of analyticity as truth in all state-descriptions, he argues, applies only to logical truths and not to narrowly analytic truths which should qualify under clause (ii)) or else turn out to depend, overtly or covertly, upon an understanding of some other intensional notion no clearer than analyticity itself. If, for example, clause (ii) is explained in terms of substitution on the basis of definitions, this involves an indirect appeal to the synonymies upon which the definitions are based; nor, again, can synonymy be explained as substitutability in all contexts *salva veritate* (i.e. without change of truth-value), unless contexts such as 'Necessarily...' are taken into account. In brief, explanations of analyticity can never break out of an 'intensional circle' of concepts no clearer than what is being explained (see fig. 6).

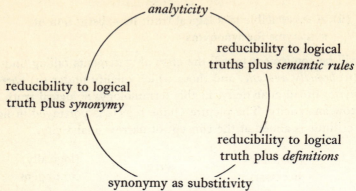

analyticity

reducibility to logical truths plus *semantic rules*

reducibility to logical truth plus *synonymy*

reducibility to logical truth plus *definitions*

synonymy as substitivity
Fig. 6   in all (including *modal*) contexts *salva veritate*

This is not the place for a full-scale discussion of the argument of 'Two dogmas' (I shall have some more to say about it in ch. 12 §3); my present object is, rather, to bring out some points which are especially relevant to Quine's attitude to modal logic.

First: Quine's attack, however successful, threatens only narrow analyticity: logical truths, which qualify as analytic under clause (i), are unaffected. The distaste Quine feels for the concept of narrow analyticity does not extend to the concept of logical truth. This will be relevant to discussion (pp. 182, 193 below) of whether the necessity operator in the usual modal logics can be understood as representing logical truth, or whether it must correspond to a broader conception of necessity.

Quine characterises a logical truth as 'a statement which is true and remains true under all reinterpretations of its components other than the logical particles' (1951 pp. 22–3; and cf. 1970 ch. 4). Here, as elsewhere, Quine is careless of the distinction between the system-relative idea of the logical truth of a wff of a formal language, and the extra-systematic idea of the logical truth of a statement of a natural language. I suggested (pp. 14–15) that the extra-systematic idea of logical truth amounts, initially, only to a none-too-precise idea of a statement which is trivially true. However, if this idea is refined in the same way that the idea of a valid argument as one whose premises couldn't be true and its conclusion false is refined by the insight that an argument is valid if there is no argument of the same form with true premises and false conclusion, the result is the idea of a statement such that no other statement of the same form is false: which is very close to Quine's characterisation.[1]

Second: Quine's objection to narrow analyticity rests, at bottom, on the idea that no explanation can be given of it except by means of other terms from the 'intensional circle', and that all such terms are unclear. This will be relevant to discussion (pp. 189–90, 193–4 below) of whether, in the interpretation of modal systems, it is realistic to hope for a non-modal explanation of modal terms.

First, though, I shall be concerned with a syntactical characterisation of modal logics.

2 Modal systems
Extensions of classical logic

One system is an extension of another if it shares the vocabulary of the first, and has the same theorems and valid inferences involving only the shared vocabulary, but also has additional vocabulary, and additional theorems and/or valid inferences involving that vocabulary essentially; an 'extended logic' is a system which is an extension of classical logic (ch. 1 §2, ch. 9 §1). Extensions of classical logic are often motivated by the belief that the standard sentence and predicate calculi are, though unobjectionable, less than fully adequate: their theorems are logically true, and their valid sequents truth-preserving, but there are other logical truths and/or valid arguments which involve operations for which they lack the vocabulary, which they cannot even express.

Modal logic adds to the classical vocabulary the 1-place operators 'L', to be read 'necessarily', and 'M', to be read 'possibly', and the 2-place operator ' $\dashv$ ', to be read 'strictly implies'. (Other extended logics, such as *epistemic logic*, which adds the operators 'K', to be read 'x knows that', and 'B', to be read 'x believes that'; *deontic logic*, which adds the operators 'O', to be read 'It ought to be the

---

[1] Strawson has urged (1957) against Quine, that the explanation of logical truth, like the explanation of narrow analyticity, requires appeal to synonymy. How is one to know that 'If he is sick then he is sick' is logically true, he asks, unless one has assurance that 'he is sick' means the same at each occurrence? The reply should be, I think, that where appeal to meaning may be necessary is, rather, with respect to the question, whether 'If he is sick then he is sick' is appropriately to be represented, formally, as '$p \to p$'.

case that', and '*P*', to be read 'It is permitted that'; and *tense logic* (ch. 9 §3) are modelled rather closely on modal logic.)

Historical remarks

The logic of modal sentences was discussed by Aristotle and by medieval logicians; in the present century Hugh MacColl (1880, 1906) contributed formal as well as philosophical proposals. But sustained formal development came in the present century, in the wake of Frege's and Russell's development of non-modal sentence calculi. The first axiomatisations of modal sentence logic were given by Lewis 1918. The extension to modal predicate logic came with Marcus 1946.

The primary motivation for Lewis's development of modal logics was dissatisfaction with the notion – central to the logic of the *Begriffsschrift* and *Principia Mathematica* – of material implication. Since '*p*' materially implies '*q*' if either '*p*' is false or '*q*' is true, one has the theorems, the so-called 'paradoxes' of material implication:

$$p \rightarrow (q \rightarrow p)$$
$$-p \rightarrow (p \rightarrow q)$$
$$(p \rightarrow q) \vee (q \rightarrow p)$$

The material implication of classical logic, Lewis held, is quite inadequate to the intuitive notion of implication, which requires, not just that '*p*' *is* not true and '*q*' false, but that '*p*' *could* not be true and '*q*' false. So he proposed that the logic of *Principia* should be enriched by a new operator, for *strict* implication, which could be defined as necessity of material implication.

A formal sketch

Only one modal operator need be added, as a primitive, to the vocabulary of classical logic; with '*L*' ('necessarily') as primitive, '*M*' ('possibly') is standardly defined as:

$$MA = \mathrm{df} \quad -L-A$$

and ' $\dashv$ ' as:

$$A \dashv B = \mathrm{df} \quad L(A \rightarrow B)$$

Or '*M*' may be taken as primitive and '*LA*' defined as ' $-M-A$ '.

In the usual modal logics the formation rules allow 'LA' as a wff whenever 'A' is a wff; this, of course, allows for *iterated modalities*, such as 'LMp' or 'LLp'.

Now there is not one, but a whole range, of modal logics, differing from each other with respect to the strength of the axioms they admit to govern the modal operators. I shall sketch some of the better-known systems, in order of increasing strength.

So·5, one of the weakest modal systems, results from the addition of the axioms:

    1. $Lp \rightarrow p$

and:

    2. $L(p \rightarrow q) \rightarrow (Lp \rightarrow Lq)$

together with the rule:

    (R) If A is a theorem of sentence calculus, then $\vdash_{S0.5} LA$

The system T results from the strengthening of (R) to:

    (RN) If $\vdash_T A$, then $\vdash_T LA$

(so that $\vdash LA$ not only when A is a theorem of sentence calculus (as with (R)) but also when it is one of the added axioms 1 and 2, etc.; another contrast with (R) is that (RN) is iterable, so that one gets $\vdash LLA$, $\vdash LLLA$, etc.).

The system S4 results from T by the addition of the axiom:

    3. $Lp \rightarrow LLp$

and the system S5 from S4 by the addition of:

    4. $Mp \rightarrow LMp$

There are other modal systems as well, weaker, stronger and in between these. The exact character of the quantified modal logic, also, may differ according to some variations in the presentation of the underlying predicate calculus. (For fuller details, consult Hughes and Cresswell 1968.)

Relations between the modal systems

The proliferation of modal systems immediately raises the question whether one is obliged to choose between them, whether, that is, each aims at – and so, at most one succeeds in – capturing just the logical truths/valid inferences involving *the* notion of necessity, or whether, perhaps, each aims – and so, all may succeed – at capturing *a* sense of 'necessary'. This, to anticipate an idea I shall discuss in more detail subsequently (ch. 12 §1), is the question, whether the various modal systems should be regarded as *rivals* of each other. Lemmon has argued (1959) for a tolerant, pluralistic approach; each of the modal systems, he thinks, can be seen as formalising a different idea of necessity: for example, So·5 the idea of tautologousness, S5 the idea of analyticity. Others, however, (e.g. Cargile 1972) doubt the feasibility of Lemmon's interpretations. Among those who believe that there is *a correct* modal logic, the stronger systems, S4 and S5, seem to be most often favoured.

3   Criticisms of modal logic

Doubts go deeper, however, than the dispute about whether there is a correct modal logic, or which modal logic is the correct one. For the feasibility, and even the intelligibility, of the whole enterprise of modal logic has been questioned; Quine, most notably, has long challenged it (but cf. also e.g. Bergmann's criticisms in 1960).

Quine's objections are threefold: that the motivation for the development of modal systems rested upon a confusion; that modal logics are anyway not needed for any of the legitimate purposes of formalisation; and that the interpretation of modal logics presents insuperable difficulties. Underlying these objections, of course, is Quine's deep-seated scepticism about the concept of analyticity. It is against this background of scepticism about the status of modal notions that one should see Quine's objections to modal logics.

Modal logic 'was conceived in sin'

' $\dashv$ ', or 'strictly implies', Lewis argued, was needed because of the excessive weakness of '$\to$' or 'materially implies'. Now Quine points out that 'materially implies' is anyway a grammatically improper reading of '$\to$'; for '$\to$' is a sentence-forming operator upon sentences, while 'materially implies' is a 2-place predicate. So modal logic was 'conceived in sin', the sin of confusing *use* (as in '$p \to q$') and *mention* (as in ''p' materially implies 'q''). It seems that Lewis did, indeed, succumb to this confusion, helped, no doubt, by Russell's bad example; it is also pretty clear, however, that this grammatical misdemeanour need not vitiate the enterprise of modal logic (and cf. Belnap 1974 for arguments why grammatical deviance may be positively desirable in logical innovations). Grammar, as Quine insists, deplores the reading of '→' as 'materially implies'; nevertheless, there is a relation that holds between two sentences 'p' and 'q' just when $p → q$, a weak relation which may, in all grammatical propriety, be referred to as 'material implication'; and modal logic formalises another relation that holds between two sentences 'p' and 'q', a stronger relation which may be referred to as 'strict implication'.

Modal logic is not needed

Modal logics are, as I explained, extensions of classical logic; Quine suggests (e.g. in 1960a §41) that such extensions are not needed. The question arises, of course, 'needed for what?'. Quine holds that the aim of formalisation, or, as he puts it, 'regimentation' of informal argument is to achieve a precise language 'adequate for science'; and for the purposes of science, he believes, modal notions are not required.

The assumption that the aim of formalisation is a language 'adequate for science' may be challenged, even though Quine, I think, understands 'science' pretty broadly, including mathematics as well as physics, chemistry, biology, psychology and the social sciences, and commonsense cognitive discourse as well as the official talk of professional scientists. Certainly some logicians regard it as part of their job to devise a language adequate, also, to represent argument in, for example, moral discourse (cf. Smiley 1963) or discourse in fiction (cf. ch. 5 §4). The claim that modal notions are inessential to scientific discourse is, again, controversial. It is particularly difficult to get an undistorted perspective on this issue, because Quine himself is – naturally enough – inclined to apply specially stringent standards when considering claims that scientific discourse requires the broad conception of necessity which he anyway rejects. In other words, Quine's claim that these concepts are not needed, and his claim that they are empty, inevitably no doubt, interact.

An example: dispositions and the subjunctive conditional

The best way to understand what is at issue here may be, therefore, to consider in some detail a case where it has been held, but where Quine denies, that certain locutions are (i) essential to scientific discourse and (ii) inexplicable except in modal terms. A family of locutions which is apparently very deeply entrenched in the language of science is the idiom of *dispositions* and its close relation, the *subjunctive conditional*. To say, for instance, that x is water-soluble, is to say that if x were placed in water, x would dissolve. The material conditional of truth-functional sentence calculus is inadequate to represent the subjunctive conditional, for '$A \to B$' is true if 'A' is false, while one does not suppose that 'x is soluble' or 'if x were placed in water, x would dissolve' need be true just because x has never been placed in water. Some writers believe that an adequate formal representation of the subjunctive conditional requires modal apparatus, specifically, appeal to possibilities. Modal analyses of subjunctive conditionals have been offered by Stalnaker 1968 and by D. K. Lewis 1973. Quine, of course, takes a somewhat dim view of such proposals, just because they use this modal apparatus; but he has also, more relevantly to the present issue, argued that subjunctive conditionals can be accommodated without it. At one time, it seems, Quine admitted that dispositional terms must be part of a language of science, and offered an extensional analysis of them: 'x is soluble', for instance, was explained along the lines of '$(\exists y)$ (x has an internal structure like y, which has been placed in water and which dissolved)'. Sometimes, Quine observed, as in the case of solubility, the relevant structure is known; sometimes, as in the case of irritability, the reference to an internal structure is no more than a 'promissory note' (see 1960a §46). It has been argued, however, that this account does not allow the surely genuine possibility that all things of a certain kind should have a given disposition, and yet none of them should ever have manifested it, as, perhaps, all nuclear power stations have a disposition to explode in certain circumstances, even though, thus far, safety precautions have ensured that those circumstances have not arisen, so that none have ever exploded (Mellor 1974). Subsequently, anyway, Quine seems to suggest that dispositional terms do not really belong, after all, to the language of science; they are essential only while the enterprise of science is uncompleted, but can be dropped once the relevant structures are known. One might feel that Quine's attempt to exclude dispositional idioms from a 'regimented theoretical language' would be more convincing had it not been preceded by an abandoned attempt to include them in an extensional guise; and one may well feel discomfort with the appeal to a finished, by contrast with an ongoing, science, for such a distinction fits especially ill with Quine's usually pragmatic approach to the philosophy of science.

As I have observed, Quine's conviction that we can do without modal notions also rests upon his belief that the interpretation of modal logic is so beset with difficulties that the use of such apparatus is not really helpful anyway. So it is time to look at these difficulties.

The interpretation of modal logic is fraught with difficulties

These criticisms fall into two groups: the difficulties which Quine finds in the interpretation of modal sentence logic, and the additional difficulties which he finds in the interpretation of modal predicate logic.

In 1953b Quine distinguishes what he calls the 'three grades of modal involvement', viz:

(i) the use of 'necessary' as a predicate of sentences. Here 'L' would apply to names of, or quoted, sentences, as in 'L '$2+2 = 4$''; it could be read '...is necessarily true' and would have a strong analogy to '...is true' in Tarski's theory, where is it treated as a predicate of sentences;

(ii) the use of 'necessarily' or 'it is necessary that' as a sentence-forming operator on sentences, as in '$L(2+2 = 4)$', where 'L' is treated as syntactically analogous to 'it is true that ...';

(iii) the use of 'necessarily' as an operator both on closed sentences, as in (ii), and on open sentences, as in '$L(2+2 = x)$' and its existential generalisation, '$(\exists x)\, L(2+2 = x)$'.

Modal sentence logic will require at most the second grade of modal involvement, whereas modal predicate logic requires the third. In 'Three grades' it is clear that Quine regards (i) and (ii) as, though by no means unproblematic, at least preferable to (iii); and this corresponds to his view of modal sentence logic as, though by no means unproblematic, at least preferable to modal predicate logic.

Difficulties in the interpretation of modal sentence logic

In modal sentence logics of the conventional kind, 'L' and 'M' are sentence operators, as in grade (ii). However, at least so long as one sticks with single modal operators, one can always regard, say, '$L(2+2 = 4)$', as a syntactic variant on 'L '$2+2 = 4$'', as in grade (i).

Since he dislikes the notion of analyticity, Quine is less than happy even about the use of 'necessary' as a sentence predicate. However, he admits the concepts of theoremhood and its semantic counterpart, logical truth, so that the interpretation of 'LA' as "'A' is logically true (a theorem)' is available to him. But this kind of interpretation allows for only a fragment of the usual modal sentence logics, since it leaves the status of iterated modalities in question. It does, however, suggest an interesting line of thought: that if 'LA' were interpreted as "'A' is a theorem (valid formula) of L', where L is some formal theory, then 'LLA' might be interpreted as "'LA' is a theorem of M', where M is the metalanguage of L. In other words, iterated modal operators would not be univocal, but each would refer to theoremhood or logical truth in one of a hierarchy of theories. Modal logics along these lines – motivated by the sorts of consideration just discussed – have been devised (Priest 1976). The usual modal logics, however, with their univocally interpreted iterated modal operators, are not amenable to this kind of approach.

Difficulties in the interpretation of modal predicate logic[1]

If the adjunction of modal operators to sentence logic is dubious, the mixture of modal operators and quantifiers is, Quine argues, disastrous.

Quine's difficulties with quantified modal logic derive, fundamentally, from the intersection of his views about quantifiers and his views about modality. According to Quine (ch. 4 §2), since singular terms are eliminable, it is the quantifiers which carry ontological commitment; the quantifiers are the basic device by means of which we talk *about things*. On the other hand, he takes modal locutions to be talk, not directly about things, but about *our ways of talking about things*: 'necessity', he comments, 'resides in the way we say things, and not in the things we talk about' (1953b p. 174). To put it another way, Quine thinks that modality, insofar as it is intelligible at all, is *de dicto* and not *de re*; 'necessary' and 'possible' are predicates of sentences, not of extra-linguistic things: "'$2 + 2 = 4$' is necessary' (grade (i)) is comprehensible, but '$2 + 2$ necessarily $= 4$' (grade (iii)) is not (cf. Plantinga 1974 ch. 1 §2 and ch. 2). Given his view of the contrasting roles of quantifiers and modal operators, the main theme of Quine's criticisms of quantified modal logic should

---

[1] A useful presentation and discussion of these criticisms is to be found in Føllesdal 1969; there is a reply by Quine in the same volume.

come as no surprise: when quantifiers and modal operators are combined, it is hopelessly unclear *what* we are talking about.

Some of the difficulties show up in the anomalous behaviour of singular terms in the scope of modal operators. Modal operators, as Quine puts it, are *referentially opaque* (or intensional); *substitutivity* (Leibniz's law) fails in modal contexts, that is to say: within the scope of a modal operator, substituting one singular term for another which denotes the very same object can change the truth-value of the resulting sentence; so singular terms within the scope of the modal operator *are not purely referential*, do not serve, that is, solely to pick out their referents. (In point of referential opacity, Quine argues, modal operators are like quotation marks or epistemic operators.) For example (Quine 1943, 1947, 1953b):

$$9 = \text{the number of the planets}$$

is true, yet substitution on the basis of this identity into the true sentence:

$$L\,(9 > 7)$$

yields the presumably false sentence:

$$L\,(\text{the number of the planets} > 7)$$

Since, however, Quine allows no very fundamental significance to singular terms, which, after all, he thinks can and should be eliminated, the core of his objection lies in the anomalous behaviour of quantifiers and bound variables within the scope of modal operators.

In non-modal predicate calculus:

$$(\exists x)\,(x > 7)$$

follows by existential generalisation from:

$$9 > 7$$

and in modal predicate calculus, analogously,

$$(\exists x)\,L\,(x > 7)$$

follows from:

$$L\,(x > 7)$$

But Quine cannot accept that *there is something which is necessarily greater than* 7 ('$(\exists x)\,L\,(x > 7)$'); the 'something', he argues, cannot be the number 9, for that is the number of the planets, and the number of the planets isn't necessarily, but only contingently, greater than 7. *Being necessarily greater than* 7, Quine urges, can't be a property of a number; it is only that that a number is greater than 7 necessarily follows if it is specified in certain ways (e.g. as the number 9, or as the sum of 5 and 4) but not if it is specified in certain other ways (e.g. as the number of the planets). If modal predicate calculus requires one to accept that the number 9 has the property of being necessarily greater than 7, it is committed to *essentialism*, the thesis that things have some of their properties necessarily, or essentially. But essentialism, according to Quine, is a 'metaphysical jungle' (1953b p. 174), to which the only appropriate response is 'puzzlement' (1960a p. 199).

The difficulties thus far discussed, Quine allows, could be avoided if one was prepared to place sufficiently stringent restrictions on the universe of discourse, specifically, to admit only objects such that any two conditions specifying them are necessarily equivalent, i.e.:

$$C: ((y) (Fy \equiv y = x) \& (y) (Gy \equiv y = x)) \rightarrow$$
$$L (y) (Fy \equiv Gy)^1$$

Condition C restores substitutivity; i.e., given C:

$$(x) (y) ((x = y \& Fx) \rightarrow Fy)$$

However Quine points out (1953b pp. 155–6) that substitutivity, together with the presumably true:

$$L (x = x)$$

yields the consequence that:

$$(x) (y) (x = y \rightarrow L (x = y))$$

that is, that all identities are necessary. And this, Quine thinks, is doubtful. (It has, for example, been held by some proponents of the physicalist theory that the identity they claim between the mind and

---

[1] Quine points out (1953a pp. 152–3, *contra* Church 1943) that restricting the universe of discourse to intensional objects, e.g. numerical concepts rather than numbers, wouldn't be sufficient to restore substitutivity. For if *a* is such an intensional object, and *p* a sentence which is true but not necessarily true, then:

$$a = (\imath x) (p \& x = a)$$

But this identity is not analytic, and its two sides are not interchangeable in modal contexts *salva veritate*.

the brain is contingent, not necessary; it is like, for instance, the identity between lightning and electrical discharges in the atmosphere. Such contingent identities, they assume, are commonplace in science.) This is rather closely related to the first problem discussed, with 'L (... = x)' replacing 'L (... > 7)'. Indeed, the 'Morning Star paradox' is another well-known version of the original problem: necessarily (presumably) the Morning Star = the Morning Star; but, though the Morning Star = the Evening Star, it is not necessary, but contingent, that the Morning Star = the Evening Star.

The further consequences of imposing condition C, anyway, are, Quine argues, even worse: modal distinctions collapse, for with condition C one can prove that:

$$p \to Lp$$

which, in view of the axiom '$Lp \to p$' means that $Lp \equiv p$, so that 'L' is redundant.[1]

So the strategy of Quine's critique is this: adjunction of modal operators leads to anomalous behaviour on the part of singular terms and bound variables; these difficulties may be avoided by a restriction on the universe of discourse, but at the cost of the collapse of modal distinctions. The collapse of modal distinctions could not, of course, be tolerated by the supporters of modal logic; the question is, therefore, whether they can avoid or explain what Quine sees as 'misbehaviour' on the part of singular terms and bound variables in modal contexts. In one way or another, their responses consist, as one would expect, in claiming that what Quine takes to be false (or perhaps doubtfully intelligible) consequences of quantified modal logic are, in fact, when properly understood, true. For instance, *de re* modalities and essentialism are defended (e.g. Plantinga 1974) and it is argued that all identities are, indeed, necessary (Marcus 1962, Kripke 1972).

I can't look at all the replies which have been made to Quine's criticisms, but will confine myself to a couple which serve quite well to illustrate what is at issue. Several writers (e.g. Smullyan 1948, Fitch 1949) argue that the apparent failure of substitutivity in modal contexts can be shown, once one takes adequate care about the

[1] The argument goes: let p be any true sentence, and let F be 'p & $y = x$' and G be '$y = x$'; then from C it follows that $L(y)$ (p & $y = x \equiv y = x$), whence, in particular, $L(p$ & $x = x \equiv x = x$), and so Lp.

distinction between names and descriptions, to be *merely* apparent. Smullyan argues thus:

9 = the number of the planets

is not a straightforward identity statement of which the two terms are *bona fide* names, but, rather, has the form:

$$9 = (\imath x)\, Fx$$

And the sentence

L (the number of the planets > 7)

which Quine takes to be straightforwardly false, is ambiguous; depending on the scope (p. 65) given to the definite description it can be understood either as:

The number of the planets is necessarily > 7

or as

It is necessary that the number of the planets is > 7.

Of these, Smullyan argues, the first follows from 'L ($9 > 7$)' and '$9 = $ the number of the planets', but that is all right, because it's true; while the second is false, but that's also all right, because it doesn't follow.

Smullyan's distinction blocks Quine's original argument in quite a neat way. However, his solution requires one to accept the truth of 'The number of the planets is necessarily greater than 7' which has, when the definite description is eliminated, the form:

$$(\exists x)\,((y)\,(y \text{ numbers the planets} \equiv x = y)\ \&\ L\,(x > 7))$$

But Quine, no doubt, would object to this, where a quantifier (the initial '$(\exists x)$') binds a variable (the 'x' in '$x > 7$') inside a modal context; this after all is just his example of the misbehaviour of bound variables in modal contexts. Smullyan's solution would be, in Quine's eyes, unacceptably essentialist.

Marcus, however, denies (1962) that there *is* really anomalous behaviour on the part of the quantifiers in modal contexts. Quine's difficulties spring from his reading the quantifier *objectually*, as 'There is at least one object, x, such that x is necessarily greater than 7', and then asking what this object could be. Marcus proposes, instead, that the quantifier be read substitutionally, as 'Some substitution instance of 'L ($x > 7$)' is true'; and this, she argues, is straightforwardly true, since '$L(9 > 7)$', for example, is a true substitution instance.

But Quine, of course, rejects the substitutional interpretation of the quantifiers. Furthermore, he assimilates proper names to contextually eliminable definite descriptions. So Quine's attitudes to quantifiers and singular terms are such that (i) they blur the distinction on which Smullyan's response depends and (ii) they assume a priority of quantifiers over singular terms which is directly opposed to Marcus' substitutional interpretation of quantification. The debate runs true to form: Quine's criticisms are answered by rejection of the premises on which they rest. Quine thinks quantifiers talk about things; according to the substitutional interpretation, quantifiers talk about talk about things. Quine thinks that modality is talk about talk about things; according to essentialism, modality is talk about things.

Quine's views about quantification and necessity aren't sacrosanct, of course – indeed, I have already expressed some reservations about them. But this doesn't make the tendency for the debate between Quine and the defenders of modal logic to degenerate into assertion and counter-assertion less disagreeable, especially in view of the fact that rival views about names, for instance, are apt to be defended by appeal to 'essentialist' intuitions (e.g. Kripke 1972, Plantinga 1974). What prospects are there for a more independent resolution?

4 Semantics for modal logics

Quine's criticisms of modal logic are to the effect, not that it is not *formally* feasible, but that its *interpretation* involves serious philosophical difficulties. These criticisms should be seen in the light of the fact that modal logic was initially developed syntactically, by the introduction of new modal vocabulary, formation rules and axioms; and that for a long time after its syntactic development no semantics was available. However, after the publication, in the 1940s and 1950s, of Quine's critique, a formal semantics was developed for modal logic (Kanger 1957a, b; Kripke 1963; Hintikka 1969); that is to say, a formal model was devised – comparable to the truth-table semantics for non-modal sentence logic, for instance. And it has, understandably enough, been thought by some that this settles the question of the interpretability of modal logic, and shows Quine's fears to have been unnecessary. It turns out, as we shall see, that this is very far from obvious.

Formal semantics – a sketch

A model structure is an ordered triple $\langle G, K, R \rangle$, where K is a set of which G is a member and on which R is a relation; for T, R is to be a reflexive relation, for S4, reflexive and transitive, for S5, reflexive, transitive and symmetrical. A quantified model structure is an ordered pair of which the first member is a model structure as already described, and the second a function $\Psi(w)$, assigning to each w in K a set of individuals. Conditions are specified for the valuation of formulae in each member w of K; and then this set-theoretical construction provides a definition of 'valid formula' for each of the systems treated: a formula A is valid in the system S iff the valuation of A is true for all w in K in the quantified model structure.

Thus far, a set-theoretical construction has been supplied in terms of which validity can be defined and the consistency of the modal systems established. More is needed, however, to establish that these systems, besides being formally feasible, have a plausible claim to represent modal reasoning, reasoning in which the notions of necessity and possibility play an essential role. Intuitively, Kripke suggests, one could think of K as a set of *possible worlds* $w_1...w_n$, of G as the *actual world*, of R as the relation of accessibility, which holds between w_1 and w_2 when w_1 is possible relative to w_2, and of $\Psi(w_i)$ as the *set of individuals* existing in the possible world w_i. On this understanding, the formal semantics tell one that, for instance, 'LA' is true just in case 'A' is true in all possible worlds, and 'MA' just in case 'A' is true in some possible world, so that one may with some plausibility take 'L' as corresponding to 'necessarily' and 'M' to 'possibly'.

'Pure' and 'depraved' semantics

I distinguished (ch. 3 §2) four aspects relevant to one's understanding of ordinary, non-modal sentence logic; the distinction applies, equally, to modal logic. One has:

(i)	(ii)	(iii)	(iv)
syntax of the formal language	informal readings of (i)	formal semantics for (i) ('pure semantics')	informal account of (iii) ('depraved semantics')

In the case of the sentence calculus, the formal semantics (iii) supplies a mathematical construction in which one of t, f is assigned to wffs of the calculus, and in terms of which (semantic) validity is defined and consistency and completeness results proved. For all the formal semantics tells one, however, the calculus could be a notation representing electrical circuits, with '*t*' standing for 'on' and '*f*' for 'off'. (Indeed (ch. 1 §2) interpretations of this kind, of 2- and of many-valued calculi, are both feasible and useful.) But the claim of the calculus *to be a sentence logic*, to represent arguments the validity of which depends upon their molecular sentential structure, depends upon one's understanding the formal semantics in such a way that '*t*' represents truth and '*f*' falsehood; it depends, in other words, on the informal account of the formal semantics – level (iv).

The questions I want to raise now concern the status of depraved semantics. First, do we need it? Well, I have already urged that the pure semantics, by itself, is not sufficient; to justify the claim of a formal system *to be a modal logic* (sentence logic) some intuitive account of the formal semantics, connecting that set-theoretical construction with the ideas of necessity and possibility (truth and falsity) seems essential. In urging this view, I am, of course, opposing a purely formalist conception, according to which logic consists of sheer uninterpreted formalism (but contrast Curry 1951; there is also some pertinent discussion, couched in less familiar terms, in Derrida 1973). Second, how seriously must we take depraved semantics? It has been suggested that it is appropriate to regard the intuitive explanation given of the formal semantics as a picture or metaphor, a heuristic device to make the pure semantics a little more palatable. But I think we need to take the intuitive account somewhat more seriously than this, to regard the explanation of possible worlds and their possible inhabitants as aspiring to literal truth (to be the 'sober metaphysical truth' in Plantinga's memorable phrase). This is clear from the non-modal case; the explanation of '*t*' and '*f*' as 'true' and 'false', after all, is scarcely to be dismissed as merely metaphorical.

A third methodological question which arises at this point is, I fear, as difficult as it is important. Perhaps the best way to introduce it is by means of D. K. Lewis' criticisms of explanations of possible worlds in terms of consistency. Such accounts, Lewis argues (1973 ch. 4) are apt to be objectionably circular. Suppose it is said that *w* is a possible world only if there is a consistent description of *w*; if this means, only if there is a description of *w* which is *possibly true*, it fails to explain 'possible' in a suitably independent fashion. Lewis claims, furthermore, that his own realist account of possible worlds is explanatory, non-circular; indeed, he proposes to use it as a test of disputed modal principles, such as the S4 principle. Critics, however, have urged that Lewis' account is no more successful, on this score, than the alternative he criticises (Richards 1975, Haack 1977a).

But, as I now see it, there is a deeper question to be asked: is one entitled to require, as Lewis does, that the intuitive account with which one is supplied at the level of depraved semantics give a non-circular, explanatory informal account of the formal semantics? What is being required, I think, is that the depraved semantics be given in terms which are, so to speak, epistemologically independent of the readings of the modal operators, that one should be able to tell *whether there is a possible world in which A* independently of one's beliefs about *whether possibly A*. But is this feasible? One's suspicions may be aroused, initially, by the fact that Lewis' account, like its rivals, seems to fail the epistemological requirement. They may be to some degree confirmed by the following considerations. The syntactical operators of a formal logical system are given both natural language readings and a formal semantics, which then has, in turn, to be 'interpreted'. At this stage, I take it, further *formal* interpretation would only postpone the issue; one needs, as I argued above, an *informal* account. But now either the informal account (I'll call it the 'patter') will be closely related to the natural language readings of the system's operators, or not. If not, one is likely to regard the patter as somewhat inappropriate (consider the suggestion that *w* is a possible world just in case it is a country in the southern hemisphere, for instance; then why should '*L*', i.e. 'true in all possible worlds', be read 'necessarily'?). But if the patter is close to the readings, it is apt to violate the requirement of epistemological independence. It is too much to ask that neither 'necessary' nor 'possible' nor any equivalents thereof appear in the patter; explanations of meaning must end somewhere. This isn't to say, of course, that there is no point in giving patter which *elaborates* on the original readings; one can after all be helped to understand something by being told the same thing another way.

Approaches to possible worlds

It is notable that even among those who take possible worlds seriously there is disagreement about what kinds of thing possible worlds are. At least three approaches can be distinguished:

(i) the linguistic approach, which construes talk about possible worlds as talk about maximally consistent sets of sentences (e.g. Hintikka 1969), and in which consistency might be understood either syntactically or semantically

(ii) the conceptualist approach, which construes talk about possible worlds as talk about ways in which we could conceive the world to be different (see Kripke 1972)

(iii) the realist approach, which takes talk about possible worlds at its face value, as talk of real, abstract entities wholly independent of our language or thought (see D. K. Lewis 1973 ch. 4).[1]

Approaches to possible individuals: transworld identity

However possible worlds are construed, some account needs to be given of when individuals in different possible worlds are to count as the same; for the truth-conditions of such sentences as:

$(\exists x)\,M\,(Fx)$ ('there is an x which is possibly F')

or:

$M(Fa)$ ('a is possibly F')

will go 'in the actual world there is an individual which in some possible world is F' and 'in some possible world a is F', respectively, and thus seem to require that one be able to identify an individual as the same in different possible worlds. Consider, for example, a sentence like 'Socrates might have been a carpenter'; its truth-conditions would be given as 'There is a possible world in which Socrates is a carpenter'. But what determines *what* individual in another possible world is *Socrates*? Suppose, for example, that in w_n there are two possible individuals, one just like Socrates but for being a cobbler instead of a philosopher, the other just like Socrates but for being a carpenter instead of a philosopher; which is to be identified with the actual Socrates? (see Chisholm 1967).

Now the problem of transworld identity has proved notably intractable, and there remains considerable disagreement about how it is best tackled. The alternatives seem to be:

(1) Certain of the properties of an individual are regarded as essential to its being that individual, and the criterion for

---

[1] The different approaches are quite strongly analogous to formalist, Intuitionist and logicist views, in the philosophy of mathematics, about the status of numbers.

an individual in another possible world being the same individual is that it possess those properties. (This is the 'net' model of ch. 5 §2.)

(2) The burden of the problem is shifted off predicates and on to names. Thus, Kripke denies that the proper names of individuals are equivalent in sense to any set of descriptions of their *denotata*, and bypasses the question, how much of such a set of descriptions an individual in another possible world would have to satisfy to be identical with, say, Socrates, in this world. Proper names are *rigid designators*, denoting the same individual in all possible worlds; the correct answer to the question which individual in another possible world is Socrates, is, simply, 'Socrates', *that* individual. (This is the 'harpoon' model.)

(3) The terms of the original difficulty are rejected. It is denied that it is necessary, in order for it to make sense to say that individuals in different worlds are one and the same, that criteria be supplied by means of which one could pick out which individual in another world is the same as a given individual in this world. The requirement that 'criteria of identity' be given is, according to proponents of such an approach (e.g. Plantinga 1974 ch. 6), both impossibly and undesirably demanding (cf. ch. 4 §2). After all, Plantinga observes, it makes sense to say that Georg Cantor was once a precocious baby, even though we may be entirely unable to 'locate' or 'pick out' that baby, or specify what properties an individual must have to be the infant Cantor.

(4) Others reject the terms of the original problem, not because they consider the requirement that criteria of identity be given if it is to be meaningful to identify individuals across possible worlds to be too stringent, but because they *deny* that the same individual can exist in different possible worlds, so that the problem doesn't arise. Leibniz, the originator of the possible-worlds metaphysic, thought that each individual exists in only one possible world.
D. K. Lewis 1968 adopts this line, but elaborates it with what he calls 'counterpart theory'. Each individual, according to this theory, exists in just one possible world, but has counterparts in other possible worlds (not

necessarily in all other possible worlds, and perhaps more than one in some possible worlds); and the truth of assertions such as 'Socrates might have been a carpenter' now depends, not upon whether there is a possible world in which Socrates is a carpenter, but upon whether there is a possible world in which a counterpart of Socrates is a carpenter.

Quine's doubts confirmed?

Quine's doubts about modal logic antedate the development of possible-worlds semantics; Quine, however, clearly doesn't think that that development justifies confidence about the philosophical, as opposed to the purely formal, feasibility of modal logic (see e.g. Quine 1976). I shall suggest, in what follows, that the philosophical problems raised by the metaphysics of possible worlds and their possible inhabitants turn out to illuminate, and to some extent to confirm, Quine's earlier doubts (and that reservations about the views of modality and quantification on which Quine's original criticisms rested can be to some extent bypassed).

(i) First, Quine had suggested that if modality were – as he urges – understood as essentially a metalinguistic concept, the standard modal systems would not be appropriate. Montague 1963 investigates in detail the restrictions which would be imposed by a syntactical treatment of modality, concluding that 'virtually all of modal logic, even the weak system S1, must be sacrificed' (p. 294). This means, furthermore, that the prospects for interpreting the conventional modal systems by understanding possible worlds in syntactic style, as suggested in the first approach to possible worlds, are poor.

(ii) Second, Quine doubted whether an account could be given of modal locutions which did not, eventually, turn out to require an understanding of just the ideas it purported to explain. Quine's refusal to be content with an explanation in terms of the 'intensional circle' (analyticity – synonymy – definition – semantic rule) of 'Two dogmas' can, I think, be seen as rather strongly analogous to an insistence on the requirement of epistemological independence, discussed above. The only account of possible worlds which shows much promise of meeting this requirement is a purely syntactic linguistic account, such that w is a possible world only if there is a consistent description of it, where 'consistent' is understood purely in syntactic terms, as 'no formula of the form '$A \;\&\; -A$' is derivable'. But such an account – as I observed under (i) above – leads to a conception of necessity weaker than that formalised by the usual modal systems. (The fact that Quine's scepticism about analyticity doesn't extent to logical truth is pertinent here.) The rival accounts of possible worlds seem all to be apt to violate the independence requirement: the semantic linguistic approach because 'consistent' is explained as 'possibly true'; the realist because (since, despite Lewis' habit of speaking of other possible worlds as if they were like distant places, Australia or Mars, we can't visit other possible worlds, nor have we, to borrow a phrase of Kaplan's, a Jules-Verne-o-scope through which to inspect them) it gives no test of which worlds are possible; the conceptualist because someone who claims to be able to imagine a world in which A is apt to be told he has wrongly described what he imagines if A is inconsistent. However, I suspect that the requirement of epistemological independence may be unacceptably stringent; and if so, those critics of Quine (e.g. Grice and Strawson 1956) who commented that, in 'Two dogmas', he has asked for the impossible and complained when it wasn't forthcoming, are, in some measure, vindicated.

(iii) Third, Quine found it hopelessly obscure what it was that quantified modal logics quantify over. Now the problems about the transworld identity of possible individuals can reasonably be seen, I think, as confirming some of Quine's suspicions on this score. For of the 'solutions' sketched above, (4) amounts rather to giving up the problem than to solving it, (3) depends upon the rejection of the requirement that one quantify only over items for which one can give adequate identity conditions, (2) depends on a distinction between names and descriptions which Quine rejects, and (1) seems to require a form of essentialism – essentialism not about *kinds* of thing, but about *individuals* (cf. Parsons 1969). If, that is, one accepts Quine's views about quantification then the problem of transworld identity of individuals is soluble only at the cost of (individual) essentialism. Of course, this leaves one with the options of rejecting Quine's views about quantification or accepting essentialism, besides the option Quine recommends, of abandoning the enterprise of modal logic.

5 Prospects

I should say, to make it quite clear that the following remarks should not be taken in the spirit of a Strawsonian critique of the inadequacies of formal languages to the subtleties of English, that formalisation, inevitably, involves a certain amount of simplification; it is a legitimate aim of modal logics to aspire to represent what is vital to reasoning about possibility and necessity while ignoring inessential features of modal discourse in ordinary language. However, in view of the metaphysical burden that conventional modal logics carry, there may be profit, I think, in a fresh look at the informal argument that they are intended to formalise.

There are many features of modal discourse in English to which these modal logics are quite insensitive. For example, 'possible' takes modifiers, as: It is perfectly (quite, entirely, distinctly, remotely, just, barely, ...) possible that...; it is a distinct (remote, real, ...) possibility that... Some of these locutions suggest a link with 'probably' or 'likely' (e.g. 'It is just possible that I shall be late' seems close in meaning to 'It is possible, but highly unlikely, that I shall be late'). 'Necessary' doesn't take the same modifiers – which may of itself occasion some doubts about '$Mp \equiv -L-p$' – but it can be qualified in other ways, as: It is absolutely necessary (quite essential...) to...

These features may turn out to be logically significant. But I feel more discomfort about logicians' disregard for some other features of English[1] modal discourse, which seem to have quite a strong *prima facie* claim to logical relevance. In English one needs to pay attention both (i) to the tense of a modal operator and (ii) to the tense and the mood of the verb in the contained sentence. The conventional modal logics are wholly insensitive to both tense and mood; yet it seems to make a difference whether one reads:

$$M (\exists x) (Fx)$$

for example, as:

It is possible that there is an F (There may be an F)

or as:

It is possible that there should be an F (There might be (have been) an F)

---

[1] It would be a pertinent question whether they are shared by other languages.

or whether one reads:

$M (Fa)$

as:

It is possible that a is F (a may be F)

or as:

It is possible that a should be F (a might be (have been) F).

Or, again, consider the difference between:

It is possible that he has had an accident

said when the visitor is late and has not yet arrived, and:

It was possible that he should have had an accident

when the visitor has arrived late, and the delay is known to have been due to a traffic jam; or, the significance of the tense of the modal operator in:

It was possible $\begin{cases} \text{that the government would save the pound} \\ \text{for the government to save the pound} \end{cases}$

but it failed to act in time.

It is notorious that philosophers find themselves unable to agree on the truth-values of formulae of modal logic, especially on those involving iterated modal operators. This is scarcely surprising in view of the fact that, without paying attention to considerations of tense and mood, one has difficulty in understanding even modal statements with single modal operators. So I conjecture that it might prove profitable for logicians to try to devise modal systems which build upon an underlying apparatus in which tense and mood can be represented. Obviously, however, there would be dangers in attempting to build on the tense logics presently available – for those systems are themselves constructed by analogy with the conventional modal logics, the inadequacies of which prompted this suggestion in the first place. And more will be needed than merely formal ingenuity, even in combination with sensibility to those complexities of unformalised modal discourse which seem to be inferentially relevant; for instance, the interplay between modality and tense may well raise metaphysical questions about determinism. But then, it is just this kind of interdependence between formalism, informal argument, and philosophical argument, that makes the philosophy of logic interesting.

6 Implication again: a postscript on 'relevance logic'
The 'paradoxes' of strict implication

An important motivation for the development of modal logic was, as we saw, to introduce a stronger implication relation, and so deflect the impact of the 'paradoxes' of material implication. And, of course, strict implication is, indeed, stronger than material implication (since $A \dashv B \equiv L\ (A \to B)$); whether it altogether meets the need for which it was introduced, however, remains controversial. For strict implication has 'paradoxes' of its own, since in the regular modal systems one has the theorems:

$$Lp \to (q \dashv p)$$
$$L-p \to (p \dashv q)$$

i.e. a necessary proposition is strictly implied by any proposition whatever, and an impossible proposition strictly implies any proposition whatever. It isn't hard to see how this happens: for one proposition strictly implies another just in case it is impossible that the first be true and the second false; and so, in particular, if it is impossible that the first be true, or if it is impossible that the second be false.

Lewis himself held that these consequences, however surprising, must be accepted as true. (In this, he is followed by e.g. Kneale 1945–6, Popper 1947, Bennett 1954.) He thought it still appropriate to identify strict implication as the formal counterpart of the intuitive idea of 'implication' or 'entailment'. For entailment, he proposed, is the converse of deducibility (A entails B iff there is a valid deduction of B from A); and the 'paradoxes' are truths about entailment since there is, he argued, a valid deduction of any necessary conclusion from an arbitrary premise, and of an arbitrary conclusion from an impossible premise; for example, in the latter case, as follows:

$(1)\ p\ \&\ -p$ [impossible premise]
$(2)\ p$ from (1)
$(3)\ p \lor q$ from (2)
$(4)\ -p$ from (1)
$(5)\ q$ from (3) and (4) [arbitrary conclusion]

(This argument is, of course, valid in the standard sentence logic. You will recall that it is just because, in standard logical systems, anything follows from a contradiction, that consistency is of such overriding importance.) Lewis' challenge to critics of strict implication is to say what step of this argument, and its twin for the other 'paradox', could possibly be rejected.

Other writers, however, find the 'paradoxes' of strict implication quite as shocking as Lewis thought the 'paradoxes' of material implication. It has been said that they are 'so utterly devoid of rationality [as to be] a *reductio ad absurdum* of any view which involves them' (Nelson 1933 p. 271), that they are 'outrageous' (Duncan-Jones 1935 p. 78). These writers won't allow that strict implication adequately represents the intuitive idea of entailment. Nelson, for instance, argues that what is required for A to entail B is not just that it be impossible for A to be true and B false, but also that there be some 'connection of meanings' between A and B.[1] However, the difficulty is to specify just when there *is* a 'connection of meanings' between propositions, and to justify the rejection of whatever step(s) of Lewis' 'proofs' of the paradoxes of strict implication are held to violate this requirement. A further problem is that manoeuvres adopted to block Lewis' proofs may ramify in perhaps unanticipated and unappealing ways; some critics, for example, found themselves obliged to deny the transitivity of entailment. Not surprisingly, perhaps, it has been doubted (e.g. Suppes 1957) whether the idea of connection of meaning, or, more generally, the idea of the *relevance* of one proposition to another, is amenable to formal treatment. Relevance logicians, however, think otherwise.

Relevance logic

As with modal logic, there is not just one, but a whole range of 'relevance logics'. I shall concentrate on R, the system of 'relevant implication' proposed by Anderson and Belnap (1962a, b, 1975) and E, the combination of R with the modal system S4 to give a system of 'entailment' (Anderson and Belnap 1975); cf. Smiley 1959 for an especially clear and helpful account of the alternatives.

Anderson and Belnap agree that entailment is, as Lewis held, the converse of deducibility; they urge, however, that the standard

[1] It may be of more than historical significance that Lewis himself made some proposals along lines similar to Nelson's in an early paper (1912) attacking Russell's notion of implication.

conception of deducibility, because it ignores considerations of relevance, is defective. Relevance logicians urge that *their* conception of deducibility, and not the 'official' notion of classical logicians, is the one that one's intuitive, uncorrupted sense of what it is for an argument to be valid requires:

> A mathematician writes a paper on Banach spaces, and...
> concludes with a conjecture. As a footnote to the
> conjecture, he writes: In addition to its intrinsic interest,
> this conjecture has connections with other parts of
> mathematics which might not immediately occur to the
> reader. For example, if the conjecture is true, then the
> first order functional calculus is complete; whereas if it is
> false, then it implies that Fermat's last conjecture is
> correct. ...the editor counters...'...in spite of what
> most logicians say about us, the standards maintained by
> this journal require that the antecedent of an "if...then –"
> statement must be *relevant* to the conclusion drawn.'
> *...the fancy that relevance is irrelevant to validity strikes*
> *us as ludicrous, and we therefore make an attempt to*
> *explicate the notion of relevance of A to B.* (Anderson and
> Belnap 1975 pp. 17–18, final italics mine)

B is deducible *from A*, by their standards, only if the derivation of B genuinely *uses*, and does not simply *take a detour via A*. The idea of a premise really being used, of course, stands in need of explanation. But it's easy enough to give examples of the kind of argument that Anderson and Belnap would describe as 'proving B *under* the assumption A' but not 'proving B *from* the assumption A'; for instance, in a system with '$p \to p$' as an axiom:

(1) q assumption
(2) $p \to p$ axiom
(3) $q \to (p \to p)$ (from (1) and (2), by the deduction
                     theorem: if $A \vdash B$ then $\vdash A \to B$)

So what Anderson and Belnap propose is, first, to put appropriate restrictions on deducibility, such that B is deducible from A only if A is used in the derivation of B; these restrictions are economically summarised by Fogelin as 'the Rule of No Funny Business'. Then they construct a system of 'relevant implication' such that A relevantly implies B just in case B is deducible, in *their* sense of 'deducible', from A. The axioms for relevant implication are (I'll write '$\Rightarrow$', to keep a clear distinction from '$\rightarrow$' and '$\dashv$'):

1. $A \Rightarrow A$
2. $(A \Rightarrow B) \Rightarrow ((C \Rightarrow A) \Rightarrow (C \Rightarrow B))$
3. $(A \Rightarrow (B \Rightarrow C)) \Rightarrow (B \Rightarrow (A \Rightarrow C))$
4. $(A \Rightarrow (A \Rightarrow B)) \Rightarrow (A \Rightarrow B)$

(This is the 'implicational fragment', i.e. the axioms involving only implication, of R.) Entailment, however, they think, requires necessity as well as relevance; so the connective representing entailment should be restricted by imposing, besides the restrictions on deducibility which ensure relevance, other restrictions characteristic of strict implication as specified by S4. The upshot is these axioms, the implicational fragment of E, for entailment (which I'll write by an obvious analogy, '$\Rrightarrow$'):

1. $A \Rrightarrow A$
2. $A \Rrightarrow B \Rrightarrow ((B \Rrightarrow C) \Rrightarrow (A \Rrightarrow C))$
3. $A \Rrightarrow B \Rrightarrow (((A \Rrightarrow B) \Rrightarrow C) \Rrightarrow C)$
4. $(A \Rrightarrow (B \Rrightarrow C)) \Rrightarrow ((A \Rrightarrow B) \Rrightarrow (A \Rrightarrow C))$

The full system E is obtained, finally, by adjoining axioms for the other sentential connectives.

It remains to show how Anderson and Belnap meet Lewis' challenge: where, according to them, does Lewis' 'proof' of 'q' from 'p & $-p$' go wrong? They don't, of course, deny Lewis' claim that 'q' is deducible from 'p & $-p$' by 'some valid form of inference', *in the 'official' sense of 'valid'*; what they deny is that 'q' is deducible from 'p & $-p$' by a valid form of inference in their sense, i.e., they take it, *the real sense of 'valid'*. Anderson and Belnap centre their criticism on the step from '$p \vee q$' and '$-p$' to 'q'. (In classical logic, of course, this step is justified, being an instance of what is sometimes known as the 'disjunctive syllogism'.) Their more detailed diagnosis of what is wrong with Lewis' argument goes as follows (Anderson and Belnap 1975 pp. 165–6). 'Or' has two senses, the truth-functional and the intensional; in the latter but not the former sense, the truth of '$p \vee q$' requires that the disjuncts be relevant to each other. Now, they argue, the step from 'p' to '$p \vee q$' is valid only if '$\vee$' is understood truth-functionally, while the step from '$p \vee q$' and '$-p$' to 'q' is valid only if '$\vee$' is understood intensionally. Once again, I should point out that by 'valid' here they mean, naturally, valid in *their* sense; they don't deny that if '$p \vee q$' (where '$\vee$' is truth-functional) is true, and '$-p$' is true, then, necessarily, 'q' is true, but they do deny that this is sufficient to show that the argument is valid.

Now, of course, in classical logic, since '$A \to B$' is equivalent to '$-A \vee B$' the disjunctive syllogism (from '$-A$' and '$A \vee B$' to infer 'B') is equivalent to *modus ponens* (from 'A' and '$A \to B$' to infer 'B'). And, indeed, as one might, in view of this equivalence, expect, *modus ponens* for material implication fails in E.

The relevance logicians, as should, by now, be apparent, challenge classical logic in more than one way.

(i) Most fundamentally, their challenge is to the classical conception of validity. Classical logicians have conceived of relevance as irrelevant to the validity of an argument; irrelevance, if it is considered at all, is apt to be relegated to the category of rhetorical defects. Consequently, relevance logicians give a stricter sense to the notion of one proposition's being deducible from another, and, hence, to its converse, the notion of one proposition's entailing another.

(ii) So, relevance logicians introduce a new entailment connective, '$\Rightarrow$', to extend the classical logical apparatus.

(iii) And finally, their diagnosis of a 'fallacy of relevance' in disjunctive syllogism, and hence, in *modus ponens* for material implication, leads them not only to add a new connective to the classical logical apparatus, but also to reject certain principles of inference *for classical connectives*.

In the case of relevance logic one has, that is, a *challenge to classical metaconcepts* (strategy 6 of ch. 9 §2), an *extension of the classical apparatus* (strategy 4) and, at the same time, a *restriction* of it (strategy 5). Of these, the challenge to the classical concept of validity is the most basic. How is one to assess this challenge? Well, it is hard to deny that, at an informal level, irrelevance is seen as a defect in an argument. The question is, rather, whether it is more properly regarded as a logical defect or as a rhetorical defect. The difference between logical and rhetorical concerns could perhaps be indicated, in a rough and ready way, by stressing rhetoric's interest in the audience for whom an argument is intended; and on this count, relevance – conceived as a relation between propositions – apparently has a claim to belong to logic. An important reason why considerations of relevance have tended to be disregarded by logicians, I think, is that they don't seem, on the face of it, very readily amenable to formal treatment. Interestingly, Schiller's comment that 'the central doctrine of the most prevalent logic still consists in a flat denial of Relevance' (1930 p. 75), quoted with approval by Anderson and Belnap, is intended as an argument against the pretensions of formal logic, not as a plea for the formalisation of relevance. If this is so, the enterprise of relevance logic would be, so to speak, vindicated by success (rather like Davidson's claims for the applicability of Tarski's methods to natural languages) – the formalisabilty of relevance would be a reason for regarding it as a logical matter. The efforts of the relevance logicians have surely gone a long way towards rebutting the suspicion that relevance is hopelessly recalcitrant to formal treatment. There may, of course, be grounds for reservations about the relevance logics presently available (and there is rivalry between them, too) – some find Anderson and Belnap's construction of E disagreeably *ad hoc*, and those, like myself, with doubts about conventional modal logics may not be altogether happy with E's close alliance with S4. (But Anderson and Belnap's suggestion, p. 28, that necessity might be understood in terms of entailment, rather than conversely, is appealing if one thinks of logic as concerned primarily with validity, secondarily with logical truth.) And relevance logic will inevitably be more complex than classical truth-functional logic; so that one is entitled to ask what advantages one might expect it to bring.

One reason why the semantic and set-theoretical paradoxes are seen as catastrophic is that, since, classically, anything and everything follows from a contradiction a formal system in which a paradox is derivable is worthless. Some writers have observed, though, that in informal argument the effects of contradiction are not taken to be so disastrously global, but are thought of as localised; and some of them, understandably enough, have hoped that a formalism in which a contradiction doesn't entail any arbitrary wff might have advantages as a 'logic of paradox'.

But the interest of relevance logic isn't to be restricted to issues in philosophy of logic (this needn't occasion surprise; remember, after all, the metaphysical issues to which tense logic is pertinent). I see some prospects for a concept of relevance in some interesting issues in epistemology, for example. Consider Quine's idea, expressed in 'Two dogmas of empiricism', that the unit of verification/falsification must be the whole of science; Quine argues, persuasively enough, that a single sentence can't be subjected to empirical test in isolation, and concludes, in what might reasonably seem rather short order, that it is the whole of science that faces 'the tribunal of experience'. It wouldn't be too fanciful to suspect that the fact that, of any two sentences, either the first materially implies the second, or else the second materially implies the first, may give an air of inevitability to the dilemma that either an isolated sentence, or else the whole of science, is the unit of empirical test; and it is interesting to speculate that a stronger notion of implication might make room for a third possibility, that a sentence is tested along with those other sentences that are relevant to it.

I observed, above, that E involves a restriction of classical logic: *modus ponens*, for material implication, fails. Many-valued logics, to which I now turn, also involve a restriction of the classical logical apparatus.

Many-valued logic

1 Many-valued systems

Restrictions of classical logic: deviant logics

One system is a deviation of another if it shares the vocabulary of the first, but has a different set of theorems/valid inferences; a 'deviant logic' is a system which is a deviation of classical logic. (A system may involve *both* an extension *and* a deviation of classical logic, if it adds new vocabulary and hence new theorems/valid inferences, but at the same time differs from classical logic with respect to theorems/valid inferences involving only shared vocabulary essentially. The system E, considered in ch. 10 §6, would be an example.) Many-valued logics are deviant; sharing its vocabulary, they characteristically lack certain theorems of classical logic, such as the 'law of excluded middle', '$p \vee -p$'. (Some also add new vocabulary and so come in the category of extensions as well.)

The many-valued logics I shall consider in this chapter were devised from two main kinds of motivation: the purely mathematical interest of alternatives to the 2-valued semantics of classical sentence logic; and – of more philosophical interest – dissatisfaction with the classical imposition of an exhaustive dichotomy into the true and the false, and, relatedly, dissatisfaction with certain classical theorems or inferences. The second kind of motivation is characteristic – as I observed in ch. 9 §2 – of proposals for restrictions of classical logic.

Historical remarks

Many-valued logics have as long a history as modal logics: Aristotle already expresses reservations about bivalence (*De interpretatione* ix); early in the present century Hugh MacColl made both formal and philosophical proposals. But as in the case of modal logics, the impetus to detailed formal development came in the wake of the formal development of 2-valued logic, specifically, of the truth-table semantics for the logic of the *Begriffsschrift* and *Principia Mathematica*, initiated by Post and Wittgenstein. The earliest many-valued systems were devised by Łukasiewicz 1920 and Post 1921 (see Rescher 1969 ch. 1 for detailed historical discussion).

However, in one respect there is an important difference between the development of modal and the development of many-valued logics: whereas in the former case the syntax (vocabulary, axioms, rules) was developed first, and semantics supplied only considerably later, in the latter case the initial development was semantic and syntax was supplied only subsequently, axiomatisations of Łukasiewicz's many-valued logics being devised by Jaśkowski 1934. Many-valued logics began, that is, with the development of many-valued truth-tables; it would be fair to say, however, that the question of the interpretation of the values of these matrices is still at best only partially answered. The problem of depraved semantics will be a major preoccupation, here as in the previous chapter.

Formal sketch

Recall (ch. 3 §1) that a system is n-valued if n is the smallest number of values which any characteristic matrix for that system has. When speaking of 'many-valued' logics I shall restrict myself to n-valued logics where $2 < n$ (so 2-valued logic isn't 'many-valued'; this follows standard usage).

Though there is just one system of 2-valued logic (in the broad sense of 'system' explained in ch. 2, in which two systems are the same if, differences of notation, primitives, and axioms/rules taken into account, they have just the same theorems/valid inferences) there are alternative systems of 3-valued (etc.) logic. This is scarcely surprising; for, once one has 3 or more values, obviously, alternative decisions are possible about the value to be assigned to compound formulae.

I shall offer only a sketch of some of the best-known many-valued logics, and shall concentrate on formal points which bear on the philosophical issues raised subsequently. (More detailed formal treatment is to be found in Rosser and Turquette 1952, Ackerman 1967, or Rescher 1969.) My presentation will be semantic rather than syntactic; this is not only consonant with the history of many-valued logics, but also, I think, brings out the differences between them in a more perspicuous way.

Łukasiewicz's 3-valued logic (Łukasiewicz 1920, 1930) is characterised by the following matrices:

A	$-A$
*t	f
i	i
f	t

A \\ B ($A \& B$)	t	i	f
t	t	i	f
i	i	i	f
f	f	f	f

A \\ B ($A \to B$)	t	i	f
t	t	i	f
i	t	t	i
f	t	t	t

A \\ B ($A \vee B$)	t	i	f
t	t	t	t
i	t	i	i
f	t	i	f

(* indicates the designated value, i.e. the value such that wffs which uniformly take it count as tautologies.)

Initially, Łukasiewicz had in mind that the third value, which he read 'indeterminate' or 'possible', was to be taken by future contingent statements, which he, following Aristotle, thought couldn't be either true or false. Neither the law of excluded middle nor the law of non-contradiction is uniformly designated on these matrices, so neither is a theorem in Ł₃; '$p \vee -p$' and '$-(p \& -p)$' take the value i when 'p' does. Since, however, the truth-table for implication gives '$A \to B$' the value t even when antecedent and consequent take i, the law of identity, '$p \to p$', is a theorem.[1]

Kleene's 3-valued logic (Kleene 1952) differs from Łukasiewicz's with respect to implication. Whereas Łukasiewicz, anxious to save the law of identity, sets $|A \to B|$ at t for $|A| = |B| = i$, Kleene has:

---

[1] This 3-valued logic can be generalised. If one represents the three values by the numbers $(1, \frac{1}{2}, 0)$, then Łukasiewicz's matrices fall under the rules:

$$|-A| = 1-|A|$$
$$|A \vee B| = \max \{|A|, |B|\}$$
$$|A \& B| = \min \{|A|, |B|\}$$
$$|A \to B| = \begin{cases} 1 & \text{if } |A| \leqslant |B| \\ 1-|A|+|B| & \text{if } |A| > |B| \end{cases}$$

('$|A|$' means 'the value of A') and these rules yield matrices for 4, 5 ... n, and infinitely many, values. Cf. p. 165.

$A \backslash B$	$A \rightarrow B$		
	t	i	f
t	t	i	f
i	t	i	i
f	t	t	t

Unlike Łukasiewicz, Kleene didn't think of i as an intermediate truth-value; rather, it was to represent 'undecidable', and to be taken by mathematical sentences which, though either true or false, are neither provable nor disprovable. Kleene's matrices are thus constructed on the principle that where the truth or the falsity of one component is sufficient to decide the truth or falsity of a compound, the compound should take that value despite having (an)other, undecidable component(s); otherwise, the compound is itself undecidable.

Bochvar's 3-valued system (Bochvar 1939) was originally intended as a solution to the semantic paradoxes (ch. 8 §2), and the interpretation he had in mind for the third value was 'paradoxical' or 'meaningless'. On the principle that a compound sentence of which a component is paradoxical is itself paradoxical, he offered matrices in which the third value is, so to speak, 'infectious':

A	$-A$
t	f
i	i
f	t

$A \backslash B$	$A \& B$		
	t	i	f
t	t	i	f
i	i	i	i
f	f	i	f

$A \backslash B$	$A \lor B$		
	t	i	f
t	t	i	t
i	i	i	i
f	t	i	f

$A \backslash B$	$A \rightarrow B$		
	t	i	f
t	t	i	f
i	i	i	i
f	t	i	t

(On these matrices, of course, there will be no wffs which take t for all assignments to their atomic components, since i input always results in i output. For in each table the central entries read 'i' throughout.) So Bochvar adds an 'assertion operator', which I'll write 'T' since it seems to mean something like 'It is true that':

A	TA
t	t
i	f
f	f

This enables him to define 'external' connectives thus:

$$-A = -TA$$
$$A \; \& \; B \; = \; TA \; \& \; TB$$
$$A \vee B \; = \; TA \vee TB$$
$$A \rightarrow B \; = \; TA \rightarrow TB$$

The matrices for the external connectives, consequently, always have t or f output; and in fact just the classical, 2-valued tautologies uniformly take t for all assignments to their components. (The matrices for the external connectives are, so to speak, 3-valued tables for 2-valued logic, with both 'i' and 'f' as kinds of falsehood.)

All the matrices considered so far are *normal* (Rescher's terminology): they resemble the familiar 2-valued matrices where only classical input is concerned – where a compound wff has only true or false components, the 3-valued matrices give the same value that the classical table would give. (That is, the 3-valued matrices are like the classical ones with respect to the corner entries.) Post's many-valued logics are an exception because of his 'cyclical' matrix for negation:

A	$-A$
t	i
i	f
f	t

2 Philosophical motivations

I shan't be able to consider all the arguments which their proponents have offered in favour of many-valued logics, but will have to restrict myself to what, I hope, is a reasonably representative sample.

Future contingents

Łukasiewicz introduces his 3-valued logic by means of an argument derived from Aristotle, to the effect that unless one allows that statements about the future are not yet true or false, one will be committed to fatalism. (Łukasiewicz's interpretation of Aristotle is disputed, but that dispute needn't concern me here; cf. Haack 1974 ch. 4 for relevant discussion.) Łukasiewicz's argument runs along the following lines. Suppose it is true now that I shall be in Warsaw at noon on 21 December next year; then I can't not be in Warsaw at noon on 21 December next year, that is to say, it is necessary that I be in Warsaw at noon on 21 December next year. Suppose on the other hand that it is false now that I shall be in Warsaw at noon on

21 December next year; then I can't be in Warsaw at noon on 21 December next year, that is to say, it is impossible that I be in Warsaw at noon on 21 December next year. So, if it is either true or false, now, that I shall be in Warsaw then, it is either necessary or impossible that I be in Warsaw then. The only way to avoid this fatalist conclusion, Łukasiewicz urges, is to deny that such future tense, contingent statements are either true or false in advance of the event. Bivalence, he concludes, must be rejected.

If this argument were valid, of course, there would remain room for disagreement about whether to take it as a proof of fatalism or a disproof of bivalence. (All arguments go, in a sense, both ways; I mean, given an argument to the effect that *B* follows from *A*, one might either accept premise and hence conclusion, or, rejecting the conclusion, reject the premise too.) However, since I believe that the argument is invalid, I needn't pause over the question of whether fatalism is or is not a tolerable conclusion. The argument is invalid, I think, because it depends on a modal fallacy, the fallacy of arguing from:

> Necessarily (if it is now true [false] that I shall be in Warsaw at noon on 21 December next year, then I shall [not] be in Warsaw at noon on 21 December next year)

which is, of course, true, to:

> If it is now true [false] that I shall be in Warsaw at noon on 21 December next year, then necessarily I shall [not] be in Warsaw at noon on 21 December next year

i.e. of arguing from:

$$L (A \to B)$$

to:

$$A \to LB$$

(If it isn't obvious that this is a fallacy, consider this clearly non-truth-preserving instance: $L ((p \,\&\, q) \to p)$, so $(p \,\&\, q) \to Lp$.)

If I am right about this, fatalism *doesn't* follow from bivalence, so, even if fatalism is an unacceptable thesis, there is no need to reject bivalence on that account, and Łukasiewicz has not provided a good reason for adopting his 3-valued logic.

However, other writers have given quite different arguments in favour of Łukasiewicz's logic.

Quantum mechanics

Reichenbach argues (1944; Putnam 1957 supports his proposal) that adoption of 3-valued logic (the one he proposes is just like Łukasiewicz's but for the addition of further negation and implication operators) would provide a solution to some problems raised by quantum mechanics. His argument has the following structure: if classical logic is used, quantum mechanics yields some unacceptable consequences, which he calls 'causal anomalies' (roughly, statements about quantum mechanical phenomena which contradict classical physical laws for observable objects); these causal anomalies can, however, be avoided, without interfering with quantum mechanics or classical physics, by using a 3- instead of the 2-valued logic. Briefly:

classical physics & quantum mechanics & *classical logic* →
causal anomalies
classical physics & quantum mechanics & *3-valued logic* →
no causal anomalies

Reichenbach, like Łukasiewicz, reads the third value as 'indeterminate'; but the kind of statement which he intends to take this value is quite different from what Łukasiewicz had in mind. Briefly, one of the peculiarities of quantum mechanics is this: although it is possible to measure the position of a particle, and possible to measure its momentum, it is impossible – it follows from the theory that it is impossible – to measure both position and momentum at once. Bohr and Heisenberg had suggested that statements indicating both the position and the momentum of a particle at a given time be regarded as meaningless or ill-formed; Reichenbach prefers to allow that they are meaningful (after all, each component is, separately, quite unproblematic) but neither true nor false, but indeterminate. Reichenbach's argument raises too many questions for me to discuss here; for example: are the difficulties on account of which Reichenbach wants to modify logic genuine? and is it methodologically proper, anyway, to modify logic to avoid difficulties in physics? (but cf. Haack 1974 ch. 9). However, there seems to be little doubt that, even if Reichenbach is right that there is a need for a non-classical logic, the particular non-classical logic he proposes doesn't meet what he takes to be the need. The motivation for the adoption of a non-classical logic was to avoid the causal anomalies without tampering with physics (see Reichenbach 1944 pp. 159–60, 166); however, since Reichenbach intends that all statements simultaneously indicating position and momentum be indeterminate, he assigns the value 'indeterminate' not only to anomalous statements, but also to certain laws (e.g. the principle of conservation of energy; 1944 p. 166).

It is doubtful, then, that Reichenbach has given good reason for the adoption of Łukasiewicz's logic. (Of course, it remains possible that developments in quantum mechanics do indeed call for the adoption of a non-classical logic, perhaps the non-truth-functional system developed by Birkhoff and von Neumann in 1936; cf. Putnam 1969.)

Semantic paradoxes

Bochvar's 3-valued logic was intended to supply a solution to the semantic paradoxes: 'this sentence is false' is true if false and false if true; Bochvar's proposal is that it be assigned neither 'true' nor 'false', but a third value, 'paradoxical' or 'meaningless'. I have already argued (ch. 8 §2) that this kind of approach to the paradoxes is apt to go from the frying pan – the Liar paradox – to the fire – the Strengthened Liar ('this sentence is either false or paradoxical', true if false or paradoxical, false or paradoxical if true). As with Łukasiewicz's logic, however, other reasons than those given by its originator have also been suggested in favour of a 3-valued logic like Bochvar's.

Meaninglessness

Halldén's (1949) 'nonsense logic', for instance, has matrices like those for Bochvar's internal connectives, in which the third value ('meaningless') infects any compound to any component of which it is assigned. But this, again, doesn't supply any very impressive reason in favour of Bochvar's logic. For, as I argued in ch. 9 §4, the whole enterprise of a 'logic of meaninglessness' seems to me fundamentally misconceived.

I have already commented on the curious, 'infectious' character of Bochvar's third value, pointing out that it has the perhaps rather dismaying consequence that there are no wffs using only the internal connectives which take the value 'true' for all assignments to their components. One proposal, however, gives this an interesting rationale.

Sense without denotation

Recall (ch. 5 §2) that Frege held that the denotation/sense of a compound expression depended upon the denotation/sense of its components; and, consequently, that a sentence containing a singular term which has no denotation itself lacks truth-value, and a compound sentence of which a component is truth-valueless is itself truth-valueless. Frege himself preferred, as we saw, to ensure that his formal language permit no denotationless terms; if such terms were allowed, however, a non-classical logic would be needed to handle them in the way Frege's theory requires. Smiley suggests (1960) that a 3-valued logic like Bochvar's would be the appropriate non-classical system. The assignment of the third value to a wff indicates, here, not that it has an intermediate truth-value, but that it has no truth-value at all. Now the fact that the matrices for the internal connectives assign no truth-value to a compound wff if any component lacks truth-value corresponds to the Fregean principle that a compound expression lacks denotation if any component lacks denotation. And with the help of the assertion operator the Fregean conception of presupposition ('A' presupposes 'B' if 'A' is neither true nor false unless 'B' is true) can be defined. Thus, I think, this proposal succeeds admirably in representing the formal system that would result from the adoption of Frege's theory of sense and denotation (contrast Woodruff's formalisation (1970), which doesn't satisfy Frege's truth-valueless input/truth-valueless output principle). Of course, whether one takes it to supply, at the same time, an argument for the adoption of Bochvar's logic, depends on whether one accepts Frege's account of denotationless expressions.

Undecidable sentences

Kleene's 3-valued logic is intended, as we saw, to accommodate undecidable mathematical statements; the third value represents 'undecidable', and the assignment of that value to a wff is not intended to indicate that it is neither true nor false, only that one can't tell which. Indeed, it is just because Kleene takes it that undecidable wffs are true or false that he adopts the principle that a compound wff with an undecidable component should be decidable if the values of the other components suffice to ensure that the whole is either true or false (e.g. if $|p| = i$ and $|q| = t$, $|p \vee q| = t$). So while the philosophical motivation for Kleene's 3-valued logic seems unexceptionable enough, what he proposes seems to be less radical, less of a challenge to classical 2-valued logic, than initially appears (cf. Kripke's insistence (1975) that his use of Kleene's valuation rules poses no threat to classical logic; see ch. 8 §2). These reflections raise some interesting questions about how the adoption of a many-valued logic may be expected to affect the theory of truth.

3 Many-valued logics and truth-values

Not surprisingly, it has sometimes been supposed that the use of a many-valued logic would inevitably involve a claim to the effect that there are more than two truth-values: a claim which has – again, perhaps not surprisingly – sometimes been a major source of resistance to many-valued logics. But in fact, I think, it is clear that a many-valued logic needn't require the admission of one or more extra truth-values over and above 'true' and 'false', and, indeed, that it needn't even require the rejection of bivalence.

The use made by Smiley of Bochvar's 3-valued logic illustrates the first point. Assignment of the third value to a wff indicates that it has *no* truth-value, not that it has a non-standard, third truth-value. (If you are tempted to think of 'neither true nor false' as a third truth-value, on a par with 'true' and 'false', McCall's observation (1970) that no-one supposes that 'either true or false' is a third truth-value, may help to stiffen your resistance.)

Sometimes, again, intermediate values are understood, not as new truth-values, but as, so to speak, epistemological variants on 'true' and 'false'. Prior suggests interpretations of the values of a 4-valued logic as:

1 = true and purely mathematical (or, true and known to be true)

2 = true but not purely mathematical (or, true but not known to be true)

3 = false but not purely mathematical (or, false but not known to be false)

4 = false and purely mathematical (or, false and known to be false)

And these examples serve to verify, also, my stronger claim, that the use of a many-valued system needn't even require denial of bivalence. For this interpretation entails that every wff is either true or else false.

Another example where the threat to bivalence turns out to be only apparent is this: Michalski *et al.* 1976 propose a 12-valued logic which is said to be useful for devising computer programmes to handle material about plant diseases. One might be excused for feeling a certain bewilderment at this point: however is one to make sense of the *ten* extra truth-values? On closer examination, however, it turns out that what is going on is a good deal less radical, and a good deal less puzzling, than at first appears. The idea is (I simplify, but I hope not misleadingly) that instead of classifying information about the appearance of symptoms in the obvious way, as, say:

> Red spots first appear in January – false
> Red spots first appear in February – true
> Red spots first appear in March – false
> etc.

one can classify it, much more economically, thus:

> Red spots appear – value 2

The 12 values amount, in effect, to 'true-in-January', 'true-in-February'...etc. Notice, here, that what the two classical truth-values were assigned to ('Red spots first appear in January', etc.) and what the 12 non-classical values are assigned to ('Red spots appear') are different.

This leads to an important, more general, point: that what looks on the face of it like the assignment of a non-standard value to a standard item may turn out to be best explicable as the assignment of a standard value to a non-standard item. This may suggest what is correct in the recurrent criticism (e.g. Lewy 1946, Kneale and Kneale 1962 pp. 51ff.) that the proponents of many-valued logics are simply confused about truth-bearers.

The interpretation suggested for Post's many-valued systems supplies an interesting illustration of this point. The idea is, briefly, to take the 'sentence letters' to stand for *sequences* of sentences, and to take assignments of values to these sequences to depend upon the proportion of their true to their false members (more accurately: in n-valued logic, P is to stand for an $(n-1)$-tuple, $\langle p_1, p_2 \ldots p_{n-1} \rangle$, of regular, 2-valued sentences, and P is to take the value i when just $i-1$ of its elements are false). This suggests that Post's logics might be regarded as giving a formal analogue of the intuitive idea of partial truth; as, a sentence is partly true if it is complex, and part of it is true (cf. p. 169 above; and Haack 1974 pp. 62–4 for more discussion).

What I have been arguing, thus far, is that many-valued logics *needn't* call for the admission of intermediate truth-values, nor even for the rejection of bivalence. This isn't to say, of course, that they *never* pose this kind of challenge to the classical view of truth. For example, the use of Bochvar's matrices to represent a Fregean account of denotationless expressions certainly calls for a denial of bivalence; assignment of the third value represents precisely the idea that the formula is neither true nor false. (Recall (ch. 7 §5) that the classical, Tarskian account of truth is bivalent, and indeed that the (T) schema threatens to rule out non-bivalent truth-theories.)

It will not, perhaps, have escaped notice that, of the philosophical arguments for the adoption of many-valued logics discussed above, the most persuasive were those which supported an understanding of the intermediate values as epistemic variants of classical truth-values (Kleene), as assignment of classical truth-values to non-classical items (Post), or as lack of classical truth-value (Smiley). This *may* be coincidence; but those who are suspicious of the intelligibility of the idea of intermediate truth-values might find in it some confirmation of their suspicions.

4 **Non-truth-functional deviant logics**

Many-valued logics, of course, like classical logic, are truth-functional; the value assigned to a compound wff depends solely upon the values assigned to its components. (Modal logics, by contrast, are not truth-functional; the truth-value of a modal formula does not depend solely upon the truth-value of its components, and the standard modal logics have no finite characteristic matrices.) Logicians' preference for truth-functional connectives (cf. ch. 3 §2) is understandable, since the truth-tables supply a simple decision-procedure for 2- and many-valued logics.

When, however, one reflects upon the motivation for Kleene's matrices, the assumption of truth-functionality may, I think, be called into question. Remember that Kleene's argument why $|p \vee q|$ should be t if $|p| = i$ and $|q| = t$ is that the truth of *one* disjunct is sufficient to determine the truth of the whole disjunction, regardless of the value of the other disjunct; i.e., that '$p \vee q$' *will be true if 'q' is, whether 'p' is true or false*. However, Kleene's matrices assign i to '$p \vee q$' when $|p| = |q| = i$; and so, in particular, they assign i to '$p \vee -p$' when $|p| = |-p| = i$. But, one may observe, whereas '$p \vee q$' can't be relied on to be true regardless of whether 'p' and 'q'

are true or false, '*p* ∨ −*p*' *will be true whether* '*p*' *is true or false*. And this suggests that Kleene's principles might justify a *different* assignment to '*p* ∨ −*p*' than to '*p* ∨ *q*', when both disjuncts have *i*. But this, of course, would require a non-truth-functional logic.

Supervaluations

Van Fraassen's non-truth-functional 'supervaluational languages' (see 1966, 1968, 1969) seem to be more consonant than Kleene's own 3-valued matrices with the principles on which Kleene argues for his assignments. The idea, briefly, is this: a *supervaluation* assigns to a compound wff some component(s) of which lack(s) truth-value that value which all classical valuations would assign, if there is a unique such value, and otherwise no value. Since all classical valuations – i.e. both those that assign 'true' and those which assign 'false' to '*p*' – would assign 'true' to '*p* ∨ −*p*', the supervaluation also gives 'true' to '*p* ∨ −*p*'. However, since the classical valuation which assigns 'false' to '*p*' and to '*q*' assigns 'false' to '*p* ∨ *q*', while all other classical valuations assign 'true' to '*p* ∨ *q*', there is no unique value assigned by all classical valuations to '*p* ∨ *q*', and the supervaluation gives it *no* value. It isn't hard to see that supervaluations will give 'true' to all classical tautologies and 'false' to all classical contradictions, but no value to contingent formulae; however, though van Fraassen's systems will thus have just the same tautologies as classical logic, they differ from classical logic with respect to the inferences which are allowed as valid – for instance, 'disjunctive dilemma' (if $A \vdash C$ and $B \vdash C$, then $A \vee B \vdash C$) fails – which is why they count as deviant.

Intuitionist logic

Another non-truth-functional deviant logic which is of substantial philosophical *and* formal interest is Heyting's Intuitionist logic.

The Intuitionists claim (see e.g. Brouwer 1952, Heyting 1966) that classical logic is, in certain respects, incorrect. It is important, however, that their disagreement goes deeper than their rejection of certain classical laws. For, first, the Intuitionist view of the scope and character of logic is quite distinctive; the Intuitionists think of logic as secondary to mathematics, as a collection of principles which are discovered, *a posteriori*, to govern mathematical reasoning. This obviously challenges the 'classical' conception of logic as the study of principles applicable to all reasoning regardless of subject-matter, as the most fundamental and general of theories, to which even mathematics is secondary. However, this different conception of logic wouldn't, of itself, explain the Intuitionists' challenge to certain laws of classical logic, if it weren't for the fact that the Intuitionists also have a distinctive view of the nature of mathematics; for classical logical laws are supposed, of course, to govern all reasoning, including classical mathematical reasoning.

According to the Intuitionists, mathematics is essentially a mental activity, and numbers are mental entities (cf. what I called in ch. 11 §4 the 'conceptualist' view of the character of possible worlds); relatedly, what it means to say that there is a number with such-and-such a property is that such a number is constructible. The Intuitionists' distinctively psychologistic, constructivist view of mathematics leads them to the conclusion that some parts of classical mathematics – those which deal with completed, infinite totalities, for example – are unacceptable. And from this restriction of mathematics there follows a restriction of logic; some principles of classical logic are not, the Intuitionists urge, universally valid. For example, Brouwer argues, there are counter-examples to the law of excluded middle. Suppose that it is possible neither to construct a number with property F, nor to prove that there can be no such number. Then, by Intuitionist standards, it isn't true that either there is a number which is F, or there isn't.

Notice, here, an interesting contrast with Kleene's attitude. Kleene does not take the fact that some mathematical statement is undecidable in principle as any reason to deny that it is, nevertheless, either true or false. The Intuitionists, by contrast, regard the idea that there might be a number which couldn't be constructed as a piece of hopelessly confused metaphysics (see Heyting 1966 p. 4). The contrast may usefully serve to draw attention to the fact that the distinction between what, in the previous section, I called *epistemological* values versus genuine *truth*-values may not be altogether neutral but may presuppose some disputable assumptions about the relations between metaphysics and epistemology.

Because he regarded mathematics as essentially mental, and hence thought of mathematical and, *a fortiori*, logical formalism as relatively unimportant, Brouwer didn't give a formal system of the logical principles which are Intuitionistically valid. However, Intuitionist logic was formalised by Heyting, who gives these axioms:

1. $p \to (p \mathbin{\&} p)$
2. $(p \mathbin{\&} q) \to (q \mathbin{\&} p)$
3. $(p \to q) \to ((p \mathbin{\&} r) \to (q \mathbin{\&} r))$
4. $((p \to q) \mathbin{\&} (q \to r)) \to (p \to r)$
5. $q \to (p \to q)$
6. $(p \mathbin{\&} (p \to q)) \to q$
7. $p \to (p \lor q)$
8. $(p \lor q) \to (q \lor p)$
9. $((p \to r) \mathbin{\&} (q \to r)) \to ((p \lor q) \to r)$
10. $\neg p \to (p \to q)$
11. $((p \to q) \mathbin{\&} (p \to \neg q)) \to \neg p$

('$\neg$' is the usual symbol for Intuitionist negation.) Notice that this list contains axioms governing each connective ('&', '$\lor$', '$\to$', '$\neg$'); in Intuitionist logic the connectives are not interdefinable, so all must be taken as primitive. This is related, of course, to the fact that Intuitionist logic has no finite characteristic matrix (cf. comments on interdefinability of connectives in ch. 3 §1). Heyting's logic lacks some classical theorems; notably, neither '$p \lor \neg p$', nor '$\neg\neg p \to p$', are theorems. However, the double negations of all classical theorems are valid in Intuitionist logic.

Heyting's is not the only, although it is the best entrenched, system of Intuitionist logic: in fact, Johansson's logic (1936), which lacks the tenth axiom, has, arguably, a better claim properly to represent the logical principles which are acceptable by Intuitionist standards. But Heyting's logic has some unexpected affinities, affinities which raise questions about the distinction between deviant and extended logic, with modal logic, which is why it will occupy my attention for the rest of this section.

There is little doubt that the Intuitionists see themselves as challenging the correctness of certain theorems of classical logic. This makes it appropriate that they should propose a restriction of classical logic, in which the disputed theorems fail. However, Heyting's calculus, though on the face of it a deviation of classical logic, may also be interpreted as an extension of classical logic. If one takes Intuitionist negation and conjunction as primitive, and defines disjunction ($p \lor q = \mathrm{df} \; \neg(\neg p \mathbin{\&} \neg q)$) implication and equivalence in the usual, classical way, in terms of them, then all classical theorems can be derived in the Heyting logic; in addition, of course, all the theorems in Intuitionist disjunction, implication, and equivalence –

which are not definable in terms of Intuitionist negation and conjunction – are also derivable. And this makes Intuitionist logic look less like a restriction, and more like an extension, of classical logic. (But not all classical inferences are preserved by the proposed translation, not e.g. MPP, for since $\neg\neg p \to p$ under the translation, the validity of MPP would imply $\neg\neg p \vdash p$.) It is also possible to interpret the Heyting calculus as a modal logic; if:

$$
\begin{aligned}
m\,(A) &= LA \text{ (for atomic sentences)} \\
m\,(\neg A) &= L - m\,(A) \\
m\,(A \vee B) &= m\,(A) \vee m\,(B) \\
m\,(A \,\&\, B) &= m\,(A) \,\&\, m\,(B) \\
m\,(A \to B) &= L\,(m\,(A) \to m\,(B))
\end{aligned}
$$

('$m\,(A)$' means 'the translation of A'; the connectives on the left-hand side are the Intuitionist, those on the right the classical, connectives) it is provable that a wff is valid in the Heyting calculus iff its translation is valid in S4 (McKinsey and Tarski 1948; cf. Fitting 1969). Of these two 'translations' of Heyting's logic, the latter seems somewhat more natural than the former; for Brouwer and Heyting do sometimes read '$\neg$' as 'it is impossible that...', as, for example, when they read '$(\exists x)\,Fx \vee \neg\,(\exists x)\,Fx$' as 'Either an F exists, or a contradiction is derivable from the assumption that an F exists'. But what, exactly, is the significance of the availability of these translations?

It is natural to expect a correlation between, on the one hand, proposals to restrict classical logic, and the idea that it is in some way mistaken, and, on the other, proposals to extend classical logic, and the idea that it is in some way inadequate. The thought is that a restricted (deviant) logic excludes some theorems/inferences expressible wholly in classical vocabulary, and thus involves the denial that some classical theorems/inferences are really valid. But now one can see that the question, whether a non-classical logic really has 'the same vocabulary' as classical logic, is not so simple as it (perhaps) seemed. The Intuitionists regard themselves as critics, and the Heyting calculus as a restriction, of classical logic; the possibility of representing Heyting's calculus as an extension of classical logic raises the question whether the Intuitionist connectives differ in meaning from their classical 'analogues'. For myself, I am inclined to think that the fact that there is more than one way to represent Heyting's as an extended logic would justify caution about the idea that the Intuitionists' critique of classical logic can be wholly explained away as the result of meaning-variance. But the general issue, about the relevance of considerations of meaning to the distinction between deviant and extended logic, will prove important to the argument of the next chapter.

12

Some metaphysical and epistemological questions about logic

1 **Metaphysical questions**

The purpose of this chapter is to tackle some of the questions about the status of logic which are raised by the existence of a plurality of logical systems – a plurality I have been exploring in previous chapters. Some of these questions are metaphysical: e.g. is there just one correct logical system, or could there be several which are equally correct? and what could 'correct' mean in this context? Others are epistemological: e.g. how does one recognise a truth of logic? could one be mistaken in what one takes to be such truths? I'll start with the metaphysical questions, since the answers to the epistemological questions are apt to depend, to some extent, upon the answers to them.

Monism, pluralism, instrumentalism

It will be useful to start by distinguishing, in a rough and ready way, three broad kinds of response to the question whether there is a uniquely correct logical system:

monism:	there is just one correct system of logic
pluralism:	there is more than one correct system of logic
instrumentalism:	there is no 'correct' logic; the notion of correctness is inappropriate

Obviously this needs elaboration and refinement. First, some comments about the conception of correctness which both monism and pluralism require: this conception depends upon a distinction between system-relative and extra-systematic validity/logical truth;

roughly, a logical system is correct if the formal arguments which are valid in that system correspond to informal arguments which are valid in the extra-systematic sense, and the wffs which are logically true in the system correspond to statements which are logically true in the extra-systematic sense. The monist holds that there is a unique logical system which is correct in this sense, the pluralist that there are several.

Now the significance of the distinction between *extensions* of classical logic and *deviations* from it can be fully appreciated. *Prima facie*, at least, the modal logician, for instance, seems to be claiming that there are valid arguments/logical truths which cannot be represented within the vocabulary of, and so are not valid arguments/ logical truths of, classical logic; so that, although classical logic is *correct as far as it goes*, it doesn't go far enough. The proponent of a 3-valued logic, by contrast, seems to claim that there are valid arguments/logical truths of classical logic the informal analogues of which aren't valid/logically true, so that classical logic is *actually incorrect*. (This explains in a more precise way the idea, first adumbrated in ch. 9 §3, that deviant logics pose a more serious challenge than extended logics to classical logic.)

If deviant logics rival classical logic, whereas extended logics supplement it, this would indicate that a monist attitude would be suitable to the former (one is obliged to choose between the classical and deviant systems) and a pluralist attitude to the latter (one could accept the classical and an extended logic as both correct). Alternatively, one might regard classical logic and extensions of it (or, again, of course, some deviant logic and extensions of that) as *together* constituting 'the correct logic'. The point is that the difference between a pluralism which admits classical logic and its extensions (or a deviant logic and its extensions) as both correct systems of logic, and a monism which admits both classical logic and its extensions (or a deviant logic and its extensions) as both fragments of *the* correct system of logic, is only verbal.

So I shall concentrate henceforth upon the choice between classical and deviant logics (similar questions arise about the choice between one deviant logic and another, and perhaps between one modal logic and another – cf. p. 178; but I shan't discuss them here), where the issue between monism and pluralism is substantial. The monist sees classical and deviant logics as making rival claims about what formalism correctly represents extra-systematically valid arguments/

logical truths; the pluralist, in brief, claims that the apparent rivalry is, in one way or another, *merely* apparent. In fact, there are several versions of pluralism, different ways of dismissing the apparent rivalry. Some pluralists share with the monist the assumption that logic should be applicable to reasoning on any subject-matter; others, however, urge that different logics may apply to reasoning on different subject-matters. So one may distinguish between *global* and *local* versions of pluralism[1]; I shall consider the local version first.

According to *local pluralism*, different logical systems are applicable to (i.e. correct with respect to) different areas of discourse; perhaps classical logic to macroscopic phenomena, and 'quantum logic' (p. 210) to microscopic phenomena, for example, rather as different physical theories may hold for macroscopic than for microscopic phenomena. The local pluralist relativises the extra-systematic ideas of validity and logical truth, and hence the idea of the correctness of a logical system, to a specific area of discourse; an argument isn't valid, period, but valid-in-*d*.

The *global pluralist*, by contrast, shares the monist's assumption that logical principles should apply irrespective of subject-matter. However, while the monist takes it that the classical and the deviant logician disagree about the validity/logical truth *in the same sense*, of *one and the same* argument/statement, the global pluralist denies either that the classical and deviant logician are really using 'valid'/'logically true' in the same sense, or else that they are really disagreeing about one and the same argument/statement. The former idea obviously relates to what I called, in ch. 9 §2, the 'challenge to classical metaconcepts'; the latter, to some ideas discussed in ch. 3 §2 about the meanings of the connectives.

Roughly, the thought in the second version of global pluralism is this: typographically identical wffs/arguments in classical and deviant logics don't have the same meaning, and hence can't both represent the very same informal statements/arguments. One argument for this view is that the meaning of the logical constants depends wholly upon the axioms/rules of the system in which they occur; consequently, when a certain wff, '$p \vee -p$', say, is logically true in one system and not in another, then those wffs, though typo-

---

[1] The contrast between Boole's idea of logic as a calculus, and Leibniz's of logic as a universal language, discussed in van Heijenhoort 1967b, may have affinities with the distinction upon which I am presently relying, between local and global approaches to logic.

graphically the same, have different meanings in the different systems, the *meaning-variance* thesis.[1] So what the wff '$p \lor -p$' says, in classical logic, *is* logically true, but what the very same wff says, in 3-valued logic (where '$\lor$' and ' $-$ ', or perhaps 'p', have non-classical meanings) is *not* logically true; so *both* the classical and the 3-valued logic are correct. From this point of view the deviant logician seems, very much like, e.g., the modal logician, not to be challenging the old, but as offering new valid arguments/logical truths – he differs from the modal logician only in his disagreeably confusing habit of using old symbols for his new conception (cf. the discussion of the translatability of Intuitionist into modal logic in ch. 11 §4).

The *instrumentalist* position results from a rejection of the idea of the 'correctness' of a logical system, an idea accepted by both monists and pluralists. On the instrumentalist view, there is no sense in speaking of a logical system's being 'correct' or 'incorrect', though it might be conceded that it is appropriate to speak of one system's being more fruitful, useful, convenient...etc. than another (perhaps: for certain purposes). The rejection of the concept of correctness is apt to be based on a rejection of the extra-systematic ideas of logical truth and validity which that conception requires; if only the concepts of *logical-truth-in*-L and *validity-in*-L are intelligible, the question, whether the wffs/arguments which are logically true/valid-in-L correspond to statements/arguments which are extra-systematically logically true/valid, simply cannot arise. An instrumentalist will only allow the 'internal' question, whether a logical system is *sound*, whether, that is, all and only the theorems/syntactically valid arguments *of the system* are logically true/valid *in the system*.

Another version of instrumentalism seems to derive from a refusal to apply *any* idea of truth, even a system-relative idea, to logic. Logic, it is argued, is not to be thought of as a set of *statements*, as a *theory* to be assessed as true or false; rather, it is to be thought of as a set of *rules* or *procedures*, to which the concepts of truth and falsity simply

---

[1] I deliberately choose this expression to recall Feyerabend's thesis that the meanings of theoretical terms in science depend upon the theories in which they occur, so that there is failure of rivalry between alternative, apparently competing, scientific theories (cf. Feyerabend 1963; and see Haack 1974 pp. 11–14 for further exploration of the analogy).

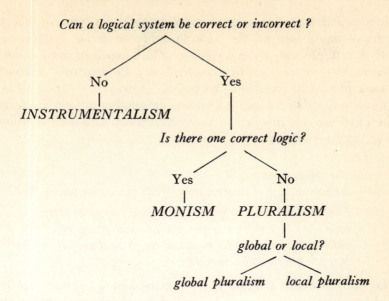

Can a logical system be correct or incorrect ?

No   Yes

INSTRUMENTALISM

Is there one correct logic?

Yes   No

MONISM   *PLURALISM*

global or local?

global pluralism   *local pluralism*

Fig. 7

don't apply.[1] However, the question of correctness would still arise, on this rule-oriented view, with respect to validity (do the arguments valid-in-L correspond to informal arguments which are extra-systematically valid?) unless the extra-systematic conception of validity is also rejected. So the initial version of the instrumentalist position, resting upon a rejection of the extra-systematic ideas in correspondence to which monists and pluralists suppose correctness to consist, is the more fundamental. These alternatives can be conveniently summarised as in fig. 7.

I have aimed rather at mapping out the alternatives in as systematic a fashion as I can, than at listing positions held by specific writers. But in fact it is possible to find examples of writers holding each of the positions I have identified. Quine seems to take for granted something like what I've called the monist position when, in the second half of 'Two dogmas' (1951), he considers the (epistemological) question of the revisability of logic; in ch. 6 of *Philosophy of Logic* (1970), however, he seems to opt for something like meaning-

---

[1] Analogously, the idea that the 'laws' of physics aren't to be thought of as true-or-false statements, but as principles of inference, is often taken to be characteristic of an 'instrumentalist' philosophy of science; see e.g. Toulmin 1953.

variance pluralism, using rather complex arguments from his theory of translation to support the claim that there is change of meaning sufficient to preclude rivalry; some quantum logicians, most clearly Destouches-Février 1951, but also, probably, Putnam 1969, support a local pluralism; Rescher's 'relativism' (1969 ch. 3) seems to be quite close to what I've called instrumentalism, but in 1977 he seems to try to combine a rule-oriented instrumentalism with the admission of an extra-systematic notion of validity.

The issues summarised

At any rate, it is clearer, now, what the major issues are:

Does it make sense to speak of a logical system as correct or incorrect? Are there extra-systematic conceptions of validity/logical truth by means of which to characterise what it is for a logic to be correct?

The instrumentalist position is characterised by a negative answer to these questions; monists and pluralists answer them positively. (It should also be clear now why I observed that some epistemological questions depend on the answers to metaphysical questions; unless there can *be* a correct logic, the question, how we tell whether a logic *is* correct, doesn't arise.)

Must a logical system aspire to global application, i.e. to represent reasoning irrespective of subject-matter, or may a logic be locally correct, i.e. correct within a limited area of discourse?

The local pluralist position is distinguished by the choice of the second of these options.

Do deviant logics rival classical logic?

The monist answers this question affirmatively, the global pluralist negatively. The issues all concern the relation between formal and informal argument, system-relative and extra-systematic validity. Thus the monist picture may be represented as in fig. 8 (p. 227). (i) aspires to represent (iii) in such a way that (ii) and (iv) correspond in 'the correct logic'. The instrumentalist rejects (iv) altogether; the local pluralist relativises (iv) to specific areas of discourse; the global pluralist either denies that the formal arguments of a deviant logic represent the same informal arguments as those of classical logic,

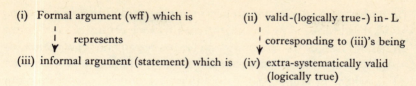

(i) Formal argument (wff) which is   (ii) valid-(logically true-) in-L

      represents   corresponding to (iii)'s being

(iii) informal argument (statement) which is   (iv) extra-systematically valid
                                         (logically true)

Fig. 8

i.e. he fragments the relation between (i) and (iii), or else he denies that validity in the deviant logic is intended to correspond to extra-systematic validity in the same sense as that to which validity in classical logic is intended to correspond, i.e. he fragments the relation between (ii) and (iv).

Comments

It is often enough the case in philosophy that asking the right questions is half the battle. However, the other half is not to be shirked; and I shall now offer some comments on what I take to be the major issues. But the questions that have been raised here are, I think, enormously difficult, and there is a serious problem about finding a starting point for the argument that begs no pertinent questions; so I should stress that the next paragraphs are tentative as well as, no doubt, inconclusive.

I indicated early on (ch. 2 §2) that I *do* take there to be an extra-systematic idea of validity to which formal logical systems aim to give precise expression. It is clear enough from the history of formal logic (consider Aristotle, for instance, or Frege) that the motivation for the construction of formal systems has been, on the basis of an initial conception of some arguments as good and others as bad, to sort out logical from other, e.g. rhetorical, features of good arguments, and to give rules which would permit only the logically good arguments and exclude the bad. This, therefore, inclines me to answer the first questions affirmatively, and so to reject the instrumentalist position. This inclination is strengthened, furthermore, by some persistent doubts about whether an instrumentalist can have anything sensible to say about how one is to choose between logical systems. The instrumentalist normally concedes that, at least for certain purposes, one logical system may be judged better than another, perhaps as more convenient, more fruitful, more appropriate, yielding the desired inferences... But no matter how convenient or fruitful it might be if one could infer '*A* and *B*' from '*A*', this would, or so it seems to me, be *no* reason to prefer a system which represented that inference as valid. I'm aware, of course, that in making such comments as this I'm in some danger of assuming an extra-systematic conception of validity, and criticising the instrumentalist for failing to take account of it, when, of course, he claims that there *is* no such conception (rather as Russell and Moore assumed the correctness of a correspondence theory of truth, and criticised the pragmatist theory on that basis). Nevertheless, I think the fact that Rescher, in presenting an instrumentalist position, in the end allows that the requirement that arguments be truth-preserving is overriding may justifiably confirm my suspicions.

I have also indicated (ch. 1 §2) that I take it to be characteristic of logic to aspire to present principles which apply to reasoning on no matter what subject; to be *global* in scope. I allowed that the notion of a principle's applying to reasoning irrespective of subject-matter wasn't perfectly clear or precise – it shares the vagueness of the extra-systematic conception of validity as holding in virtue of form rather than content. Still, though I think there is room for doubt about whether 'believes', say, or 'prefers', may legitimately be counted as form rather than content, I nevertheless feel pretty confident that principles that held for reasoning about biological subject-matter, but not for reasoning about physics, for example, wouldn't be logical (but, I suppose, biological) principles. Consequently, I should answer the second question affirmatively, and am disinclined to accept a local pluralism. If, for example, it turns out, as Birkhoff and von Neumann claimed (1936), that where quantum phenomena are concerned, '*A* and (*B* or *C*) iff (*A* and *B*) or (*A* and *C*)' isn't invariably true, then classical logic, in which the distributive laws are theorems, isn't correct. (I'm entirely willing to concede that it might be that while classical principles are, strictly, incorrect, they hold for all ordinary reasoning about macroscopic phenomena, so that it would be as reasonable to use classical logic for purposes of ordinary reasoning as to use Euclidean geometry for surveying purposes, despite the fact that Euclidean geometry isn't, strictly, true of our space. However, I now doubt whether this concession will appease the local pluralist.)

This leaves the options of monism, on the one hand, and some form of global pluralism, on the other. But at this stage, I think, the character of the argument changes; I mean, that while the first two questions concern the nature and aspirations of logic, and can be answered generally, the last concerns the relations between classical and deviant logics, and so it may have no general answer, but perhaps different answers for different deviant logics. It may be, that is, that *some* deviant logicians are using different metaconcepts from the classical logician, and others the same; or that the meaning-variance thesis is true of *some* deviant logics but not of others; or, indeed, both. A more piecemeal approach is appropriate from here on. Of course, though, monism and pluralism are *asymmetric* in a way which is relevant; even *one* instance of a deviant logic which could be correct *as well as* classical logic would tip the balance to pluralism.

Now, although I urged that there is an extra-systematic idea of validity which formal systems of logic aspire to represent, I also observed (pp. 14–15) that that idea is by no means fully precise, and that it may be refined and perhaps modified as logic develops. The relevance logician (ch. 10 §6) rejects the principle, from 'A' and '$A \to B$' to infer 'B'; *modus ponens*, he urges, is invalid. He makes it plain, furthermore, that he is speaking of *modus ponens* for ordinary, classical, material, implication. However, he doesn't deny that if 'A' and '$A \to B$' are true, then, necessarily, 'B' is true; what he means, when he says that MPP *isn't* valid, isn't what the classical logician means, when he says that MPP *is* valid, since the relevance logician would agree that MPP is valid *in the classical sense of 'valid'*. This case, I think, gives some grounds for a global pluralism (and it may be that there is also something to be said for the idea that, in Intuitionist logic, a non-classical conception of logical truth is being employed).

However, to opt unqualifiedly for global pluralism at this point would be, I think, to take much too lightly the relevance logicians' insistence that the classical logicians' conception of validity is not just *different* from theirs, but also *inadequate*. There is real competition, genuine rivalry, here, not over which arguments are valid in an agreed sense of 'valid', but over what conception of validity is most proper and adequate. (Recall the suggestion made earlier, p. 201, that relevance logicians could be seen as urging that relevance of premises to conclusions, which classical logicians regard as a *rhetorical* feature of good by contrast with bad arguments, is really a *logical* feature of good arguments, a matter of validity.) Due regard for the significance of this disagreement seems to require that one combine a kind of global pluralism about logical systems with a recognition that there may be real competition at the level of metaconcepts.

What, now, of the meaning-variance argument for pluralism? It is not plausible, to my mind, to say that when Łukasiewicz, for instance, denies that '$p \vee -p$' represents a logical truth, his apparent disagreement with the classical logician can be wholly accounted for as the result simply of his giving a novel meaning to '$\vee$' or '$-$' or both. I deliberately put the point in this guarded way; what I am denying is not that any deviant logic ever involves any change of meaning of the logical constants – it is reasonable to suspect some idiosyncrasy in the meaning of Intuitionist negation and quantification, for example – but that any deviance from classical logic inevitably involves such wholescale meaning-variance as necessarily to preclude real rivalry. (I have argued this in detail, with specific reference to Quine's arguments from translation, in 1974 pp. 14–21 and 1977c.)

The question is tricky because there are reasons both for and against meaning-variance. I argued in ch. 3 §2 that the meaning of the connectives can be thought of as deriving in part from the axioms/ rules of the system in which they occur and from its formal semantics, and in part, also, from the informal readings given to the connectives and the informal explanation of the formal semantics. The axioms/ rules and the formal semantics of deviant systems are, of course, different from the classical, and the informal semantics may differ too (cf. the discussion of whether intermediate values in many-valued systems must be regarded as truth-values, ch. 11 §3); this argues for some meaning-variance. On the other hand, deviant logicians usually employ the same informal readings of their connectives ('not', 'and', 'or', 'if') as the classical logician, which, on the other hand, seems to be a *prima facie* indication that they intend to offer rival representations of the same informal arguments.

But this suggests a thought which has tended to be overlooked in the debate about meaning-variance (but cf. Quine 1973 pp. 77ff.). Formalisation involves a certain abstraction from what are taken to be irrelevant or unimportant features of informal discourse; the logician feels free to ignore the temporal connotations of 'and', say, or the plurality implied by 'some'. And this leaves scope for, so to speak, alternative formal projections of the same informal discourse; i.e. scope for the idea that, for instance, material implication, strict implication, relevant implication, and other formal conditionals might all have some claim to represent some aspect of 'if', or that 2-valued and 3-valued and non-extensional disjunctions might all be possible projections of (some) uses of 'or'. And this supplies more support for a pluralist approach, according to which, however, rather than different formalisms aspiring to represent different informal arguments, they may be giving different representations of the same arguments.

Once again, it is likely that there will be disagreement between deviant and classical logicians – even if their rivalry at the level of the logical systems can be mitigated as I have suggested – about what is the best, or perhaps, the proper, way to represent informal arguments. However, I am sceptical of the idea that one can expect there to be a unique, ideally perspicuous formal notation in which the unique logical form of every informal argument is correctly represented (hence my preference for 'a logical form' over 'the logical form' of an argument, ch 2 §4). Some formal representations may be better than others, either absolutely, or, for certain purposes, but I'm not confident that there is a unique best. (It is possible, also, that one formal representation should be preferable in one area of discourse and another in another; and if so perhaps something of local pluralism could be salvaged.)

So, I am inclined to favour a global pluralist position: there can be several logical systems which are correct in the sense I have explained. The monist picture (fig. 8 above) should be replaced by something more along the lines of fig. 9:

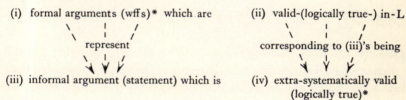

(i) formal arguments (wffs)* which are

represent

(iii) informal argument (statement) which is

(ii) valid-(logically true-) in-L

corresponding to (iii)'s being

(iv) extra-systematically valid
(logically true)*

Fig. 9

where informal arguments may be represented formally in more than one way, and when validity-/logical truth-in-L may correspond to different extra-systematic conceptions of validity/logical truth. However, I stress first that this does not mean that one *never* has to choose between a deviant and the classical logic, only that one *sometimes* need not (so my pluralism is, so to speak, piecemeal although global); and second that, even in those cases where a deviant and the classical logic may be both correct, there may nevertheless be competition between them at the metalogical level, e.g. about how the idea of validity may properly be understood, or how certain informal arguments may best be formally represented. (The stars in fig. 9 indicate when such metalogical rivalry is to be located.)

It may be worthwhile to point out that this position is able to accommodate at least some of the considerations which have been taken to indicate monism, local pluralism or instrumentalism. I have allowed – what the monist primarily stresses – that some logical systems may really compete with each other, in the strong sense that they cannot both be correct; I have denied only that logical systems must always compete in this way. I have also urged recognition of metalogical competition where I think that logical rivalry can be defused. And the suggestion that different formal representations may be best for different purposes perhaps offers some comfort to the local pluralist. I've less, at this stage, to offer by way of concessions to the instrumentalist. In the next section, however, I shall be arguing for a quite radical approach to the epistemology of logic, an approach which would be quite congenial to an instrumentalist.

2   Epistemological questions

> ...no statement is immune from revision. Revision even of the law of the excluded middle has been proposed as a means of simplifying quantum mechanics; and what difference is there in principle between such a shift and the shift whereby Kepler superseded Ptolemy, or Einstein Newton, or Darwin Aristotle? (Quine 1951 p. 43)

Quine is claiming that *logic is revisable*. I think he is right; but the epistemological issues that this claim raises are far more complex than one might suspect from the elegant but rather perfunctory treatment they receive in 'Two dogmas'.

One needs, first, to get clear just what is meant by the claim that logic is revisable – and, equally importantly, what is *not* meant by it. What I mean, at any rate, is not that the truths of logic might have been otherwise than they are, but that the truths of logic might be other than we take them to be, i.e. *we could be mistaken about what the truths of logic are*, e.g. in supposing that the law of excluded middle is one such.

So a better way to put the question, because it makes its epistemological character clearer, is this: does fallibilism extend to logic? Even this formulation, however, needs further refinement, for the nature of fallibilism is often misunderstood.

What is fallibilism?

To say that a person (or group of people, 'the scientific community', for instance) is fallible – I'll use 'fallible' in the sense of 'cognitively fallible', that is to say, fallible *with respect to beliefs*, and not, for instance, with respect to promises, resolutions, etc. – is to say that he is liable to hold false beliefs; to say that a method is fallible is to say that it is liable to produce false results; of course, a person may be fallible because he uses fallible methods – consultation of entrails or horoscopes, perhaps – of acquiring beliefs. It seems to me to be undeniable that people are fallible – we are all liable to hold at least some false beliefs; we know of beliefs that people used to hold that they are false – once, for instance, people believed that the sun moves round the earth, that the earth is flat...etc. – and it is reasonable, as well as modest, to suppose that we, too, believe things that are false, though, of course, we don't know which of the things we believe are the false ones, and we should naturally stop believing them if we did.

However, epistemologists have often thought that, with respect to certain *kinds* of belief – beliefs about one's own immediate sense-experience are a favoured example – people may be *in*fallible: they are liable to have false beliefs about astronomy, geography...etc., but they are not liable to be mistaken about whether they are in pain, seeing a red patch...etc. And neither, some writers have argued, are we liable to be mistaken about the truths of logic; logic, they think, has a special epistemological security. Popper, for example, though he stresses our fallibility where scientific conjectures are concerned, nevertheless seems confident that logic is safe; see 1960 for his fallibilism, and cf. 1970 for his refusal to extend fallibilism to logic.

Does fallibilism extend to logic?

(i) *necessity*. Now why should one find willingness to admit that we might be mistaken in what we take to be the laws of physics, but unwillingness to admit that we might be mistaken in what we take to be the laws of logic? One important reason – important at least because it's based on a significant confusion – derives from the presumed necessity of logical laws. The argument would somewhat like this: the laws of logic are necessary, that is to say, they couldn't be otherwise than true; so, since a logical law can't be false, one's belief in a logical law can't be mistaken, and so, is infallible. I have little doubt that this argument is unsound. (The truths of

mathematics are, also, supposed to be necessary. But nevertheless
we are apt to hold false mathematical beliefs, the result of mistakes in
calculation for example. And if the laws of physics are, as some suppose, physically necessary, this is not usually thought to entail that
we are able infallibly to tell what the laws of physics *are*.) But what
is wrong with the argument that, since the laws of logic are necessary,
fallibilism does not extend to logic?

The argument goes wrong in two ways. First, it depends on using
'fallible' as a predicate, not of persons, but of propositions: a predicate meaning, presumably, 'possibly false'. Now it is quite true that,
if the laws of logic are necessary, they are not possibly false, and
hence, in this sense, they are 'infallible'. But the thesis that some
propositions are possibly false (which I'll call 'proposition fallibilism') is an uninteresting logical thesis, which should not be confused with the interesting epistemological thesis that we are liable to
hold false beliefs (which I'll call 'agent fallibilism'). And proposition
infallibilism doesn't entail agent infallibilism; even if the laws of
logic are not possibly false, this by no means guarantees that we are
not liable to hold false logical beliefs. In claiming that we are fallible
in our logical beliefs (that agent fallibilism *does* extend to logic) I am
not, of course, asserting the contradictory thesis that though, say,
'$p \vee -p$' is necessary, we might falsely believe that $p \vee -p$; rather,
I am claiming that, though '$p \vee -p$' is necessary, we might falsely
believe that $-(p \vee -p)$, or else, perhaps, though '$p \vee -p$' is not
necessary, we falsely believe that it is. (I deliberately choose excluded
middle as an example of a purported logical law, since there is, of
course, dispute about its status.) Secondly, the argument is given a
deceptive plausibility by the ease with which the thesis that some
propositions are possibly false is confused with the thesis that some
propositions are contingent. If the laws of logic are necessary, our
logical beliefs will, indeed, not be contingent, but either necessarily
true or necessarily false. But 'possibly false' should not be equated
with 'contingent', for *necessarily false* beliefs are possibly false.[1]

[1] If I am right that an interesting, genuinely epistemological fallibilism
will make 'fallible' a predicate of persons rather than propositions, this
has the consequence that Popper's attempt to accommodate fallibilism
within an 'epistemology without a knowing subject' (see his paper of
that title in 1972) is misguided. And if I am right that agent fallibilism
can quite consistently extend to subject-matters the truths of which are
necessarily true there is no need for embarrassment (such as even a
'contrite fallibilist' like C. S. Peirce manifests) about extending
fallibilism to mathematics.

Faith that logic is unalterable has often enough been the basis for denying that logic is revisable. Once it is clear – as I hope it is by now – that the necessity of logical principles does not show us to be logically infallible, it will be clear, also, that if logic *is* unrevisable, it is *not* because it is unalterable.

Now one reason for believing that we are fallible where our beliefs about the world are concerned is that we know that people once confidently believed what we now (we think) know to be false; and, though we're sure that they were wrong to think, for instance, that the earth is flat, the fact that their beliefs turned out to be false is a reason for us to admit that some of our beliefs may, also, turn out to be mistaken. And similar reasons operate, I should have thought, for a comparable modesty about our logical beliefs. For example: Kant wrote that 'In our own times there has been no famous logician, and indeed we do not require any new discoveries in Logic...' (1800 p. 11); his confidence that logic was a completed science seems to us – with the benefit of hindsight, after the enormous advances made in logic since the last quarter of the nineteenth century – to exhibit a curious and remarkable over-confidence. (Kant's confidence in Aristotelian logic was based on the belief that logic embodies the 'forms of thought', that we can't but think in accordance with these principles. Discussion of these ideas will be taken up below.) Or, again: Frege thought that the reduction of arithmetic to logic would guarantee arithmetic epistemologically, because he took the truths of logic to be self-evident; we, however, knowing that Frege's 'self-evident' axioms were inconsistent, are apt to find his confidence misplaced. (Lakatos 1963–4, in a splendid philosophical essay on the history of mathematics, similarly subverts the tendency to place mathematics on an epistemological pedestal.) Another reason against epistemological over-confidence is the knowledge that other people hold, with as much confidence, beliefs incompatible with one's own. And this motive operates in the sphere of logic, too; the very plurality of logical systems speaks against our possession of any infallible capacity to ascertain the truths of logic.

(ii) *self-evidence*. Still, the idea that the truths of logic are self-evident needs closer examination. What does it mean to claim that some proposition is self-evident? Presumably, something to the effect that it is obviously true. But once it has been put like this, the difficulty with the concept of self-evidence cannot be disguised. The fact that a proposition is obvious is, sadly, no guarantee that it's true. (It is pertinent that different people, and different ages, find different and even incompatible propositions – that some men are naturally slaves, that all men are equal... – 'obvious'.) Whether one says that Frege's inconsistent axioms only *seemed* self-evident, but couldn't really have been, or that they *were* self-evident but unfortunately weren't true, self-evidence must fail to supply an epistemological guarantee; because either (on the latter assumption) a proposition may be self-evident but false, or else (on the former assumption) though if a proposition is self-evident then it is, indeed, true, one has no certain way to tell when a proposition is really self-evident.[1]

(iii) *analyticity.* Another reason for doubting the revisability of logic seems to derive from the idea, first, that logical truths are analytic and then, that analytic truths are, so to speak, manifest. If *A* is true in virtue of its meaning, the thought is, then no-one who understands it can fail to see that it *is* true. There is room, I think, for doubt about whether a really convincing argument could be developed along these lines; for the idea of 'truth in virtue of meaning' is far from transparent, not only because (as Quine has long urged) of the 'meaning', but also because of the 'in virtue of'. And even supposing that it could, there is room for further doubt about whether its conclusion would seriously damage fallibilism, for even if, if one understood a logical truth correctly, one could not but recognise its truth, this would guarantee the correctness of one's logical beliefs only if one *also* had some foolproof way to be sure that one had correctly understood a candidate logical truth. (The structural similarity between this comment and the previous criticism of the 'self-evidence' argument is worth noticing.)

A digression: 'Two dogmas' again

This seems the appropriate place for some observations about the structure of Quine's argument in 'Two dogmas'. The paper opens (I simplify, but not, I hope, misleadingly) with an attack on the analytic/synthetic distinction, and closes with a plea for the revisability of logic. What is the connection between the two?

One may interpret Quine as urging the revisability of logic as an argument against the logical positivists' conception of analyticity.

---

[1] My comments have much in common with Peirce's very shrewd critique (1868) of the infallible faculty of 'intuition' which Descartes supposed us to possess.

The positivists take the meaning of a sentence to be given by its verification conditions; and hence, take a statement to be analytic, or true in virtue of its meaning, just in case it is verified come what may. They run together the metaphysical idea of analyticity with the epistemological idea of *a priority*; which is why it would be appropriate for Quine to attack the claim that logic is analytic, in this sense, by arguing that logic is revisable. On this interpretation, the revisability of logic is not a conclusion, but a premise, of the argument of 'Two dogmas'.

Another possibility is to see the attack on analyticity as premise and the plea for the revisability of logic as conclusion. However, if the argument is: if the laws of logic were analytic they would be unrevisable, but since there are no analytic truths, the laws of logic aren't analytic, and so, they are revisable – it would be a bad one. It is invalid, having the form '$A \to -B$, $-A$, so B'. One premise is false, since, as I've just argued, A's being analytic doesn't preclude our being mistaken about it. And the other premise hasn't been established; Quine attacks the second disjunct of the 'Fregean' definition of an analytic truth as either a logical truth, or reducible to a logical truth by substitution of synonyms, but this can scarcely show that logical truths aren't analytic, for they qualify under the first disjunct.

Nevertheless, this interpretation is worthy of some attention; because it enables one to understand Quine's more recent increasing conservatism about logic. The attack in 'Two dogmas' on synonymy etc. *would* threaten an account of logical truths as analytic because *true in virtue of the meaning of the logical constants*. Now in *Word and Object* Quine renews his sceptical attack on meaning notions, but makes an exception in the case of the logical connectives, which, he claims, do have determinate meaning (1960a ch. 2); and this paves the way for his acceptance (1970 ch. 6) of a meaning-variance argument to the effect that the theorems of deviant and classical logics are, alike, true in virtue of the meaning of the (deviant or classical) connectives; which, in turn, seems to lead him to compromise his earlier insistence that fallibilism extends even to logic.

Revision of logic

If fallibilism *does* extend to logic, if, as I have claimed, we *are* apt to be mistaken in our beliefs about logic, then it would be prudent to be prepared, if need be, to revise our logical opinions.

But this isn't to say that revisions of logic should be lightly under-taken, for the extreme generality of logical principles means that such revisions will have the most far-reaching consequences; logic *is* revisable, but the reasons for revision had better be good. As I argued in ch. 11 §3, the arguments offered in favour of deviant logics have, too often, been rather weak.

3   Logic and thought

Kant's confidence in the unrevisability of Aristotelian logic rested on the idea that logical principles represent 'the forms of thought', that we can't but think in accordance with them: an idea that raises a host of intriguing questions about just what logic has to do with 'the way we think'.

Although at one time it was quite usual to suppose that the prin-ciples of logic are 'the laws of thought' (see Boole 1854), Frege's vigorous critique was so influential that there has been rather little support, of late, for 'psychologism' in any shape or form. However, Frege's arguments against psychologism are, I suspect, less con-clusive, and at least some form of psychologism more plausible, than it is nowadays fashionable to suppose. A full-scale re-assessment of psychologism would require, however, a fuller and more sophisti-cated account of the nature of thought than I am able to offer; so what follows can be sketchy at best.

One can begin by distinguishing – the distinction is pretty crude, but nevertheless may be serviceable as a starting-point – three kinds of position:

(i) logic is descriptive of mental processes (it describes how we *do*, or perhaps how we *must*, think)
(ii) logic is prescriptive of mental processes (it prescribes how we *should* think)
(iii) logic has nothing to do with mental processes

One might call these *strong psychologism*, *weak psychologism* and *anti-psychologism*, respectively. Examples: Kant held something like (i); Peirce a version of (ii); Frege, (iii).

In what follows I shall present some arguments for a form of weak psychologism rather close to that adopted by Peirce (1930–58, 3, 161ff.): that logic is normative with respect to reasoning. I shall then go on to point out some advantages of weak psychologism as against anti-psychologism, on the one hand, and strong psychologism, on the other.

Logic is primarily concerned with *arguments*: how, then, can it relate to the mental processes which constitute *reasoning*? I'll tackle this question in two stages, offering, first, a Platonist answer, and then a nominalist version of that answer; the reason for this strategy is that the connection between logic and thought is thrown into sharper relief by the Platonist account, but I think that it is better, though less simply, explained in the nominalist version.

The Platonist answer: Logic is concerned with the (in)validity of arguments, with the connection between premises and conclusion; logical relations are relations, such as entailment or incompatibility, between propositions. Reasoning is a (certain sort of) mental process, such as, coming to believe that q on the strength of one's belief that p (inferring q from p), or, coming to recognise that if p were the case, then q would be the case; and to believe that p, or to wonder whether, or what if, p, is to stand in a certain relation to a proposition. Hence, logic is normative with respect to reasoning in this sense: that if, e.g., one infers q from p, then, if the argument from p to q is valid, the inference is *safe*, in that it is guaranteed not to result in one's holding a false belief on the basis of a true one.

The nominalist version: that s believes that p, or wonders whether, or what if, p, can be analysed, ultimately, in terms of a complicated relation between s and the sentence 'p'; and Platonist talk of belief in or entertainment of a proposition is to be regarded as a convenient shorthand for this complicated analysis. Logic is concerned with the validity of arguments, which, however, are to be conceived (ch 2 §1) as stretches of discourse/strings of sentences; and Platonist talk of logical relations between propositions is, again, to be regarded as a convenient shorthand (specifically, for quite complicated qualifications about what sentences are to be regarded as inter-substitutable, ch. 6 §4). Once again, it follows that logic is normative, in the sense explained above, with respect to reasoning.

The nominalist version of weak psychologism is, I think, preferable to the Platonist, for reasons which will emerge from a consideration of an argument of Frege's against psychologism.

Frege's objections to psychologism are quite complex, and I shall only consider the argument which is most relevant to the position I have defended.[1] This argument runs as follows. Logic has nothing to do with mental processes; for logic is objective and public, whereas the mental, according to Frege, is subjective and private. This is why Frege is so concerned to stress (see especially Frege 1918; and cf. p. 61n above) that the sense of a sentence is not an idea (a mental entity), but a thought (*Gedanke*: an abstract object, a proposition). Since ideas are mental, they are, Frege argues, essentially private; you can no more have my idea than you can have my headache. If the sense of a sentence were a private, mental entity, an idea in Frege's sense, there would be a mystery about the relation between one person's idea and another's:

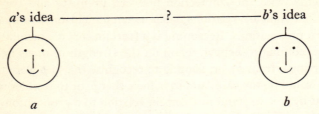

Propositions, however, are public; you and I can both 'grasp' the same proposition, and this is what makes it possible for there to be objective, public knowledge.[2]

This argument could be questioned on more than one score: e.g. why does Frege assume that everything mental is subjective and private? Is it relevant that the psychology with which he was familiar was introspectionist? But it is, anyway, pretty clear that the argument does *not* oblige one to divorce logic from mental processes in the way Frege supposes. For the postulation of propositions will only guarantee the publicity of knowledge if propositions are not only *objective*, but also *accessible*, if we can 'grasp' them; and this is just what the Platonist version of the argument for weak psychologism requires.

In fact, however, Frege has nothing very substantial to say to mitigate the mysteriousness of our supposed ability to 'grasp' his *Gedanken*:

---

[1] I shall ignore altogether Frege's arguments against psychologistic accounts of number, except to observe that, in view of his logicism, he would have taken these arguments to bear indirectly on psychologism with respect to logic.

[2] Popper's reasons for divorcing epistemology from psychology are very similar.

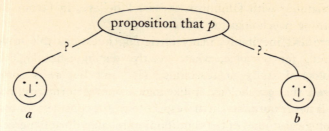

But this mystery *can* be dispelled by concentrating, not on ideas (which create a problem about objectivity), nor on propositions (which create a problem about accessibility), but on *sentences*; for the verbal behaviour of users of a language is both *objective and accessible*:

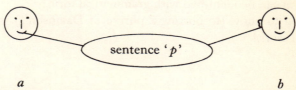

(Dewey saw this: see 1929 p. 196.) And this supplies a reason for preferring, as I urged, the nominalist version of the argument for weak psychologism.

Logic, I suggested, is prescriptive of reasoning in the limited sense that inference in accordance with logical principles is safe. (Of course, safety needn't be an overriding consideration; one might, quite rationally, prefer fruitful but risky to safe but relatively uninteresting procedures; cf. de Bono's championship, e.g. in 1969, of 'lateral thinking'.) It is important, however, that on the weak psychologistic view, though logic is applicable to reasoning, the validity of an argument consists in its truth-preserving character; it is in no sense a psychological property. Consequently, weak psychologism avoids the main difficulty of strong psychologism, the problem of accounting for logical error: for, since people surely do, from time to time, argue invalidly, how could the validity of an argument consist in its conformity to the way we think? This isn't to say that strong psychologism is flatly incompatible with logical mistakes; but that the two can be reconciled only by means of some explanation of such mistakes as the result of some irregularity or malfunction of our reasoning powers. (According to Kant, logical mistakes are the result of the unnoticed influence of sensibility on judgment.) Nevertheless, its much readier reconcilability with fallibilism speaks, I believe, in favour of weak over strong psychologism.

There are, inevitably, many intriguing questions this leaves un-answered: for instance, what, exactly, distinguishes logical from psychological study of reasoning? (It can't be, as is sometimes supposed, that psychology, unlike logic, is never normative, nor even that it is never normative with respect to truth; consider, for instance, psychological studies of the conditions of reliable/illusory perception.) What consequences would psychologism about logic have for questions about the relations between epistemology and psychology? What has logic to tell us about rationality? What would the consequences for psychologism be (in view, especially, of Chomsky's claim that certain grammatical structures are innate) of the conjecture that logical form can be identified with grammatical form?

It's good to know (to borrow a phrase of Davidson's) we shan't run out of work!

GLOSSARY

* by a term indicates that it has a separate entry. For terminology not explained here, the reader may find it useful to consult the *Dictionary of Philosophy* (Runes 1966), or the entry under *Logical terms, glossary of* in Edwards 1967.

Analytic/synthetic

An *analytically* true judgment is one such that the concept of its predicate is contained in its subject, or, such that its negation is contradictory (Kant); an analytically true proposition is either a logical truth*, or else reducible to a logical truth by means of definitions in purely logical terms (Frege: and see *logicism**); an analytically true statement is true solely in virtue of the meaning of its terms (logical positivists*). 'Analytic' is generally used equivalently with 'analytically true'; the negation* of an analytic truth is analytically false. 'Synthetic' is generally used equivalently with 'neither analytically true nor analytically false'. See discussion of Quine's critique of analyticity, pp. 172–4 and 236–7.

A priori/a posteriori

A proposition is *a priori* if it can be known independently of experience, otherwise *a posteriori* (an epistemological distinction, by contrast with the metaphysical *analytic/synthetic** distinction). See discussion of fallibilism with respect to logic, ch. 12 §2.

Atomic   An atomic wff* of sentence calculus is a sentence letter (e.g. 'p'), by contrast with a compound, or 'molecular' wff (e.g. '$p \lor q$'). An atomic wff of predicate calculus is an n-place* predicate letter followed by n variables* or singular terms. An atomic statement, analogously, is a statement which contains no statements as components.

Axiom   A wff* A is an *axiom* of L if A is laid down, its truth unquestioned, in the system L (trivially, all axioms of L are theorems* of L). An axiomatic presentation of logic uses axioms as well as rules of inference*. See ch. 2 §3.

Bivalence

Every wff* (sentence, statement, proposition) is either true or else false; see also *excluded middle**. See ch. 11 §3.

Characteristic matrix

A *matrix* is a set of truth-tables. A matrix M is *characteristic* for a system S iff all and only the wffs* uniformly designated* (*tautologous**) on M are theorems* of S. A system is *n*-valued if it has an *n*-valued characteristic matrix and no characteristic matrix with fewer than *n* values; *many-valued* if it is *n*-valued for $n > 2$, *infinitely many-valued* if *n-valued* for infinite *n*. See ch. 3 § 1 and ch. 11.

Combinatory logic

A branch of formal logic in which variables* are eliminated in favour of function symbols. See discussion of Quine's ontological criterion, ch. 4 §2.

Complete

(i) A formal system is *weakly complete* if every wff* which is logically true* in the system is a theorem* of the system; or *strongly complete* if, if any new independent* axiom* were added, it would be inconsistent*. Examples: sentence calculus is strongly complete; the usual modal systems are weakly complete; set theory, arithmetic are incomplete. See the discussion of completeness as a criterion for counting a system as a system of logic, ch. 1 § 2.

(ii) For *functional completeness*, see under *truth-functional**.

Conditional

The operators '$\rightarrow$' '$\dashv$', etc.

A wff* of the form '$A \rightarrow B$', (or statement of the form 'If A then B') is also called a conditional or hypothetical wff. 'A' is called the *antecedent*, 'B' the *consequent* of the conditional. A *subjunctive* conditional is one with a subjunctive verb (as 'If income tax were to be halved, we should all be delighted'); a *counterfactual* conditional is a subjunctive conditional which implies that its antecedent is false (as 'Had income tax been halved in the last budget, we should all have been delighted'). See ch. 3 §2; ch. 10 §6.

Conjunction

A wff* (statement) of the form 'A & B' ('A and B').

Consequence

A wff* (statement) B is a logical consequence of A iff there is a valid* argument from A to B.

Consistent

A formal system is *consistent* iff no wff* of the form 'A & $-A$' is a theorem*; or, iff not every wff of the system is a theorem; or (in the sense of Post, applicable to sentence calculus) iff no single sentence letter is a theorem.

Constant

A *constant* is a symbol employed always to stand for the same thing (as, singular terms such as 'a', 'b', ... etc., or operators such as '&', '$\lor$'...etc.) by contrast with variables* (as, 'x', 'y', 'z' ... etc.), which range over a domain* of objects.

Contradiction

Wff* of the form 'A & $-A$'; statement of the form 'A and not A'. *Principle of non-contradiction*: $-(A$ & $-A)$; or: no wff (sentence, statement, proposition) is both true and false.

Contradictory

The contradictory of a wff* (statement) A is a wff* (statement) which must be false if A is true and true if A is false.

Contrary

Wffs* (statements) A and B are contrary if they can't be both true but may be both false.

Decidable

A system is *decidable* if there is a mechanical procedure (a 'decision procedure') for determining, for any wff* of the system, whether or not that wff is a theorem*. Examples: sentence calculus is decidable; the full predicate calculus (including polyadic* as well as monadic* predicates) is not. *Truth-tables* supply the decision procedure for sentence calculus; a truth-table test determines whether a wff is a tautology*, and, by the soundness* and completeness* results, all and only tautologies* are theorems*.

Deduction

A sequence of wffs* (of L) is a deduction (in L) of B from $A_1 \ldots A_n$ iff it is a valid* argument (in L) with $A_1 \ldots A_n$ as premises and B as conclusion.

Deduction theorem

If, in a formal system L, if

$$A_1 \ldots A_n \vdash_L B, \quad \text{then} \quad \vdash_L A_1 \to (A_2 \to (\ldots(A_n \to B)))$$

then the deduction theorem holds for L.

Definite description

Expression of the form 'The so-and-so', written, formally, '$(\imath x)\, Fx$'. See ch. 5 §3.

Definition

An *explicit* definition defines one expression (the *definiendum*) by means of another (the *definiens*) which can replace the first wherever it occurs. A *contextual* definition supplies a replacement for certain longer expressions in which the *definiendum* occurs but not an equivalent for that expression itself. (If xs can be contextually defined in terms of ys, xs are sometimes said to be *logical constructions* out of ys, and 'x' to be an *incomplete symbol**.) A *recursive* definition gives a rule for eliminating the *definiendum* in a finite number of steps. A set of axioms* is sometimes said to give an *implicit* definition of its primitive* terms. See ch. 3 §1 for the interdefinability of connectives; ch. 4 §3 for Russell's contextual definition of definite descriptions; ch. 7 §5 for Tarski's recursive definition of satisfaction; pp. 103–4 for formal conditions on definitions.

Designated value

Truth-like value, such that all compound wffs* which take a designated value for all assignments to their components are *tautologies**.

Deviation

L_1 is a deviation of L_2 if it has a different set of theorems/valid inferences essentially involving vocabulary shared with L_2. A deviation of classical logic is a *deviant logic*. See chs. 9, 11, 12.

Disjunction

Wff* (statement) of the form '$A \lor B$'. *Disjunctive dilemma* is the form of argument: if $A \vdash C$, $B \vdash C$, then $A \lor B \vdash C$.

Dispositional

A dispositional predicate ascribes a tendency or 'habit'; in English many such predicates end in '-ble' (as: 'irritable', 'soluble'). Dispositional statements ('this sugar lump is soluble') are equivalent to *subjunctive conditionals** ('if this lump of sugar were to be placed in water, it would dissolve'). See ch. 10 §3.

Domain

(Universe of discourse) – range of the variables* of a theory. See ch. 4 §1.

Double negation, principle of

$A \equiv --A$. See discussion of Intuitionist logic, ch. 11 §4.

Enthymeme

Argument with a suppressed premise.

Epistemology
> Theory of knowledge.

Equivalence
> Two wffs (statements) are *logically equivalent* if they necessarily have the same truth-value. They are *materially equivalent* if they have the same truth-value.

Excluded middle
> $p \lor -p$ (cf. *bivalence**). See ch. 11 §3.

Extension
> L_1 is an extension of L_2 if it contains new vocabulary, over and above vocabulary shared with L_2, and has new theorems*/valid inferences* involving the new vocabulary essentially. An extension of classical logic is an *extended logic*. See chs. 9, 10, 12.

Extension/intension
> *Reference (extension)* versus *sense (intension)* of an expression. For a singular term, the extension is its referent, for a predicate, the set of things it is true of, for a sentence, its truth-value. Two expressions with the same extension are *co-extensive*. Related terminology: *Bedeutung* (= extension) versus *Sinn* (= intension) of an expression (Frege); *denotation* versus *connotation* (Mill); *extensional* versus *intensional** contexts. See discussion of Frege's theory of sense and reference, ch. 5 § 2; cf. Quine's distinction between theory of reference and theory of meaning, p. 119.

Extensional/intensional
> A context is *extensional* if co-referential expressions – singular terms with the same denotation, predicates with the same extension, or sentences with the same truth-value – are substitutable within it without changing the truth-value of the whole, '*salva veritate*', i.e. if *Leibniz' law* holds for it; otherwise, it is *intensional*. Examples: 'It is not the case that...' is extensional, 'Necessarily...' or '*s* believes that...' are intensional. Related terminology: *oblique* (= intensional) context (Frege); *referentially transparent* (= extensional) versus *referentially opaque* (= intensional) context, *purely referential occurrence* (i.e. occurrence in an extensional context) of a singular term (Quine); *truth-functional** connective (= extensional sentence-forming operator on sentences). See discussion of Davidson's programme, ch. 7 §5; cf. Quine's critique of the analytic/synthetic distinction, ch. 10 §1.

Finite/infinite
> A set is *infinite* if it has a proper subset such that its members can be put in one–one correspondence* with the members of that proper subset. A set is finite if it is not infinite. A set is *denumerably* infinite if it can be put in one–one correspondence with the natural numbers.

Formalism
> School in the philosophy of mathematics (Hilbert, Curry) characterised by the view that numbers may be identified with marks on paper. See discussion of the formalist approach to logic, p. 224.

Gödel's (incompleteness) theorem
> Arithmetic is incomplete; there is an arithmetical wff which is true but neither provable nor disprovable (Gödel 1931). See p. 139 for comments on the role of self-reference in Gödel's proof.

Goldbach's conjecture
> Hypothesis that every even number greater than 2 is the sum of two primes.

Implication

(i) '*p*' *materially implies* '*q*' ('*p* → *q*') if it is not the case that *p* and not *q*; '*p*' *strictly implies* '*q*' ('*p* ⥽ *q*') if it is impossible that *p* and not *q* (*p* ⥽ *q* ≡ *L*(*p* → *q*)). See ch. 3 §2 on '→' and 'if, then'; ch. 10 §6 on relations between material, strict, and relevant conditionals, and the intuitive idea of *entailment*.

(ii) 'Implies' is also used in another way, as '*s* implied that *p*' (where it is a relation between speakers and propositions, rather than, as above, between propositions). In this use it means something like '*s* hinted, though he didn't exactly say, that *p*'. Compare discussion of Grice's 'conversational implicature', p. 36.

Incomplete symbol

Contextually defined* expression. See ch. 5 §3, ch. 7 §7.

Independent

The axioms* of a formal system are independent of each other if none is a logical consequence* of the others.

Indexical

Expression the reference of which depends on the time, place or speaker, e.g. 'now', 'I', 'here'. See ch. 7 §6(c).

Induction

(i) An argument is *inductively strong* if the truth of its premises makes the truth of its conclusion probable. See ch. 2 §2.

(ii) *Mathematical induction*: a form of (deductively valid) argument used in mathematics, to show that all numbers have a property by showing that 0 has that property, and that if a number has that property, its successor also has it.

Inference

A person *infers q* from *p* if he comes to accept *q* on the strength of *p*, or comes to accept that if *p* were the case, then *q* would be the case. See ch. 12 § 3 on the relevance of logic to inference; and ch. 2 §3 on *rules of inference*.

Interpretation (of a formal system)

A set (the domain*, *D*) and a function assigning elements of *D* to singular terms*, *n*-tuples of elements of *D* to *n*-place predicates, and functions with *n*-tuples of elements of *D* as argument and elements of *D* as value to function symbols. See interpreted and uninterpreted systems, pp. 3ff; chs. 4 and 5; ch. 10 §4 on 'pure' versus 'depraved' semantics.

Intuitionism

School in the philosophy of mathematics (Brouwer, Heyting), characterised by the view that numbers are mental constructions; leads to a restricted arithmetic and to a non-standard logic. See ch. 11 §4.

Logical atomism

School of philosophy (early Wittgenstein, Russell) seeking logically to analyse the structure of the world into its most fundamental components (the 'logical atoms'). See discussion of the correspondence theory of truth, ch. 7 §2; of affinities with Davidson's programme, p. 124n.

Logical positivism

School of philosophy centred on the *Vienna Circle* (Schlick, Carnap); characterised by the *verification principle*, according to which the meaning of a statement is given by its verification-conditions, and unverifiable statements are meaningless. See discussion of Quine's attack on the *analytic/synthetic** distinction, ch. 10 § 1.

Logical truth

A wff* is logically true in L iff it is true in all interpretations of L. See ch. 2 §2.

Logicism

School in philosophy of mathematics, characterised by the thesis (Frege, Russell) that the truths of arithmetic are reducible to logic (or, *analytic** in the Fregean sense); numbers are reducible to sets. See discussion of the logicist programme and the question of the scope of logic, ch. 1 §2; of the effect of Russell's paradox, p. 137.

Mass term

Expression denoting a kind of stuff or material (as: 'water', 'snow', 'grass') rather than, like a 'singular term', an individual object (as: 'glass of water'). See ch. 7 §6(c).

Metalogic

Study of formal properties – e.g. consistency*, completeness*, decidability*, – of formal logical systems. See discussion of relations between philosophy of logic and metalogic, ch. 1 §1; of modal logic conceived of as a metalogical calculus, p. 182.

Metaphysics

Traditionally, 'the science of being as such'. I use 'metaphysical' primarily to emphasise the distinction between questions about the way things are (e.g. 'Is there one correct logic?') from epistemological questions, questions about our knowledge of how things are (e.g. 'Might the laws of logic be other than we take them to be?'). See ch. 12.

Modus ponens (MPP)

The rule of inference*, from 'A' and '$A \to B$' to infer 'B'. See discussion of the failure of MPP in relevance logic, ch. 10 §7.

Monadic/dyadic/polyadic

An open sentence/connective is monadic (1-place) if it has one, dyadic (2-place) if it has two, polyadic (many-place) if it has more than two argument(s); e.g. '...is red' is a monadic, '...is larger than —' a dyadic open sentence. See the discussion of the role of sequences of objects in Tarski's definitions of satisfaction/truth, pp. 105ff.

Monism/pluralism/instrumentalism

(i) In metaphysics*, monism is the thesis that there is only one ultimate kind of thing, dualism the thesis that there are two, pluralism the thesis that there are more than two.

(ii) Monism about logic is the thesis that there is only one correct logical system, pluralism the thesis that there is more than one correct logical system, instrumentalism the thesis that the notion of 'correctness' doesn't apply to logical systems. See ch. 12 §1.

Natural deduction

A natural deduction presentation of a logical system relies on rules of inference* rather than axioms*. See ch. 2 §3.

Necessary/sufficient conditions

A is a *necessary condition* for B, if B can't be the case unless A is; A is a *sufficient condition* for B, if, if A is the case, B is.

Negation

The negation of 'A' is '$-A$'.

Nominalism/Platonism/ conceptualism

The *nominalist* denies, the *Platonist* asserts, that there are *real universals* (e.g. redness, squareness etc.); the *conceptualist* claims that universals are mental entities. Related terminology: reism, materialism, pansomatism (forms of nominalism) versus realism (form of Platonism). See the discussion of second-order quantifiers*, ch. 4 §3; of Davidson's extensionalism* and Kotarbiński's nominalism, p. 124n; of the status of possible worlds, ch. 10 §4.

Object language/metalanguage

In talking about systems, the system being talked about is known as the *object language*, the system being used to talk about it, the *metalanguage*. (N.B. this is a relative rather than an absolute distinction; e.g. one might use French (the metalanguage) to talk about English (the object language) or English to talk about French.) Thus, metalogic*, the study of logical systems. See discussion of Tarski's use of the distinction in the definition of truth, ch. 7 §6; cf. its relevance to the semantic paradoxes*, ch. 8 §2.

One–one correspondence

Two sets* x and y are in one–one correspondence if there is a *one–one relation**, R, by which each member of x is related to exactly one member of y, and each member of y to exactly one member of x.

Ontology

Part of metaphysics concerned with the question, what kinds of thing exist. See ch. 4 §2 for discussion of relations between logic and ontology.

Oratio obliqua

Indirect (reported) speech, as: 's said that p'. See ch. 7 §6(c).

Paradoxes

(i) (Also known as 'antinomies'.) Contradictions derivable in semantics* and set* theory; they include the *Liar* ('This sentence is false') and *Russell's paradox* ('The set of all sets which are not members of themselves is a member of itself iff it is not a member of itself'). See ch. 8.

(ii) The 'paradoxes' of material and strict implication* are theorems* of classical, 2-valued and modal logic ('$p \to (-p \to q)$', '$L-p \to (p \dashv 3\ q)$)' which seem rather counterintuitive with '$\to$' or '$\dashv 3$' when read 'if...'. I use scare quotes because these 'paradoxes' involve no contradiction. See ch. 10.

Peano postulates

Set of axioms for the theory of natural numbers:

1. 0 is a number.
2. The successor of any number is a number.
3. No two numbers have the same successor.
4. 0 is not the successor of any number.
5. If 0 has a property, and, if any number has that property, then the successor of that number has that property, then all numbers have that property. (Induction* axiom.)

Pragmatism

American school of philosophy initiated by Peirce and James (other pragmatists include Dewey and F. C. S. Schiller); characterised by the 'pragmatic maxim', according to which the meaning of a concept is to be sought in the empirical or practical consequences (Kant – *pragmatische* – empirically conditioned; Greek *praxis* – action) of its application. See discussion of pragmatist theory of truth, ch. 7 §4.

Presupposition

'A' presupposes 'B' if 'A' is neither true nor false unless 'B' is true. See ch. 5 §3.

Primitive
> Undefined term (see definition*).

Proof A proof (in L) of A is a deduction* (in L) of A from no premises except the axioms* (of L), if any. A wff* A is provable (in L) if there is a proof (in L) of A; it is disprovable if its negation* is provable.

Propositional attitude
> Verbs such as 'knows', 'believes', 'hopes' etc., which take the construction 's Φs that p', are known as verbs of propositional attitude (Russell).

Quantifier
> Expression ('$(\exists\ldots)$' – the *existential* quantifier – or '$(\ldots)$' – the *universal* quantifier) binding variables*. See ch. 4.

Quantum mechanics
> A physical theory concerned with atomic structure, emission and absorption of light by matter. See discussion of 'quantum logic', ch. 11 §2.

Refute Show a thesis (or theory etc.) to be false. N.B. to deny that p is *not* to refute 'p'.

Relation
> A 2- or more-place predicate is called a *relation* symbol; its extension* – the set* of ordered pairs (triples … n-tuples) of which it holds – is known as a *relation-in-extension*. A relation R is *transitive* if, if (x) (y) (z) Rxy and Ryz, then Rxz; *symmetric* if (x) (y), if Rxy then Ryx; *reflexive* if (x) Rxx.

Salva veritate
> Without change of truth-value.

Satisfaction
> (i) In Tarski's definition of truth (ch. 7 §5): relation between open sentences and sequences* of objects (as e.g. $\langle$Edinburgh, London, …$\rangle$ satisfies 'x is north of y').
> (ii) In imperative logic (p. 85): analogue of truth-value, assigned to imperative sentences (as e.g. 'Shut the door!' is satisfied iff the door is shut).

Sequence
> Ordered pair, triple … n-tuple of objects (i.e. like a set*, except that the order matters; while $\{a, b\} = \{b, a\}$, $\langle a, b \rangle \neq \langle b, a \rangle$). See the role of sequences of objects in Tarski's definition of satisfaction*, ch. 7 §5.

Set 'any collection into a whole…of definite, distinguishable objects' (Cantor); however, set-theory includes the null set, which has no members. See Russell's paradox*, p. 136. '$\{a, b, c\}$' means 'the set consisting of a, b, c'; '$\{x\,|\,Fx\}$' means 'the set of things which are F'; '$a \in \{x\,|\,Fx\}$' means 'a is a member of the set of things which are F'. (In Gödel–von Neumann–Bernays set-theory a distinction is drawn between sets, which can both have members and themselves be members, and classes, which have members but can't themselves be members.)

Skolem–Löwenheim theorem
> Every theory that has a model (is consistent*) has a denumerable (see entry under finite/infinite*) model. See p. 51 for its bearing on substitutional quantification.

Sound
> (i) An *argument* is *sound* if (i) it is valid* and (ii) its premises, and hence, its conclusion, are true.
> (ii) A *logical system* is *sound* iff all its theorems are logically true*; soundness is the converse of completeness*.

Syntax/semantics/pragmatics

Syntax is the study of formal relations between expressions; thus, the vocabulary, formation rules and axioms*/rules of inference* of a system are called the syntax of the system. *Semantics* is the study of relations between linguistic expressions and the non-linguistic objects to which they apply; thus, the interpretation* of a system is called the semantics of the system. (Roughly, the distinction between syntax and semantics could be compared to that between grammar and meaning.) *Pragmatics* is the study of relations between expressions and the use or users of these expressions. See syntactic and semantic accounts of validity, ch. 2 §2; syntactic, semantic and pragmatic approaches to propositions etc., ch. 6 §1; pragmatic relations of conversational implicature, p. 36; and presupposition*, pp. 67ff.

Tautology

Technical sense: a wff* is a *tautology* if it takes the value 'true' for all assignments of truth-values to its atomic* components (extended, in the case of many-valued logics, to: if it takes a designated* value for all assignments to its atomic components). The soundness* proof for sentence calculus shows that only tautologies* are theorems*; the completeness* proof that all tautologies are theorems.

Non-technical sense: a statement is *tautologous* if it says the same thing twice, and so is trivially true. See the discussion of the pre-systematic idea corresponding to the technical notion of logical truth*, pp. 14–15.

Theorem

A wff* *A* is a theorem of L iff *A* follows from the axioms* of L, if any, by the rules of inference* of L. See ch. 2 §2, ch. 12 §1.

Theory of types

Russell's formal solution to the paradoxes*; the *simple theory of types* avoids the set*-theoretical, the *ramified theory of types* avoids the semantic* paradoxes. See ch. 8 §2.

Truth-functional

A *connective* (sentence-forming operator on sentences) is *truth-functional* if the truth-value of a compound of which it is the main connective depends solely upon the truth-values of its components; in which case a *truth-table* can be given for that connective. A *logical system* is *truth-functional* if all its constants are truth-functional. An *n*-valued system is *functionally complete* – has an *adequate set of connectives* – if it has enough connectives to express all *n*-valued truth-functions. Examples: the connectives of classical and finitely many-valued sentence calculi are truth-functional; modal operators and epistemic operators are not. See discussion of logicians' preference for truth-functional connectives, ch. 3 §2; of many-valued and non-truth-functional calculi, ch. 11.

(T) schema

Tarski's material adequacy condition requires that any acceptable definition of truth have as consequence all instances of the (T) schema:

$$S \text{ is true iff } p$$

where '*S*' names the sentence on the right-hand side. See ch. 7 §§5 and 6.

Valid   A formal argument is:

syntactically valid-in-L iff its conclusion follows from its premises and the axioms* of L, if any, by means of the rules of inference* of L,
semantically valid-in-L iff its conclusion is true in all interpretations of L in which all its premises are true.

An informal argument is:

valid iff its premises could not be true and its conclusion false. See ch. 2 §2; ch. 10 §6.

Variable Expression, as: '*x*', '*y*' ... (in first-order predicate calculus), *ranging over* a *domain** of objects; by contrast with constants*, as: '*a*', '*b*' ..., each of which denotes a specific element of the domain. An expression which can be substituted for a variable is called a *substituend* for the variable; the elements over which it ranges, its *values*. A *bound* variable is one within, a *free* variable one without, the scope of a quantifier*. See ch. 4.

Verisimilitude

Nearness to the truth (Popper); see ch. 7 §6(b).

Vicious circle principle

Poincaré and Russell diagnose the paradoxes* as resulting from violations of the vicious circle principle (V.C.P.): 'whatever involves all of a collection cannot be a member of that collection'. See ch. 8 § 2.

Wff Well-formed formula, i.e. string of symbols of a formal language correctly constructed with respect to its *formation rules*. A *formula* is any string of symbols of a formal language.

ADVICE ON READING

I have given full references in the text, to enable the reader to locate relevant literature on specific issues. The point of the present section is to give those new to the subject some suggestions about where to begin reading.

I have taken for granted an acquaintance with *elementary formal logic*, as presented in, say, Lemmon 1965, or Quine 1950, which is somewhat harder but a good deal richer. A compact presentation of *metalogical* results can be found in Hunter 1971 or Boolos and Jeffrey 1974. For the *history of logic*, consult Kneale and Kneale 1962.

Although there are several '*introductions*' *to the philosophy of logic*, they are generally harder, and require more sophistication in the reader, than their titles suggest: Strawson's *Introduction to Logical Theory* (1952) presents a sustained critique of formal logic from the point of view of ordinary language philosophy, and should be read in conjunction with Quine's review (1953c); Quine's *Philosophy of Logic* (1970) is, though short, rich and wide-ranging, but it takes for granted a good deal of distinctively 'Quinean' philosophy, and is more suitable for the advanced than the beginning student; Putnam's *Philosophy of Logic* (1971) is devoted to a single issue, the need for abstract entities in logic.

There are several valuable *collections* of papers. Van Heijenhoort 1967a contains the classic papers from Frege's initiation of modern logic with the *Begriffsschrift* (1879) to Gödel's incompleteness theorem (1931). Other useful collections of more recent philosophical papers include Copi and Gould 1967, Strawson 1967, Iseminger 1968.

If you want to find reading on a specific subject, but don't know where to begin looking, you may find the articles on logic and philosophy of logic in the *Encyclopaedia of Philosophy* (Edwards 1967) useful; they are generally informative, and have helpful bibliographies. The reviews in the *Journal of Symbolic Logic* of (philosophical as well as formal) articles from other journals may also be found valuable. I recommend, in general, that you begin with primary rather than secondary materials – that you read Frege's own papers before commentators on Frege, for example; you will find that secondary material is generally much more useful if you've already some acquaintance with the work on which it's based.

Some suggestions about where to begin your reading on topics discussed in the present book:

Chapter

1 On the aims of formalism: Frege 1882a, b.
On the scope of logic: Kneale 1956; Quine 1970 ch. 5.

2 On induction and deduction: Skyrms 1966 ch. 1.
On *logica utens* and *logica docens*: Peirce, 'Why study logic?' in 1930–58 vol. 2, especially 2.185ff.
On validity and logical form: Cargile 1970; Davidson 1970; Harman 1970.

3 On '*tonk*': Prior 1960, 1964; Belnap 1961; Stevenson 1961.
On 'if' and '→': Faris 1962.

4 On the development of quantifiers: Frege 1891.
On substitutional versus objectual interpretations: Belnap and Dunn 1968.
On non-standard treatments of quantifiers: Montague 1973.

5 Frege 1892a; Russell 1905; Strawson 1950; Quine, 'On what there is' in 1953a; Kripke 1972.

6 Frege 1918 (and cf. Popper, 'Epistemology without a knowing subject' in 1972); Quine 1970 ch. 1; Putnam 1971; Lemmon 1966.

7 Definitions versus criteria: Rescher 1973 chs. 1 and 2.
Correspondence theories: Russell 1918; Austin 1950; Prior in Edwards 1967.
Coherence theories: Bradley 1914; Hempel 1935; Rescher 1973.
Pragmatist theories: Peirce 1877; James 1907; Dewey 1901; Rescher 1977 ch. 4.
The semantic theory: Tarski 1944 (and cf. Quine 1970 ch. 3, Rogers 1963); Popper, 'Truth, rationality and the growth of scientific knowledge' (in 1963); 'Philosophical comments on Tarski's theory of truth' (in 1972); Davidson 1967.
The redundancy theory: Ramsey 1927; Prior 1971; Grover *et al.* 1975.

8 Russell 1908a; Mackie 1973 ch. 7; Kripke 1975.

9 On temporal logic: Quine 1960a §36; Prior 1957, 1967; Lacey 1971; Geach 1965.
On fuzzy logic: Zadeh 1975; Gaines 1976.

10 On necessary truth: Quine 1951.
Formal presentation of modal logics: Hughes and Cresswell 1968.
Philosophical issues: Quine 1953b; Linsky 1971; Plantinga 1974.

11 Rescher 1969; Haack 1974.

12 On metaphysical questions: van Heijenhoort 1967b; Rescher 1977 chs. 13, 14.
On epistemological questions: Quine 1951; Putnam 1969; Popper 1970.
On psychologism: Mill 1843 book II; Frege (on mathematics) 1884 especially § 26; (on logic) 1918; Peirce 1930–58, 3.161ff.; Russell 1938.

BIBLIOGRAPHY

* by an entry indicates to which edition page numbers in the text refer.

Ackerman, R. 1967. *Introduction to Many-Valued Logics* (Routledge and Kegan Paul)

Alston, W. P. 1958. Ontological commitments, *Philosophical Studies* 9; and in Iseminger 1968

Altham, J. E. J. 1971. *The Logic of Plurality* (Methuen)

Anderson, A. R. 1970. St Paul's epistle to Titus, in *The Paradox of the Liar*, ed. Martin (Yale U.P.)

Anderson, A. R. and Belnap, N. D., Jr 1962a. Tautological entailments, *Philosophical Studies* 13

– 1962b. The pure calculus of entailment, *Journal of Symbolic Logic*, 27 (1962a and b are partly reprinted in Iseminger 1968)

– 1975. *Entailment*, vol. 1 (Princeton U.P.)

Anscombe, G. E. M. 1957. *Analysis* puzzle, 10, *Analysis* 17

– 1959. *An Introduction to Wittgenstein's Tractatus* (Hutchinson)

Austin, J. L. 1950. Truth, *Proceedings of the Aristotelian Society, Supplement* 24; and in Urmson and Warnock (eds.) 1961; and Pitcher 1964

Ayer, A. J. 1958. *The Problem of Knowledge* (Macmillan)

Baker, A. J. 1967. 'If' and '⊃', *Mind* 76

Bar-Hillel, Y. 1957. New light on the Liar, *Analysis* 18

Barker, S. F. 1965. Must every inference be either inductive or deductive?, in *Philosophy in America*, ed. Black (Allen and Unwin)

Belnap, N. D., Jr 1961. Tonk, plonk and plink, *Analysis* 22; and in Strawson 1967

– 1974. Grammatical Propaedeutic, in *The Logical Enterprise*, ed. Anderson, Marcus and Martin (Yale U.P.); and in Anderson and Belnap 1975

Belnap, N. D., Jr and Dunn, M. 1968. The substitution interpretation of the quantifiers, *Noûs* 2

Belnap, N. D., Jr and Grover, D. L. 1973. Quantifying in and out of quotes, in *Truth, Syntax and Modality*, ed. Leblanc (North Holland)

Bennett, J. 1954. Meaning and implication, *Mind* 63

Bergmann, G. 1960. The philosophical significance of modal logic, *Mind* 69

Binkley, R. 1970. Quantifying, quotation, and a paradox, *Noûs* 4

Birkhoff, G. and van Neumann, J. 1936. The logic of quantum mechanics, *Annals of Mathematics* 37

Black, M. 1937. 'Vagueness', *Philosophy of Science* 4; and in *Language and Philosophy* (Cornell U.P. 1949)
– 1948. The semantic definition of truth, *Analysis* 8; and in MacDonald 1954.*
Blanché, R. 1962. *Axiomatics*, trans. Keene (Routledge and Kegan Paul)
Blanshard, B. 1939. *The Nature of Thought* (Allen and Unwin)
Blumberg, A. 1967. Logic, modern, in Edwards 1967
Bochvar, D. A. 1939. On a three-valued logical calculus and its application to the analysis of contradictories, *Matematiceskij sbornik* 4
de Bono, E. 1969. *The Mechanism of Mind* (Cape; Pelican 1971)
Boole, G. 1854. *An Investigation of the Laws of Thought* (Dover 1951)
Boolos, G. S. and Jeffrey, R. C. 1974. *Computability and Logic* (Cambridge U.P.)
Bradley, F. H. 1914. *Essays on Truth and Reality* (Oxford U.P.)
Brandom, R. 1976. Truth and assertibility, *Journal of Philosophy* 73
Brouwer, L. E. J. 1952. Historical background, principles and methods of Intuitionism, *South African Journal of Science* 49
Burge, T. 1973. Reference and proper names, *Journal of Philosophy* 70
Bynum, T. Ward (ed.) 1972. *Conceptual Notation* (Oxford U.P.)
Cargile, J. 1970. Davidson's notion of logical form, *Inquiry* 13
– 1972. On the interpretation of T, S4 and S5, *Philosophia* 2
Carnap, R. 1931. The logicist foundations of mathematics, in *Philosophy of Mathematics*, ed. Putnam and Benacerraf (Blackwell 1964)
– 1934. *Logische Syntax der Sprache* (Julius Springer); English translation, *The Logical Syntax of Language* (Kegan Paul 1937)
– 1942. *Introduction to Semantics and Formalisation of Logic* (Harvard U.P.)
– 1947. *Meaning and Necessity* (Chicago U.P.)
– 1950. *The Logical Foundations of Probability* (Chicago U.P.)
Cartwright, R. 1954. Ontology and the theory of meaning, *Philosophy of Science* 4
– 1960. Negative existentials, *Journal of Philosophy* 56; and in Caton 1963
– 1962. Propositions, in *Analytical Philosophy*, vol. 1, ed. Butler (Blackwell)
Caton, C. (ed.) 1963. *Philosophy and Ordinary Language* (Illinois U.P.)
Chihara, C. 1972. Russell's theory of types, in *Bertrand Russell*, ed. Pears (Anchor)
– 1973. *Ontology and the Vicious-Circle Principle* (Cornell U.P.)
Chisholm, R. 1967. Identity through possible worlds, *Noûs* 1
Chomsky, N. 1957. *Syntactic Structures* (Mouton)
Church, A. 1943. Review of Quine, W. V. O., 1943, *Journal of Symbolic Logic* 8
Clark, M. 1971. Ifs and hooks, *Analysis* 30
Cohen, L. J. 1962. *The Diversity of Meaning* (Methuen)
Copi, I. 1971. *The Theory of Logical Types* (Routledge and Kegan Paul)
Copi, I. and Gould, J. A. (eds.) 1967. *Contemporary Readings in Logical Theory* (Macmillan)
Curry, H. 1951. *Outline of a Formalist Philosophy of Mathematics* (North Holland)
Dauer, F. 1974. In defence of the coherence theory of truth, *Journal of Philosophy* 71
Davidson, D. 1967. Truth and meaning, *Synthese* 17; and in Davis, Hockney and Wilson 1969
– 1968a. The logical form of action sentences, in *The Logic of Decision and Action*, ed. Rescher (Pittsburgh U.P.)
– 1968b. On saying that, *Synthese* 19
– 1970. Action and reaction, *Inquiry* 13
– 1973. In defense of convention T, in *Truth, Syntax and Modality*, ed. Leblanc (North Holland)

‒ 1974. Belief and the basis of meaning, *Synthese* 27

Davidson, D. and Hintikka, J. (eds.). 1969. *Words and Objections: Essays on the Work of W. V. Quine* (Reidel)

Davis, J. W., Hockney, D. J. and Wilson, W. K. (eds.) 1969. *Philosophical Logic* (Reidel)

Derrida, J. 1973. *Speech and Phenomena*, ed. Garver (Northwestern U.P.)

Destouches-Février, P. 1951. *La structure des théories physiques* (Presses Universitaires de France)

Dewey, J. 1901. A short catechism concerning truth, in *The Influence of Darwin on Philosophy* (Henry Holt)

‒ 1929. *Experience and Nature* (Open Court; and Dover 1958*)

‒ 1938. *Logic, the Theory of Inquiry* (Henry Holt)

Donnellan, K. 1966. Reference and definite descriptions, *Philosophical Review* 75; reprinted in Steinberg and Jakobovits 1971

Duhem, P. 1904. *La théorie physique: son objet, sa structure*; page references to *The Aim and Structure of Physical Theory*, trans. Wiener from the 2nd edition (1914) (Atheneum 1962)

Dummett, M. A. E. 1959. Truth, *Proceedings of the Aristotelian Society* 59; and in Pitcher 1964

‒ 1973. *Frege, Philosophy of Language* (Duckworth)

Duncan-Jones, A. E. 1935. Is strict implication the same as entailment? *Analysis* 2

Edwards, P. (ed.) 1967. *Encyclopaedia of Philosophy* (Collier-Macmillan)

Faris, J. A. 1962. *Truth-Functional Logic* (Routledge and Kegan Paul); appendix on 'if' reprinted in Iseminger 1968

Feigl, H. and Sellars, W. 1949. *Readings in Philosophical Analysis* (Appleton-Century-Crofts)

Feyerabend, P. K. 1963. How to be a good empiricist, in *Delaware Seminar in the Philosophy of Science*, vol. 2 (Interscience); and in Nidditch 1968

Field, H. 1972. Tarski's theory of truth, *Journal of Philosophy* 69

Fitch, F. 1949. The Problem of the Morning Star and the Evening Star, *Philosophy of Science* 17; and in Copi and Gould 1967

Fitting, M. C. 1969. *Intuitionistic Logic, Model Theory and Forcing* (North Holland)

Flew, A. G. N. (ed.) 1956. *Essays in Conceptual Analysis* (Macmillan)

‒ 1975. *Thinking About Thinking* (Fontana)

Føllesdal, D. 1965. Quantification into causal contexts, *Boston Studies in the Philosophy of Science*, vol. 2, ed. Cohen and Wartofsky (Reidel); and in Linsky 1971

‒ 1969. Quine on modality, in Davidson and Hintikka 1969

van Frassen, B. C. 1966. Singular terms, truth-value gaps, and free logic, *Journal of Philosophy* 63

‒ 1968. Presupposition, implication and self-reference, *Journal of Philosophy* 65

‒ 1969. Presuppositions, supervaluations and free logic, in *The Logical Way of Doing Things*, ed. Lambert (Yale U.P.)

Frege, G. 1879. *Begriffsschrift* (Nebert); English translations in Heijenhoort 1967a, and in Bynum 1972

‒ 1882a. Über den wissenschaftliche Berechtigung einer Begriffsschrift (On the scientific justification of a conceptual notation), *Zeitschrift für Philosophie und philosophische Kritik*, 81; English translations by Bartlett, *Mind* 73, 1964; and Bynum 1972

1882b. Über den Zweck der Begriffsschrift (On the aims of the conceptual notation), *Sitzungsberichte der Jenaischen Gesellschaft für Medizin und*

Naturwissenschaft 16, 1882–3; English translations by Dudman, *Australasian Journal of Philosophy* 46, 1968; and Bynum 1972

– 1884. *Die Grundlagen der Arithmetik* (Koebner 1884); English translation by Austin, *The Foundations of Arithmetic* (Blackwell 1950)

– 1891. Function and Concept, *Jenaische Gesellschaft für Medizin und Naturwissenschaft*, 1891; trans. Geach in Geach and Black 1952

– 1892a. Über Sinn und Bedeutung, *Zeitschrift für Philosophie und philosophische Kritik*, 100; trans. Feigl in Feigl and Sellars 1949; and reprinted in Copi and Gould 1967; trans. Black in Geach and Black 1952

– 1892b. Concept and object, *Vierteljahrsschrift für Wissenschaftliche Philosophie* 16; trans. Geach in Geach and Black 1952

– 1893. *Grundgesetze der Arithmetik* 1 (H. Pole); partial English translation in Furth *The Basic Laws of Arithmetic* (California U.P. 1964)

– 1903. *Grundgesetze der Arithmetik* 2 (H. Pole); partial English translation in Geach and Black 1952; the Geach and Black selection includes Frege's response to Russell's paradox

– 1918. The thought: a logical inquiry, *Beitrage zur Philosophie der Deutschen Idealismus*; trans. Quinton and Quinton *Mind* 65, 1956; reprinted in Klemke 1968*

Gaines, B. 1976. Foundations of fuzzy reasoning, *International Journal of Man-Machine Studies* 8

Garver, N. 1970. The range of truth and falsity, in *The Paradox of the Liar*, ed. Martin (Yale U.P.)

Geach, P. T. 1956. On Frege's way out, *Mind* 65

– 1962. *Reference and Generality* (Cornell U.P.)

– 1965. Some problems about time, *Proceedings of the British Academy* 51

– 1967. Intentional identity, *Journal of Philosophy* 64

– 1976. *Reason and Argument* (Blackwell)

Geach, P. T. and Black, M. 1952. *Translations from the Philosophical Writings of Gottlob Frege* (Blackwell)

Gentzen, G. 1934. Untersuchungen über das logische Schliessen, *Mathematische Zeitschrift* 39; English translation by Szabo, *American Philosophical Quarterly* 1, 1964 and 2, 1965

Gochet, P. 1972. *Esquisse d'une théorie nominaliste de la proposition* (Librairie Armand Colin)

Goodman, N. 1955. *Fact, Fiction and Forecast* (Harvard U.P.)

– 1970. Seven strictures on similarity, in *Experience and Theory*, ed. Foster and Swanson (Massachussets U.P.)

Grice, P. and Strawson, P. F. 1956. In defense of a dogma, *Philosophical Review* 65

Grover, D. L. 1972. Propositional quantifiers, *Journal of Philosophical Logic* 1

– 1973. Propositional quantification and quotation contexts, in *Truth, Syntax and Modality*, ed. Leblanc (North Holland)

Grover, D. L., Camp, J. and Belnap, N. D., Jr 1975. A prosentential theory of truth, *Philosophical Studies* 27

Haack, R. J. 1971. On Davidson's paratactic theory of oblique contexts, *Noûs* 5

Haack, R. J. and S. 1970. Token sentences, translation, and truth-value, *Mind* 79

Haack, S. 1974. *Deviant Logic* (Cambridge U.P.)

– 1975. Mentioning expressions, *Logique et Analyse* 67–8

– 1976a. The justification of deduction, *Mind* 85

– 1976b. Critical Notice of Woods, J., 1974, *Canadian Journal of Philosophy* 6

- 1976c. The pragmatist theory of truth, *British Journal for the Philosophy of Science* 27
- 1976d. Is it true what they say about Tarski?, *Philosophy* 51
- 1977a. Lewis's ontological slum, *Review of Metaphysics* 30
- 1977b. Two fallibilists in search of the truth, *Proceedings of the Aristotelian Society* Supplement 51
- 1977c. Analyticity and logical truth in *The Roots of Reference*, *Theoria* 43
- 1977d. Pragmatism and ontology: Peirce and James, *Revue Internationale de Philosophie* 121–2

Hacking, I. M. 1979. What is logic?, *Journal of Philosophy* 76
Halldén, S. 1949. *The Logic of Nonsense* (Uppsala Universitets Arsskrift)
Harman, G. 1970. Deep structure as logical form, *Synthese* 21
- 1971. Substitutional quantification and quotation, *Noûs* 5
- 1975. Moral relativism defended, *Philosophical Review* 84
Harris, J. H. 1974. Popper's definitions of verisimilitude, *British Journal for the Philosophy of Science* 25
Heidelberger, H. 1968. The indispensability of truth, *American Philosophical Quarterly* 5
van Heijenhoort, J. (ed.) 1967a. *From Frege to Gödel* (Harvard U.P.)
- 1967b. Logic as calculus and logic as language, *Synthese* 17
Hempel, C. G. 1935. On the logical positivists' theory of truth, *Analysis* 2
Herzberger, H. 1970. Paradoxes of grounding in semantics, *Journal of Philosophy* 17
Heyting, A. 1966. *Intuitionism* (North Holland)
Hintikka, J. 1962. *Knowledge and Belief* (Cornell U.P.)
- 1969. *Models for Modalities* (Reidel)
- 1973. *Logic, Language Games and Information* (Oxford U.P.)
- 1976. Quantifiers in logic and quantifiers in natural language, in Körner 1976
Hughes, G. and Cresswell, M. 1968. *Introduction to Modal Logic* (Methuen)
Hunter, G. 1971. *Metalogic* (Macmillan)
Iseminger, G. (ed.) 1968. *Logic and Philosophy* (Appleton-Century-Crofts)
James, W. 1907. *Pragmatism* (Longman's, Green)
- 1909. *The Meaning of Truth* (Longman's, Green; and Michigan U.P. 1970*)
Jaśkowski, S. 1934. On the rules of supposition in formal logic, *Studia Logica* 1
Johannson, I. 1936. Der Mininmalkalkül, ein reduzierter intuitionistischer Formalismus, *Compositio Mathematica* 4
Johnson, W. E. 1921. *Logic* (Cambridge U.P.)
Kanger, S. 1957a. The Morning Star paradox, *Theoria* 23
- 1957b. A note on quantification and modalities, *Theoria* 23
Kant, I. 1800. *Logik*; trans. Abbott *Kant's Introduction to Logic* (Longman's, Green 1885*)
Kleene, S. C. 1952. *Introduction to Metamathematics* (North Holland)
Klemke, E. D. (ed.) 1968. *Essays on Frege* (Illinois U.P.)
Kneale, W. C. 1945–6. Truths of logic, *Proceedings of the Aristotelian Society* 46
- 1956. The province of logic, in *Contemporary British Philosophy*, ed. Lewis 3rd Series (Allen and Unwin); page references to 2nd, 1961 edition
- 1962a. Universality and necessity, *British Journal for the Philosophy of Science* 12
- 1962b. Modality, *de dicto* and *de re*, in *Logic, Methodology and Philosophy of Science: Proceedings of the 1960 International Congress* (Stanford U.P.)
- 1971. Russell's paradox and some others, *British Journal for the Philosophy of Science* 22
Kneale, W. C. and Kneale, M. 1962. *The Development of Logic* (Oxford U.P.)

Körner, S. 1966. *Experience and Theory* (Routledge and Kegan Paul)
– (ed.) 1976. *Philosophy of Logic* (Blackwell)
Kotarbiński, T. 1955. The fundamental ideas of pansomatism, *Mind* 64
Kripke, S. 1963. Semantical considerations on modal logic, *Acta Philosophica Fennica* 16; and in Linsky 1971.
– 1972. Naming and necessity, in *Semantics of Natural Language*, ed. Harman and Davidson (Reidel)
– 1975. Outline of a theory of truth, *Journal of Philosophy* 72
– 1976. Is there a problem about substitutional quantification?, in *Truth and Meaning*, ed. Evans and McDowell (Oxford U.P.)
Lacey, H. 1971. Quine on the logic and ontology of time, *Australasian Journal of Philosophy* 49
Lakatos, I. 1963–4. Proofs and refutations, *British Journal for the Philosophy of Science* 14; and edited by Worrall and Zahar (Cambridge U.P. 1976)
Lemmon, E. J. 1959. Is there only one correct system of modal logic?, *Proceedings of the Aristotelian Society* Supplement 23
– 1965. *Beginning Logic* (Nelson)
– 1966. Sentences, statements and propositions, in *British Analytical Philosophy*, ed. Williams and Montefiore (Routledge and Kegan Paul)
Lewis, C. I. 1912. Implication and the algebra of logic, *Mind* 21
– 1918. *A Survey of Symbolic Logic* (California U.P.)
Lewis, D. K. 1968. Counterpart theory and quantified modal logic, *Journal of Philosophy* 65
– 1973. *Counterfactuals* (Blackwell)
Lewy, C. 1946. How are the calculuses of logic and mathematics applicable to reality?, *Proceedings of the Aristotelian Society* Supplement 20
Linsky, L. (ed.) 1952. *Semantics and the Philosophy of Language* (Illinois U.P.)
– (ed.) 1971. *Reference and Modality* (Oxford U.P.)
– 1972. Two concepts of quantification, *Noûs* 6
Łukasiewicz, J. 1920. On 3-valued logic, in McCall, *Polish Logic* (Oxford U.P. 1967)
– 1930. Many-valued systems of propositional logic, in McCall, *Polish Logic* (Oxford U.P. 1967)
McCall, S. 1970. A non-classical theory of truth, with an application to Intuitionism, *American Philosophical Quarterly* 7
MacColl, H. 1880ff. Symbolic reasoning, 1–8, *Mind* 5, new series 6, 9, 11, 12, 14 (two papers), 15
– 1906. *Symbolic Logic and Its Applications* (Longman's, Green)
MacDonald, M. (ed.) 1954. *Philosophy and Analysis* (Blackwell)
McDowell, J. 1977. On the sense and reference of a proper name, *Mind* 86
Mackie, J. L. 1973. *Truth, Probability and Paradox* (Oxford U.P.)
McKinsey, J. C. C. and Tarski, A. 1948. Some theorems about the sentential calculus of Lewis and Heyting, *Journal of Symbolic Logic* 13
MacTaggart, J. M. E. 1908. The unreality of time, *Mind* 17; and in *Philosophical Studies* (Arnold 1934)
Marcus, R. Barcan 1946. A functional calculus of first order based on strict implication, *Journal of Symbolic Logic* 11
– 1962. Modalities and intensional languages, *Synthese* 27; and in Copi and Gould 1967
– 1967. Essentialism in modal logic, *Noûs* 1
– 1972. Quantification and ontology, *Noûs* 6
Martin, R. L. (ed.) 1970. *The Paradox of the Liar* (Yale U.P.)

Massey, G. 1974. Are there any good arguments why bad arguments are bad?, *Philosophy in Context* 4

Meinong, A. 1904. The theory of objects, in *Untersuchungen zur Gegenstands-theorie und Psychologie*; trans. Levi, Terrel and Chisholm in Iseminger 1968

Mellor, D. H. 1974. In defense of dispositions, *Philosophical Review* 82

Mendelson, E. 1964. *Introduction to Mathematical Logic* (van Nostrand)

Michalski, R. S., Chilansky, R. and Jacobsen, B. 1976. An application of variable-valued logic to inductive learning of plant disease diagnostic rules, *Proceedings of the Sixth International Symposium on Multiple-Valued Logic* (Utah State University)

Mill, J. S. 1843. *A System of Logic* (Longman's)

Miller, D. W. 1974. Popper's qualitative theory of verisimilitude, *British Journal for the Philosophy of Science* 25

Molnar, G. 1969. Kneale's argument revisited, *Philosophical Review* 77

Montague, R. 1963. Syntactical treatments of modality, *Acta Philosophica Fennica* 16; and in Thomason 1974

– 1973. The proper treatment of quantification in ordinary English, in *Approaches to Natural Language*, ed. Hintikka, Moravcsik and Suppes (Reidel); and in Thomason 1974

Moore, G. E. 1908. Professor James' 'Pragmatism', *Proceedings of the Aristotelian Society* 8; and in Moore 1922

– 1922. *Philosophical Studies* (Routledge 1922, 1960)

– 1952. *Commonplace Book*, ed. Lewy (Allen and Unwin)

– 1953. *Some Main Problems of Philosophy* (Macmillan)

Nagel, E. and Newman, J. R. 1959. *Gödel's Proof* (Routledge and Kegan Paul)

Nelson, E. J. 1933. On three logical principles in intension, *Monist* 43

– 1946. Contradiction and the presupposition of existence, *Mind* 55

Nerlich, G. 1965. Presupposition and entailment, *American Philosophical Quarterly* 2

Ness, A. 1938. 'Truth' as conceived by those who are not professional philosophers, *Skrifter utgitt av Der Norske Videnkaps-Akademi; Oslo* II: *Hist-Filos Klasse*, 4

Neurath, O. 1932. Protocol Sentences, in *Logical Positivism*, ed. Ayer (Free Press 1959)

Nidditch, P. H. (ed.) 1968. *Philosophy of Science* (Oxford U.P.)

O'Connor, D. J. 1975. *The Correspondence Theory of Truth* (Hutchinson)

Parsons, T. 1969. Essentialism and quantified modal logic, *Philosophical Review* 77; and in Linsky 1971

– 1974. A prolegomenon to Meinongian semantics, *Journal of Philosophy* 71

Pears, D. F. (ed.) 1972. *Bertrand Russell* (Anchor)

Peirce, C. S. 1868. Questions concerning certain faculties claimed for man, *Journal of Speculative Philosophy* 2; and in Peirce 1930–58, 5.213ff.

– 1877. The fixation of belief, *Popular Science Monthly* 12; and in Peirce 1930–58, 5.358ff.

– 1885. On the algebra of logic, *American Journal of Mathematics* 7; and in Peirce 1930–58, 3.210–38

– 1930–58. *Collected Papers*, ed. Hartshorne, Weiss and Burks (Harvard U.P.) (Reference to the collected papers is by volume and paragraph no., as, e.g., 3.117 = volume 3, paragraph 117.)

Pitcher, G. (ed.) 1964. *Truth* (Prentice-Hall)

Plantinga, A. 1974. *The Nature of Necessity* (Oxford U.P.)

Popper, K. R. 1947. New foundations for logic, *Mind* 56

– 1954. Self-reference and meaning in ordinary language, *Mind* 63

– 1960. On the sources of knowledge and ignorance, *Proceedings of the British Academy* 46; and in Popper 1963*
– 1961. *The Open Society and Its Enemies* (1945), vol. 2, 2nd edition (Routledge and Kegan Paul)
– 1963. *Conjectures and Refutations* (Routledge and Kegan Paul)
– 1970. A realist view of physics, logic and history, in *Physics, Logic and History*, ed. Yourgrau and Breck (Plenum)
– 1972. *Objective Knowledge* (Oxford U.P.)
– 1976. *Unended Quest* (Fontana)
Post, E. 1921. Introduction to the general theory of elementary propositions, *American Journal of Mathematics* 43; and in Heijenoort 1967
Prawitz, D. 1965. *Natural Deduction* (Almqvist and Wiksell)
Priest, G. G. 1976. Modality as a meta-concept, *Notre Dame Journal of Formal Logic* 17
Prior, A. N. 1955. *Formal Logic* (Oxford U.P.)
– 1957. *Time and Modality* (Oxford U.P.)
– 1958. Epimenides the Cretan, *Journal of Symbolic Logic* 23
– 1960. The runabout inference ticket, *Analysis* 21; and in Strawson 1967*
– 1964. Conjunction and contonktion revisited, *Analysis* 24
– 1967. *Past, Present and Future* (Oxford U.P.)
– 1968. *Papers on Time and Tense* (Oxford U.P.)
– 1971. *Objects of Thought*, ed. Geach and Kenny (Oxford U.P.)
Putnam, H. 1957. Three-valued logic, *Philosophical Studies* 8
– 1969. Is logic empirical?, in *Boston Studies in the Philosophy of Science* 5, ed. Cohen and Wartofsky (Reidel)
– 1971. *Philosophy of Logic* (Harper Torchbooks)
Quine, W. V. O. 1934. Ontological remarks on the propositional calculus, *Mind* 43; and in Quine 1966a
– 1940. *Mathematical Logic* (Harper and Row)
– 1943. Notes on existence and necessity, *Journal of Philosophy* 40; and in Linsky 1952
– 1947. The problem of interpreting modal logic, *Journal of Symbolic Logic* 12; and in Copi and Gould 1967
– 1950. *Methods of Logic* (Holt, Rinehart and Winston); third edition 1974 (Routledge and Kegan Paul)
– 1951. Two dogmas of empiricism, *Philosophical Review* 60; and in Quine 1953a*
– 1953a. *From a Logical Point of View* (Harper Torchbooks)
– 1953b. Three grades of modal involvement, *Proceedings of the XIth International Congress of Philosophy* 14; and in Quine 1966a
– 1953c. Review of Strawson, P. F., 1952, *Mind* 62; and in Copi and Gould 1967
– 1955. On Frege's way out, *Mind* 64
– 1960a. *Word and Object* (Wiley)
– 1960b. Variables explained away, *Proceedings of American Philosophical Society*; and in *Selected Logic Papers* (Random House 1966)
– 1966a. *Ways of Paradox* (Random House)
– 1966b. Russell's ontological development, *Journal of Philosophy* 63; and in Pears (ed.) 1972
– 1968. Ontological relativity, *Journal of Philosophy* 65; and in *Ontological Relativity* (Columbia U.P. 1969)
– 1969. Replies, in *Words and Objections*, ed. Davidson and Hintikka (Reidel)
– 1970. *Philosophy of Logic* (Prentice-Hall)
– 1973. *The Roots of Reference* (Open Court)

- 1976. Worlds away, *Journal of Philosophy* 73
Quine, W. V. O. and Ullian, J. 1970. *The Web of Belief* (Random House)
Ramsey, F. P. 1925. The foundations of mathematics, *Proceedings of the London Mathematical Society*, Series 2, 25; and in Ramsey 1931
- 1927. Facts and propositions, *Proceedings of the Aristotelian Society* Supplement 7; and in Ramsey 1931*; and, in part, in Pitcher 1964.
- 1931. *The Foundations of Mathematics* (Routledge and Kegan Paul)
Reichenbach, H. 1944. *Philosophic Foundation of Quantum Mechanics* (California U.P.)
Rescher, N. 1969. *Many-Valued Logic* (McGraw-Hill)
- 1973. *The Coherence Theory of Truth* (Oxford U.P.)
- 1974. Bertrand Russell and modal logic, in *Studies in Modality* (American Philosophical Quarterly Monograph)
- 1975. *A Theory of Possibility* (Blackwell)
- 1977. *Methodological Pragmatism* (Blackwell)
Richards, T. 1975. The worlds of David Lewis, *Australasian Journal of Philosophy* 53
Rogers, R. 1963. A survey of formal semantics, *Synthese* 15
Ross, A. 1968. *Directives and Norms* (Routledge and Kegan Paul)
Rosser, J. B. and Turquette, A. R. 1952. *Many-Valued Logics* (North Holland)
Routley, R. 1963. Some things do not exist, *Notre Dame Journal of Formal Logic* 7
- 1966. On a significance theory, *Australasian Journal of Philosophy* 44
- 1969. The need for nonsense, *Australasian Journal of Philosophy* 47
Runes, D. B. 1966. *Dictionary of Philosophy* (Littlefield, Adams)
Russell, B. 1903. *The Principles of Mathematics* (Allen and Unwin)
- 1905. On Denoting, *Mind* 14
- 1906. Review of McColl, 1906, *Mind* 15
- 1908a. Mathematical logic as based on the theory of types, *American Journal of Mathematics* 30; and in Russell 1956*; and in Heijenhoort 1967a
- 1908b. James's conception of truth, *Albany Review*; and in Russell 1910
- 1910. *Philosophical Essays* (Allen and Unwin 1910, 1916)
- 1918. The philosophy of logical atomism, in Russell 1956
- 1919. On propositions: what they are and how they mean, in Russell 1956
- 1923. Vagueness, *Australasian Journal of Philosophy and Psychology* 1
- 1938. The relevance of psychology to logic, *Proceedings of the Aristotelian Society* Supplement 17
- 1956. *Logic and Knowledge*, ed. Marsh (Allen and Unwin)
- 1959. *My Philosophical Development* (Allen and Unwin); § on Strawson's criticisms of the theory of descriptions reprinted in Copi and Gould 1967
Russell, B. and Whitehead, A. N. 1910. *Principia Mathematica* (Cambridge U.P.)
Russell, L. J. 1970. 'If' and '⊃', *Mind* 79
Ryle, G. 1949. *The Concept of Mind* (Hutchinson)
- 1952. Heterologicality, *Analysis* 11; and in MacDonald 1954
- 1954. Formal and informal logic, in *Dilemmas* (Cambridge U.P.)
Salmon, W. 1967. *Foundations of Scientific Inference* (Pittsburgh U.P.)
Scheffler, I. 1954. An inscriptionalist approach to indirect quotation, *Analysis* 14
- 1967. *Science and Subjectivity* (Bobbs-Merrill)
Scheffler, I. and Chomsky, N. 1958. What is said to be, *Proceedings of the Aristotelian Society* 59
Schiller, F. C. S. 1912. *Formal Logic: a Scientific and Social Problem* (Macmillan)
- 1930. *Logic for Use* (Harcourt, Brace)

Schlick, M. 1934. The foundation of knowledge, trans. Rynin in *Logical Positivism*, ed. Ayer (Free Press 1959)

Schock, R. 1968. *Logics Without Existence Assumptions* (Almqvist and Wiksell)

Searle, J. 1969. *Speech Acts: An Essay on the Philosophy of Language* (Cambridge U.P.); pp. 162–74 reprinted in Steinberg and Jakobovits 1971*

– 1975. The logical status of fictional discourse, *New Literary History* 6

Sellars, W. 1967. *Science, Perception and Reality* (Routledge and Kegan Paul)

Skyrms, B. 1966. *Choice and Chance* (Dickenson)

– 1970a. Return of the Liar: three-valued logic and the concept of truth, *American Philosophical Quarterly* 7

– 1970b. Notes on quantification and self-reference, in Martin 1970

Smiley, T. J. 1959. Entailment and deducibility, *Proceedings of the Aristotelian Society* 59

– 1960. Sense without denotation, *Analysis* 20

– 1963. The logical basis of ethics, *Acta Philosophica Fennica* 16

Smullyan, A. 1948. Modality and description, *Journal of Symbolic Logic* 13

Smullyan, R. M. 1957. Languages in which self-reference is possible, *Journal of Symbolic Logic* 22

Stalnaker, R. 1968. A theory of conditionals, in *Studies in Logical Theory*, ed. Rescher (Blackwell)

Stebbing, S. 1939. *Thinking to Some Purpose* (Penguin)

Steinberg, D. D. and Jakobovits, L. A. (eds.) 1971. *Semantics* (Cambridge U.P.)

Stevenson, J. T. 1961. Roundabout the runabout inference ticket, *Analysis* 22

Strawson, P. F. 1949. Truth, *Analysis* 9; and in MacDonald 1954

– 1950. On referring, *Mind* 59; reprinted in Flew 1956; in Copi and Gould 1967; and in Strawson 1971

– 1952. *Introduction to Logical Theory* (Methuen)

– 1954. Reply to Mr. Sellars, *Philosophical Review* 63

– 1957. Propositions, concepts and logical truth, *Philosophical Quarterly* 7; in Strawson 1967; and in Strawson 1971

– 1959. *Individuals* (Methuen)

– 1961. Singular terms and predication, *Journal of Philosophy* 57; and in Strawson 1971

– 1964. Identifying reference and truth-values, *Theoria* 30; reprinted in Steinberg and Jakobovits 1971

– (ed.) 1967. *Philosophical Logic* (Oxford U.P.)

– 1971. *Logico-Linguistic Papers* (Methuen)

Suppes, P. 1957. *Introduction to Logic* (van Nostrand)

Tarski, A. 1931. The concept of truth in formalised languages, in Tarski 1956

– 1936. The establishment of scientific semantics, in Tarski 1956

– 1944. The semantic conception of truth, *Philosophy and Phenomenological Research* 4, and in Feigl and Sellars 1949*

– 1956. *Logic, Semantics and Metamathematics*, trans. Woodger (Oxford U.P.)

Tarski A. and Vaught, R. L. 1957. Arithmetical extensions of relational systems, *Compositio Mathematica* 13

Thomason, R. (ed.) 1974. *Formal Philosophy* (papers of Richard Montague) (Yale U.P.)

Thouless, R. H. 1930. *Straight and Crooked Thinking* (Hodder and Stoughton, 1930; Pan, 1953)

Tichý, P. 1974. On Popper's definitions of verisimilitude, *British Journal for the Philosophy of Science* 25

Toulmin, S. 1953. *Philosophy of Science* (Hutchinson)

Urmson, J. O. and Warnock, G. J. (eds.) 1961. *Philosophical Papers of J. L. Austin* (Oxford U.P.)

Wallace, J. 1970. On the frame of reference, *Synthese* 22

– 1971. Convention T and substitutional quantification, *Noûs* 5

– 1972. Positive, comparative, superlative, *Journal of Philosophy* 69

Weinstein, S. 1974. Truth and demonstratives, *Noûs* 8

Weston, T. S. 1974. Theories whose quantification cannot be substitutional, *Noûs* 8

White, A. R. 1970. *Truth* (Anchor)

White, M. G. 1950. The analytic and the synthetic, in Hook, S. (ed.), *John Dewey, Philosopher of Science and Freedom* (Dial)

– 1956. *Toward Reunion in Philosophy* (Harvard U.P.)

Whitehead, A. N. 1919. *The Concept of Nature* (Cambridge U.P.)

Williams, C. J. F. 1976. *What is Truth?* (Cambridge U.P.)

Wittgenstein, L. 1922. *Tractatus Logico-Philosophicus*, trans. Ogden (Routledge and Kegan Paul); and trans. Pears and McGuinness (Routledge and Kegan Paul, 1961)

– 1953. *Philosophical Investigations*, trans. Anscombe (Blackwell)

Wolf, R. 1977. Are relevant logics deviant?, *Philosophia* 7

Woodruff, P. 1970. Logic and truth-value gaps, in *Philosophical Problems in Logic*, ed. Lambert (Reidel)

Woods, J. 1974. *The Logic of Fiction* (Mouton)

von Wright, G. H. 1957. *Logical Studies* (Routledge and Kegan Paul)

– 1963. *Norm and Action* (Routledge and Kegan Paul)

Zadeh, L. A. 1963. On the definition of adaptivity, *Proceedings of the Institute of Electrical and Electronic Engineers* 51

– 1964. The concept of state in system theory, in *Trends in General Systems Theory*, ed. Mesarovic (Wiley)

– 1965. Fuzzy sets, *Information and Control* 8

– 1972. Fuzzy languages and their relation to human intelligence; *Proceedings of the International Conference, Man and Computer* (S. Karger)

– 1975. Fuzzy logic and approximate reasoning, *Synthese* 30

– 1976. Semantic inference from fuzzy premises, *Proceedings of the Sixth International Symposium on Multiple-Valued Logic* (Utah State University)

Zadeh, L. A. and Bellman, R. E. 1977. Local and fuzzy logic, in *Modern Uses of Multiple-Valued Logic*, ed. Epstein and Dunn (Reidel)

Ziff, P. 1960. *Semantic Analysis* (Cornell U.P.)

INDEX

* indicates glossary entry